FINANCE
First Levels of Competence

John Harrison

Pitman

PITMAN PUBLISHING
128 Long Acre, London WC2E 9AN

A Division of Longman Group UK Limited

© John Harrison 1990

First published in Great Britain 1990

British Library Cataloguing in Publication Data
Harrison, John
  Finance: first levels of competence.
  1. Business. Firms. Finance
  I. Title
  338.6041

  ISBN 0–273–03225–9

Typeset by ⎇ Tek Art Ltd, Croydon, Surrey

Printed in England by Clays Ltd, St Ives plc

Contents

Preface

This is a practical activity book designed for students training for employment as accounts or wages clerks, as well as providing a sound preparation for basic level examination awards. These include the BTEC First Unit in Finance, RSA Stage I Book-keeping, PEI and LCCI Elementary examinations.

In addition I have taken into account the financial record-keeping competences and associated skills and knowledge identified by the Administrative, Business and Commercial Training Group of the Training Agency to enable students to qualify for a Level II National Vocational Qualification. I have also included performance checks based on the NVQ performance criteria to assist students in measuring their work against what is expected for the achievement of competent standards. These stress the importance of accuracy, legibility and speed in the performance of office tasks. For self-assessment, as a further guide to students, abbreviated answers to the first two tasks in each unit are provided on pages 182–4.

I have adopted a case-study approach, with the text and many of the tasks centred around P Faulkner & Sons, a sole trader engaged in the business of manufacturing and marketing camping equipment. The study of finance and accounts is more realistic when linked with office procedures, and office procedures are more meaningful when the financial and accounting aspects are understood. The approach integrates these two important subjects, showing how business documents supply data for financial records. The tasks will give practice in looking up information from business records, completing business documents and using this data to prepare ledger accounts and eventually to calculate profit and loss. Several of the tasks are linked together from one unit to the next to provide ongoing and complete office procedures, and priority 'in-tray' and telephone tasks reflect realistic office conditions. The reference sources for many of the activities are provided in the database in Unit 1 (see pages 4–6).

I have recognised the need to adapt conventional systems to computer techniques, suggesting appropriate tasks which may be worked on a computer, and the use of calculators and computers will enhance the value of all the activities. However, I have also been conscious of the need to give an introduction to the principles of accounts, essential for both fully computerised offices and those still operating manual systems.

Integrated assignments are suggested in each main unit of the book, with the aim of integrating finance with other units. These place the study of finance in the context of the BTEC First core unit 'Working in Organisations' for the development and assessment of the core skills:

- organising and learning
- working with others
- communicating
- information gathering
- using information technology
- identifying and tackling problems
- numeracy
- design and visual discrimination

The accounting format of using columns for debit, credit and balance has been adopted in this book. In order to make the balances clearer to the student during the period of accounting training, all final entries in accounts containing credit balances are indicated by a 'Cr' and all other balances, i.e. the majority for assets and expenses, are assumed to be debit.

JH

Acknowledgments

The author and publisher would like to thank the Royal Society of Arts for permission to reproduce questions from past examination papers, and Midland Bank plc, Barclays Bank plc, National Westminster Bank plc and the Controller of Her Majesty's Stationery Office for documents reproduced.

The author is particularly grateful to Mr Ron Dawber, a former co-author, for the important part he played in earlier accounting publications which have provided the basic structure and philosophy for this book.

Finance: First Levels of Competence Lecturer's Manual

A *Lecturer's Manual* for this book, containing answers, blank forms and income tax and national insurance tables, is available to lecturers by writing on school/college headed paper to:

Order Processing Department
Pitman Publishing
12/14 Slaidburn Crescent
SOUTHPORT
PR9 9YF

1 The organisation

Introduction

The accounting and office procedures of a firm of camping equipment manufacturers, P Faulkner & Sons, form the central theme of this book. Although the systems outlined apply to Faulkners, you should appreciate that businesses use procedures which suit their own particular needs so that no two will necessarily be the same. However, the principles are common to them all.

Peter Faulkner started his business as a hardware retailer 25 years ago and, with the growing popularity of camping, he became involved with selling and hiring camping equipment. The firm quickly established itself in the trade and, as the volume of business increased, so did the number of people it employed. It now employs nineteen people (as detailed in the organisation chart below). Peter Faulkner's daughter, Sarah, and son, David, assist him in running the business, which now manufactures the 'Faulkner' range of tents and accessories.

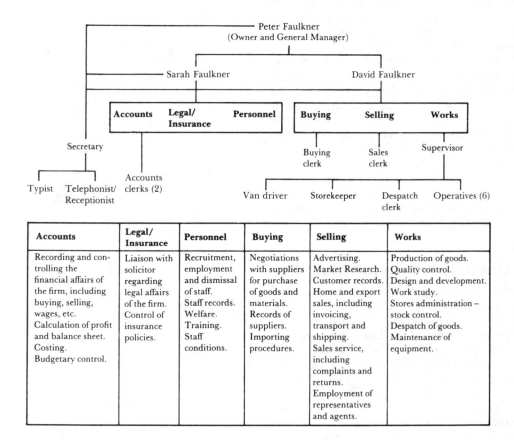

Accounts	Legal/ Insurance	Personnel	Buying	Selling	Works
Recording and controlling the financial affairs of the firm, including buying, selling, wages, etc. Calculation of profit and balance sheet. Costing. Budgetary control.	Liaison with solicitor regarding legal affairs of the firm. Control of insurance policies.	Recruitment, employment and dismissal of staff. Staff records. Welfare. Training. Staff conditions.	Negotiations with suppliers for purchase of goods and materials. Records of suppliers. Importing procedures.	Advertising. Market Research. Customer records. Home and export sales, including invoicing, transport and shipping. Sales service, including complaints and returns. Employment of representatives and agents.	Production of goods. Quality control. Design and development. Work study. Stores administration – stock control. Despatch of goods. Maintenance of equipment.

Fig 1.1 Organisation chart of P Faulkner & Sons

Sarah and David receive a salary as employees while they are learning the business. They expect to become partners or directors in about three years' time, when it is hoped that the present sole trader business will be converted into either a partnership or a limited company. Sarah is currently studying to qualify for membership of the Institute of Chartered Secretaries and Administrators, whilst David hopes to sit the finals of the Chartered Institute of Management Accountants examination next year. Their duties are shown in the organisation chart, drawn up with the long-term plan of dividing the work into departments as the business grows.

At present, as a sole trader, Peter Faulkner has to accept total responsibility for the business liabilities, even by contributing his personal possessions to meet them, but he is also entitled, of course, to receive any profits that are made. He was able to find the necessary capital to set up in business on his own because of a legacy received from a relative and when he expanded the business he took out some of his savings which he had accumulated during previous employment. He also borrowed money from the bank to finance some of his major acquisitions.

Peter Faulkner owes the success of his business to his policy of always providing his customers with good service and quality products at affordable prices. He recognises the need for his business to keep pace with new technology and constantly to adapt products to meet the needs of a changing market.

A variety of delivery methods are used to ensure that orders arrive on time. These include an efficient nationwide delivery service, Royal Mail and the firm's own delivery van.

1.1 The accounting function

Your study of this subject is concerned mainly with the work of the accounts department and the financial record-keeping tasks of other departments. Figure 1.2 shows how all the departmental activities are linked and controlled by the accounting function. For example, the orders received by the sales department result in income (incoming money which is recorded in a sales ledger by the accounts department) and this money pays for goods bought by the purchases department and wages for staff in all departments.

By keeping accounts for business transactions

the firm has the necessary information to:

a calculate the amount of profit or loss made each year;
b calculate the cost of manufacturing its products, i.e. camping equipment;
c know what its customers (debtors) owe to the firm as well as the amounts it owes to its suppliers (creditors);
d be aware of its cash position at any time, i.e. cash flow;
e draw up a balance sheet which reveals the firm's possessions (assets), debts (liabilities) and the amount invested in the firm by the owner (capital);
f conform with the legal requirements for employees' wages, value added tax and personal income tax.

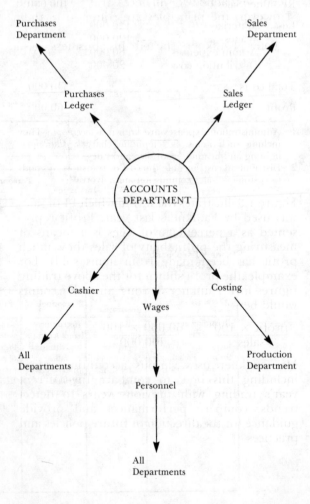

Fig 1.2 The relationship of the accounts department with other departments

1.2 Calculation of profit

Profit is what remains from sales income (called *revenue*) after all expenses have been paid, as explained below. The amount of profit received is important to the firm so that employees can receive wage increases, bonuses, and benefits such as canteen and social amenities. It also provides for replacement of machinery and the future expansion of the firm. The major factors involved in calculating profit for a small business operating as a sole trader are shown in the annual accounts of P Faulkner & Sons for last year.

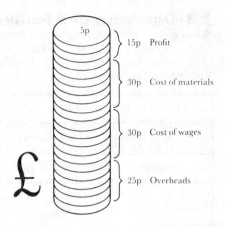

Fig 1.3

P Faulkner & Sons: annual accounts

		£	£
Revenue (Sales)			400 000
Less:	Materials	120 000	
	Wages	120 000	
	Admin expenses[1]	80 000	
	Distribution costs[2]	20 000	
Total costs			340 000
Profit			60 000

1 Administration expenses are known as *overheads*. They include such items as telephone charges, stationery, lighting and heating, insurance and rates.
2 Distribution costs include the cost of transport of goods to customers, sales commission and advertising.

Figure 1.3 illustrates the way in which £1 of sales was used by Faulkners last year. Profit represented as a percentage of sales is a means of measuring the profitability of sales (how much profit has been made from items sold). For example, the profit shown for the above trading figures in P Faulkner & Sons' annual accounts would be:

$$\frac{\text{profit} \times 100}{\text{sales}} = \frac{60\ 000 \times 100}{400\ 000} = 15\%$$

Mr Faulkner uses various accounting ratios, including this one, to compare the current year's trading with previous years to detect trends, compare performances and provide guidance for the direction of future policies and practices.

1.3 Database of P Faulkner & Sons

(Providing the data for many of the tasks set in this book.)

Material	Suppliers	A/C ID
Aluminium tubing	NKG plc, Hall Lane, Sheffield, Yorks SD5 3AP	NKG 01
Brass sheeting	NKG plc, Hall Lane, Sheffield, Yorks SD5 3AP	NKG 01
Foam	Insulation Supply Co Ltd Albert Street, Kettering Northants KG8 6ML	INS 02
Kapok filling	Insulation Supply Co Ltd Albert Street, Kettering Northants KG8 6ML	INS 02
Latex	Insulation Supply Co Ltd Albert Street, Kettering Northants KG8 6ML	INS 02
Netting (nylon)	Tape Works Ltd, Netter Lane, Nottingham NM1 8OR	TAP 03
Nylon (proofed)	CIC plc, Lanchester, Co Durham DM4 9SA	CIC 04
Nylon sheeting	CIC plc, Lanchester, Co Durham DM4 9SA	CIC 04
PVC	CIC plc, Lanchester, Co Durham DM4 9SA	CIC 04
PVC (nylon reinforced)	CIC plc, Lanchester, Co Durham DM4 9SA	CIC 04
Springs	Fettlenold & Sons, Birch Lane, Birmingham B29 2BR	FET 05
Steel rods	Fettlenold & Sons, Birch Lane, Birmingham B29 2BR	FET 05
Tape	Tape Works Ltd, Netter Lane, Nottingham NM1 8OR	TAP 03
Tent cloths	Outdoor Fabrics plc, Manchester Road, Bolton, Lancs BN3 2BT	OUT 06
Terylene filling	Insulation Supply Co Ltd, Albert Street, Kettering, Northants KG8 6ML	INS 02
Thread	Sam Beller & Sons, Pickwick Works Church Bank, Bradford, Yorks BD4 1AW	BEL 07
Twine	Sam Beller & Sons, Pickwick Works Church Bank, Bradford, Yorks BD4 1AW	BEL 07
Zips (tent)	Darling & Son Ltd, Mawney Road, Romford, Essex RD7 2OP	DAR 08

Fig 1.4 Supplier/material records

Section: A to D

Name	Address	Account ID	Credit limit £	Account balance £	Area	Area Code
Aldous N K & Sons	14 High Street, Winchester, Hants WR4 5QP	ALD 01	3500	3000	South	2
Andrews J G	129 Market Street, Bradford, West Yorks BD1 7AS	AND 02	3500	3511	North	1
Arnold & Baker	The Headrow, Leeds, West Yorks LS8 4ST	ARN 03	6000	2070	North	1
Attwood Camping Distributors plc	48 Desborough Road, Eastleigh, Hants SO4 4AG	ATT 04	4500	3000	South	2
Bailey Brothers	School Lane, Littlemelton, Norwich, Norfolk NH8 1AD	BAI 05	6000	4930	Midlands	3
Baldwin Stores Ltd	Hipperholme, Halifax, West Yorks HX7 3MN	BAL 06	6000	3000	North	1
Bell & Sons	400 Princes Street, Edinburgh, Scotland EH3 9AS	BEL 07	12 000	4000	North	1
Bostock (DIY)	4 High Street, Abingdon, Oxford OX4 2VC	BOS 08	3500	2000	South	2
Brentfords plc	Weston House, Piccadilly, London W1V 9PA	BRE 09	20 000	16 000	South	2
Brown & Co Ltd	140 Deansgate, Manchester MR3 1AT	BRO 10	4000	3074	North	1
Carters Sports	57 Victoria Street, Wolverhampton WN7 1DE	CAR 11	5000	4267	Midlands	3
Charles Hugh	'Outdoor Centre', Shakespeare Street, Nottingham NM5 5AD	CHA 12	3500	3000	Midlands	3
Chudleigh & Sons	Edgbaston Shopping Arcade, Hagley Road, Birmingham BM6 8AK	CHU 13	5000	4000	Midlands	3
Clarke Brothers Ltd	40 Blandford Street, Sunderland, Durham SD8 4GF	CLA 14	5000	4000	North	1
Coleman, David (Sports Equipment) Ltd	Torrington, North Devon, TN5 7BN	COL 15	10 000	9150	South	2
Credit I N & Co	Ruxley Corner, Sidcup, Kent SP9 4SD	CRE 16	500	34	South	2
Davies Edna	2347 High Street, Swansea, S Wales SA6 3JH	DAV 17	500	460	South	2
Dentford Donald	1 High Road, Wormley, Broxbourne, Herts BE3 8AS	DEN 18	2000	1500	South	2
Dreamland Ltd	8 Kings Road, Brentwood, Essex BD3 1TY	DRE 19	6000	4600	South	2
Dunn (Sports Outfitters) Ltd	25 Saville Row, London W1X 2AY	DUN 20	15 000	14 404	South	2
	Total Debtors			£90 000		

Fig 1.5 Customer records

Name	ID	Position	Tax Code	Weekly pay rates (ordinary time – 38 hours) £	Savings £	Social Club £
B Brown	1	Operative	430	152.00	5.00	1.00
J Brown	2	Sales clerk	430	200.00	2.00	1.00
J T Bull	3	Accounts clerk	320	182.40	4.00	1.00
W Cap	4	Telephonist/receptionist	278	114.00	–	1.00
C Capable	5	Operative	278	152.00	–	1.00
D Davis	6	Operative	320	152.00	2.00	1.00
E Evans	7	Operative	450	152.00		1.00
D Faulkner	8	Assistant proprietor				
S Faulkner	9	Assistant proprietor				
F Forecast	10	Operative	278	171.00	8.00	1.00
G Grant	11	Operative	320	171.00	5.00	1.00
R Mace	12	Storekeeper	292	152.00	2.00	1.00
R Martin	13	Typist	278	133.00	5.00	1.00
S T Pratt	14	Van driver	278	175.00	–	1.00
T Rawlings	15	Accounts clerk	294	190.00	5.00	1.00
J Russell	16	Supervisor	437	266.00	10.00	1.00
L O Watson	17	Buying clerk	282	150.00	3.00	1.00
S Watson	18	Despatch clerk	278	95.00	1.00	1.00
J Wyatt	19	Secretary	409	190.00	8.00	1.00

Fig 1.6 Employee records

P FAULKNER & SONS
Chestnut Avenue, Southampton SO2 4AG

Telephone: 0703 7654321   Telex: 51 7812

19__ Price List (excluding VAT)

	Cat No.	£
Caravans		
Faulkner ACE	FA15	5,000.00
" KING	FK13	3,500.00
" QUEEN	FQ11	2,500.00
Frame Tents		
Faulkner Major	734T	298.00
Faulkner Minor	754T	268.00
Faulkner Cadet	774T	238.00
Ridge Tents		
Faulkner Expedition	523T	157.00
Faulkner Ranger	553T	130.00
Faulkner Hiker	583T	112.00
Sleeping Bags (Terylene filled)		
Arctic 44	13SB	16.50
Temperate 38	14SB	14.25
Junior 36	15SB	13.10
Rucksacks		
Mount Farley (frame)	27R	22.50
Rover	29R	17.25
Guider	31R	15.10
Camp Beds		
Resteasy	79C	15.75
Sleepwell	81C	13.50

Terms: All prices include delivery anywhere on the United Kingdom mainland

Trade Discount: 10% on orders of £12 000 and over

Payment due one month after delivery

Analysis codes

Commodity		Area	
Caravans	01	North	01
Tents	02	South	02
Other	03	Midlands	03

1.4 Computer applications

A computerised accounting system is made up of files and records, as in manual accounting. A computer file is a collection of records for a particular topic, such as the sales ledger (see Unit 5), whereas a computer record holds the data on one item within the file, e.g. a customer. Information relating to several files may be brought together to form a database so that this can be accessed for different uses, such as sales order processing, credit control, invoicing, sales ledger and sales analysis. It allows the data to be sorted and re-sorted in a variety of ways using different 'fields', e.g. invoice numbers, customer names, regions, products.

The procedures in computerised accounts are similar to many of those used in traditional manual accounting. However, an obvious advantage is that, once the transactions have been entered into a computerised system, reports and management control information can be obtained much faster and more accu-

Fig 1.7 Price list

rately. All accounting packages enable users to print out results (called 'hard copy') at key points in the accounting cycle.

There are many accounting software packages on the market which can be bought 'off the shelf'. They are of a general nature and conform to standard practice, although some packages are tailored to the needs of a particular trade or industry. A small business, such as Faulkners, could use computer applications for ordering, purchases ledger, sales ledger, credit control, sales forecasting, sales analysis, stock control, cash book/cash flow statements, payroll, profit and loss statements and balance sheets. These applications will all be described in the Units which follow.

A computer applications program, known as a spreadsheet, which is in the form of a computerised analysis sheet, can be used to make rapid calculations to help with financial planning and decision-making. A spreadsheet program displays a chart divided by columns of vertical and horizontal lines (a matrix). The screen is a window through which any part of the matrix may be viewed and data can be entered to give a rapid means of forecasting and financial planning. For example, it can reveal the effects of an increase in wages or raw materials on the cost of finished products, profit margins, etc. Hard copy (paper records) of the spreadsheet figures can be printed out at any stage. Spreadsheet programs are particularly useful if amendments have to be made quickly or there is a need for columns of figures to be updated regularly.

A computer screen is illustrated below showing a spreadsheet for Task 1 and the previous year's figures which were given in Unit 1.2. Note that it includes headings (referred to as columns) with the different elements of the calculation; side headings (referred to as rows) for each year; and 'cells' of data within the chart identified by the column letters and row numbers, e.g. G5.

A spreadsheet and accompanying notes for its construction are given in Task 5 of Unit 5.3 (page 80).

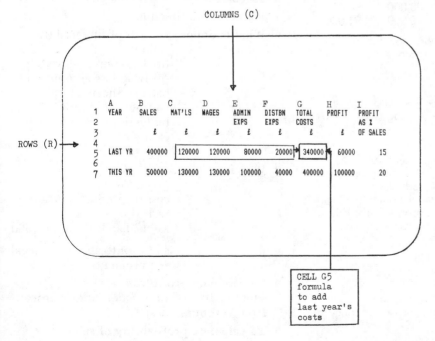

Columns A–F: entered by keying the data into the computer

Columns G–I: calculated automatically according to the formula entered

TASKS

1

a Calculate the profit made by P Faulkner & Sons for this year if sales were £500 000 and costs were: wages £130 000, materials £130 000, administration expenses £100 000 and distribution costs £40 000.

b Construct a diagram to illustrate what happened to £1 of sales in this year, using the information from (a) above.

c Calculate the profit arrived at in (a) above as a percentage of sales and compare it with the figure for last year's trading. Do you think Mr Faulkner would be pleased with the result?

2

Calculate the profit for your group of students if each member sold two articles at £10 each. The costs per article were: wages £2, materials £2.50, other expenses £3.50.

3

The following trading figures are extracted from the accounts of P Faulkner & Sons for the years 19–1 and 19–2:

	19–1 £	19–2 £
Sales	320 000	330 000
Materials	80 000	83 000
Wages	80 000	90 000
Overhead expenses	90 000	91 000

Calculate the profit for each year, show the profits as a percentage of sales and comment on the significance of these figures.

4

Design a chart similar to the one illustrated on page 3 to show how your own weekly wages or allowances are used.

5  **Priority**

You are required to assist in the mailroom of P Faulkner & Sons. The mail is sorted initially into two trays – one for Sarah Faulkner and the other for David Faulkner – according to their responsibilities. Which tray would you use for each of the following items of mail?

a invoice for purchase of tent cloth
b quotation for supplying foam
c cheque from a customer
d catalogue and price list from a supplier
e application form from an applicant for a vacancy in the sales office
f letter from an insurance company concerning fire insurance
g order from a customer
h printer's proof for a new catalogue

Assignment – Unit 1

Select a local organisation (full-time students may wish to use the firm where they are employed on work experience and part-time students may use their own organisation) and find out:

1 a What business unit is employed, e.g. sole trader, partnership, limited company, local authority, central government, etc.

b What are the advantages and disadvantages of this type of business unit.

c Why Mr Faulkner intends to convert his sole trader business into either a partnership or a limited company.

d Which of these business units Mr Faulkner should be advised to adopt and why.

2 a Who is responsible for supplying the finance in your organisation.

b How it differs from the way in which Mr Faulkner's firm is financed.

3 a The departmental structure of your organisation – draw an organisation chart showing your position in it.

b How the finance/accounts department affects the activities of the other departments.

Choose an appropriate format in which to supply this information to your course tutor.

TO SUM UP

The accounting function:

- **What is done:** records of financial transactions
  final accounts – trading, profit & loss account and balance sheet
  costing
  budgeting
  cash control
  wages

- **Why it is done:** *to calculate:*
  profit/loss
  cost of production/trading
  cash flow
  assets, liabilities and capital

  and conform with legal requirements

- **To calculate profit/loss**
  subtract cost of production and overheads from revenue (sales)

- **To calculate profitability of sales**
  use the ratio: $\dfrac{\text{profit} \times 100}{\text{sales}}$

2 Purchases: order and delivery procedures

Introduction

When you buy goods from a shop, you normally pay for them immediately in cash or by cheque and the only paperwork involved is the till receipt which you are given for your payment. The process of purchasing goods on credit (i.e. to be paid for later) in a business transaction is very different, involving many more operations and as many as eight pieces of paper. These are necessary for the reasons given below:

		Document
1	to request the purchase of the goods	requisition
2	to request the seller to supply the goods	order
3	to confirm that the goods have been delivered to the firm	delivery note
4	to notify the purchaser and accounts department of the arrival of the goods	goods received note
5	to inform the purchaser of the cost of the goods supplied – for entry in the accounts	invoice
6	if the goods are returned or an allowance is made, to inform the purchaser of the credit given – for entry in the accounts	credit note
7	to notify the purchaser of the amount due to be paid and request payment	statement
8	to pay the seller the amount owing	cheque or alternative method of payment

These documents are necessary for:

- communicating data between buyer and seller and to the various departments within organisations
- providing written evidence of transactions
- supplying data for entry in accounts, stock records, etc.

2.1 Requisitioning goods

A requisition is an internal request for goods to be drawn from stock (stores requisition) or for goods to be purchased (purchases requisition).

Before any materials can be taken from the stock room, a stores requisition must be made out (see Fig 2.1). It is an instruction to the storekeeper to release the items listed. The stores requisition must be signed by the person receiving the materials as well as the supervisor. Details of the materials issued on the stores requisition are entered on stock control cards (see Unit 8).

If the goods are not in stock or if the quantity of stock falls to the ordering level, the storekeeper issues a purchases requisition (Fig 2.2) requesting the buyer to place an order for the goods.

Flow of requisition documents

Document	Department requiring goods	Stores	Buyer
Stores requisition	→———→		
Purchases requisition		→———→	

Example

On 2 July 100 metres of Grade A gold tent cloth were required for production in the Works Department.

a Prepare a stores requisition to draw this item from stock. As a result of withdrawing the cloth from stores, the quantity of cloth left in stock is reduced to the reorder level.
b Complete a purchases requisition for 400 metres of this cloth to replenish the stock and bring it up to the maximum quantity required to be stored.

```
┌─────────────────────────────────────────────────────────────┐
│              Stores Requisition      No 811                  │
│                                                              │
│ Section: Works                    Date  2 July 19—           │
│ ┌──────────────┬──────────────────┬───────────────────────┐ │
│ │  Quantity    │   Description    │    Stock Ref No        │ │
│ ├──────────────┼──────────────────┼───────────────────────┤ │
│ │ 100 metres   │ Grade A tent     │   60 TC A/G            │ │
│ │              │ cloth (Gold)     │                        │ │
│ └──────────────┴──────────────────┴───────────────────────┘ │
│                                                              │
│ Signed...J Rose......  Storekeeper's initials.....P.L.       │
│                                                              │
│ Authorised by...K Martin...                                  │
└─────────────────────────────────────────────────────────────┘
```

Fig 2.1

```
┌─────────────────────────────────────────────────────────────┐
│              Purchases Requisition   No 816                  │
│                                   Date  2 July 19—           │
│ ┌──────────┬───────────┬────────┬─────────┬────────────────┐ │
│ │ Quantity │Description│Supplier's│Purchase│   Supplier     │ │
│ │          │           │ Cat No  │Order No │                │ │
│ ├──────────┼───────────┼────────┼─────────┼────────────────┤ │
│ │ 400      │Grade A1   │ S 800  │         │ Outdoor        │ │
│ │ metres   │tent cloth │        │         │ Fabrics PLC    │ │
│ │          │(Gold)     │        │         │                │ │
│ └──────────┴───────────┴────────┴─────────┴────────────────┘ │
│                                                              │
│ Signed ....B Lo...ny....    Approved ...J McDonald...        │
│                                                              │
│ Authorised by ...D Falkner...      Buyer                     │
└─────────────────────────────────────────────────────────────┘
```

Fig 2.2

PERFORMANCE CHECK

Completed requisitions must:

- contain the correct information
- be legible
- have the current date
- be signed and authorised

TASKS

1

a Prepare stores requisitions for tent zips (size 2 metres), stock reference No 35 TZ, issued from stores on the following dates:

	Quantity	Job No	Reqn No
Dec 4	60	5861	134
7	30	5920	157
15	50	6004	183
20	40	6102	196

b Complete a purchases requisition (No 1470) on 31 December for 300 of these tent zips to be ordered from Darling & Son Ltd (catalogue No AB119). (*Continued: Task 1, Unit 2.2.*)

2

Refer to Outdoor Fabrics' price list (Fig 2.6) and prepare a purchases requisition dated 31 December (No 1471) for 100 metres of Grade A2 green tent cloth. (*Continued: Task 1, Unit 2.2.*)

3

Refer to Outdoor Fabrics' price list (Fig 2.6) and prepare a purchases requisition dated 31 December (No 1472) for the following items:

Catalogue No	Quantity required	Colour
S804	3	green
S806	2	orange

(*Continued: Task 1, Unit 2.2.*)

4

After issuing the materials in the stores requisition (Fig 2.3), you are required to replenish the stock of 5 mm brown webbing with a further 20 bobbins (Catalogue No 41692). Arrange for the buyer to issue an order to Tape Works Ltd on 2 November. (*Continued: Task 2, Unit 2.2*)

5 📞

Reply to the following telephone enquiry from a new employee in the Works Office:

'The Works Supervisor has a query concerning the nylon reinforced PVC in stock. Do you know the name and address of the manufacturer who supplied it?'

Stores Requisition	No 93	
Section: Works		Date: 1 November 19—

Quantity	Description	Stock Ref No
4 bobbins	5 m/m Brown webbing	42 RP

Signed ....J.Rose.......... Storekeeper's initials.............P.L.............

Authorised by:....J.Martin..........

Fig 2.3

2.2 Ordering goods

When a purchases requisition is received in the buying department it is submitted for approval to the head of the department, usually the purchasing manager or buyer. If the supplier is not specified, the buyer must decide where to place the order. The buyer keeps an index of approved suppliers for the various materials required and Fig 1.4 on page 4 is an extract of the strip index kept by Faulkner for this purpose. (This index contains information for the various examples and tasks which follow.) When a new supplier has to be selected, the buyer will take account of the following factors:

- price of the goods;
- quality of the goods;
- delivery costs, if any (e.g. carriage paid means delivery costs will be paid by the supplier; carriage forward (fwd) means these costs will be paid by the buyer);
- delivery date;
- VAT – is it included in the price?
- trade discount – this is an allowance taken off the invoice or list price of goods; it is deducted on the invoice;
- cash discount – this is an allowance made for the prompt settlement of an account within a stated period (e.g. 30 days); it is deducted when payment is made;
- guarantee;
- after-sales service;
- reputation of the firm, i.e. your previous experience with the firm.

In order to compare the quotations offered by different suppliers, the buyer calculates the suppliers' net prices, as follows:

List price
   deduct: trade discount
                cash discount
   add: delivery charges
               VAT

to arrive at Net Price

The buyer has to negotiate the amount of trade discount with the supplier in order to secure the 'best' net price. In the example given Outdoor Fabrics plc was selected because Faulkner was satisfied with the quality of the tent cloth supplied previously; the list price was comparable with the prices offered by other suppliers; they were able to deliver the goods without any delay and a good trade discount of 15% was offered.

The approved purchases requisition is passed for typing of an order (see Fig 2.5). The information supplied in this order is extracted from the purchases requisition and the supplier's price list (Fig 2.6). Five copies of the order are prepared for the reasons given in Fig 2.4.

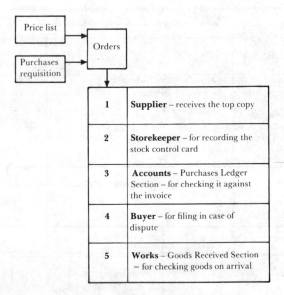

Fig 2.4

Example
Prepare an order for the purchases requisition
in Fig 2.2.

P FAULKNER & SONS	ORDER	No P97324

P FAULKNER & SONS
Chestnut Avenue
Southampton
SO2 4AG

Tel: 0703 7654321

Telex: 517812

Date: 5 July 19—

To:

> Outdoor Fabrics plc
> Manchester Road
> Bolton
> Lancs
> BN3 2BT

Please supply:

Quantity	Description	Your Cat No	Price each £
400 metres	Grade A tent cloth (gold)	S 800	£2.40 per metre
			Payment 1 month after statement
	Carriage ~~paid~~/forward		

Deliver by: Road/~~Rail~~ promptly to:

to: P FAULKNER & SONS,
CHESTNUT AVENUE,
SOUTHAMPTON

For P FAULKNER & SONS

D Faulkner
....
Buyer

Fig 2.5 Order

Price List

OUTDOOR FABRICS PLC, 90 MANCHESTER ROAD, BOLTON, LANCS BN3 2BT

Cat No	Description	Price (ex-warehouse)
S800	Grade A1 tent cloth – supplied in blue, gold, green and orange (width: 1 metre)	£2.40 per metre
S801	Grade A2 tent cloth – supplied in blue, gold, green and orange (width: 1 metre)	£2.10 per metre
S802	Grade A3 tent cloth – supplied in blue, gold, green and orange (width: 1 metre)	£1.80 per metre
S803	Extra strong tarpaulin – supplied in blue and green (4 metres×4 metres)	£120
S804	Extra strong tarpaulin – supplied in blue and green (4 metres×5 metres)	£144
S805	Extra strong tarpaulin – supplied in blue and green (4 metres×6 metres)	£168
S806	Canopy with Grade A1 tent cloth – supplied in orange, green and blue (2 metres×4 metres)	£240
	Note: All prices exclude VAT	

Fig 2.6 Price list

PERFORMANCE CHECK

Orders must:

- record the correct details from the purchases requisition and supplier's price list, i.e.
  - name and address of supplier
  - quantity, description, catalogue number and price of each item
  - method of delivery
  - delivery address
- be legible
- have the current date
- be signed by the buyer or buyer's representative

TASKS

1

Complete orders dated 2 January for the following purchases requisitions prepared in Unit 2.1:

1470 (Task 1) Order No P89216 (*Continued: Task 1, Unit 8.*)
1471 (Task 2) Order No P89217 (*Continued: Task 1, Unit 2.3.*)
1472 (Task 3) Order No P89218

Arrange for these orders to be delivered by road to P Faulkner & Sons at their Southampton address.

2

Prepare an order for brown webbing (No P88219) dated 2 November, requisitioned in Task 4 of Unit 2.1. It is required urgently and should be delivered by British Rail to P Faulkner & Sons at their Southampton address. (*Continued: Task 2, Unit 2.3.*)

3

Prepare an order form dated 3 January for the purchases requisition in Fig 2.7 (on page 15) and arrange for delivery to be made not later than 31 January to P Faulkner & Sons at Southampton. (*Continued: Task 3, Unit 2.3.*)

4

You receive quotations from the following firms to supply the materials you require for manufacturing a special type of tent:

Firm	Price of materials £	Trade discount	VAT (15%)	Carriage cost (approx £20)	Delivery
CBE Products	120	nil	not included	forward	2 weeks
Parson Manufacturing Limited	140	5%	included	paid	4 weeks
Watson (UK) plc	160	10%	not included	forward	4 weeks
YRA Europe Ltd	180	15%	included	paid	2 weeks

a Assuming that the quality of the materials is the same from all manufacturers, select the firm offering the lowest net price.

b If it is essential to receive the materials within 2–3 weeks, which firm would you then choose?

5 Reply to a telephone request from David Faulkner who asks you to look in your file for the date when the gold tent cloth was ordered from Outdoor Fabrics, as it has not yet arrived and is required for an urgent job. David intends to telephone the firm to chase up the order. What other information will you give him to assist the firm in tracing the order?

<table>
<tr><td colspan="5" align="center">Purchases Requisition</td></tr>
<tr><td colspan="3">Date ....2. January 19–</td><td colspan="2">No: 1287</td></tr>
<tr>
<td>Quantity</td>
<td>Description</td>
<td>Supplier's
Cat No</td>
<td>Purchase
Order No</td>
<td>Supplier</td>
</tr>
<tr>
<td>1</td>
<td>Blue canopy
with Grade A1
tent cloth
(2m × 4m)</td>
<td>S806</td>
<td>P89284</td>
<td>Outdoor
Fabrics plc</td>
</tr>
<tr><td colspan="3">Signed ....B Lang....</td><td colspan="2">Approved ....J. McDonald....
Buyer</td></tr>
<tr><td colspan="5">Authorised by ....D Faulkner....</td></tr>
</table>

Fig 2.7

2.3 Receiving goods

An advice/despatch note (see Unit 4.3) may be sent by the supplier to inform the customer that goods have been despatched or are ready for despatch.

When the goods arrive at Faulkner's loading bay, the driver hands over two copies of a delivery note or consignment note (Fig 2.8). One is for signature by the receiving clerk and is returned to the driver; the other is retained as a record of the delivery. Only authorised personnel at Faulkner may sign a delivery note, and then only if the correct number of packages are present and they are not damaged in any way.

Example

Prepare a delivery note for the goods despatched from Outdoor Fabrics by Bolton Carriers on 15 July in respect of Order No P97324.

Delivery Note		
BOLTON CARRIERS LIMITED		
Cheshire Road, Bolton, Lancashire BN4 3AL		
Delivered to:	P Faulkner & Sons Chestnut Avenue Southampton	
By order of:	Outdoor Fabrics plc Manchester Road Bolton	
Date despatched:	15 July 19—	
Number of packages	Description	Comments
8 rolls (50 metres each)	Tent cloth	Ref Order No P97324 dated 5/7/19—
Received in good order and condition Customer's signature.........T Jones....................		

Fig 2.8 A delivery note

At this point a goods received note has to be made out in triplicate (three copies) by the clerk in the goods received section, but copies are not distributed until the goods have been checked in, and signed for, by the storekeeper. Copies are distributed as follows:

1 **Accounts** (purchases ledger section) to await the receipt of the invoice and provide evidence of the safe arrival of the goods.
2 **Storekeeper** for entering the receipt of goods on the stock control card and for recording the new stock position.
3 **Buyer** to attach to their copy of the order.

Example

Prepare a goods received note for the gold tent cloth received with the delivery note in Fig 2.8.

Goods Received Note		No 7629
Supplier: Outdoor Fabrics plc Manchester Road, Bolton BN3 2BT		Date: 15/7/19--

Quantity	Description	Order No
400 metres	Grade A tent cloth (Gold)	P97324

Carrier Bolton Carriers Ltd	Received by *L Stone*	Checked by *J Stockwell*	Bay No 13

Condition of goods: Satisfactory / ~~Unsatisfactory~~

Distribution: Accounts ✓
Storekeeper
Buyer

Fig 2.9 Goods received note

TASKS

1

Prepare:

a a delivery note for the tent cloth supplied in respect of Order No P89217; (Task 1, Unit 2.2)

b Faulkner's goods received note when the goods were delivered on 12 January.

(*Continued: Tasks 3 and 10, Unit 3.1.*)

2

Prepare:

a a delivery note for the brown webbing supplied in respect of Order No P88219 (Task 2, Unit 2.2);

b Faulkner's goods received note when the goods were delivered on 17 November. (*Continued: Task 5, Unit 3.1.*)

3

Complete a goods received note to record the receipt on 20 January of the blue canopy ordered in Task 3 (Unit 2.2). (*Continued: Tasks 4 and 10, Unit 3.1.*)

4

Prepare a goods received note for the goods delivered with the delivery note in Fig 2.10 (page 18).

5

Reply to the following telephone call from Miss J Mason of Outdoor Fabrics:

'Has the gold tent cloth for order No P97324 been delivered yet, and if so, when did it arrive? Another of our customers has complained that their order has not been delivered on time and I am anxious to find out whether your consignment has arrived.'

```
                    Delivery Note

            SPEEDFORDS LIMITED

         Snowhill Place, Aston, Birmingham
                    B15 1BT

Delivered to:          P Faulkner & Sons,
                       Chestnut Avenue,
                       Southampton


By order of:           Fettlenold & Sons,
                       Birch Lane,
                       Birmingham 29


Date despatched:       15 July 19—
```

Number of packages	Description	Comments
2 (50 in each)	Steel rods	Ref Order No S19874 dated 8/7/19—

```
     Received in Good Order and Condition

     Customer's Signature...J Baker............................
```

Fig 2.10

3 Purchases: accounting procedures

3.1 Checking and recording purchases invoices

As soon as an invoice for purchases is received at Faulkner's accounts office the following procedure is adopted:

1 A rubber-stamp impression is made on the invoice to help with checking and to establish who has carried out the work. The invoice in Fig 3.1 has already been stamped.
2 A check is made to ensure that the goods have arrived, by taking out the copy of the appropriate goods received note from the file.
3 The price and terms are checked with the copy of the order in the copy order file.
4 The extensions are checked. (Extensions are the various calculations, such as the quantity of goods multiplied by the rate per article; addition of the different items, carriage and VAT; and deduction of trade discount.)
5 If there is an error, a request is made to the supplier (by telephone or letter) for a credit note to be issued (if too much has been charged) or an amended invoice (if too little has been charged).

If all is in order, the space for 'extensions' on the rubber-stamp impression is initialled. The copy goods received note and copy order are stapled to the invoice and passed to the purchases ledger clerk, who numbers it and enters it in the purchases day book.

The invoice provides a large number of important facts and figures, shown by the following key numbers from Fig 3.1:

1 The name of the document – invoice.
2 Supplier's name, address and telephone number.
3 Customer's name and address.
4 Supplier's invoice serial number – invoices are issued in numerical order.
5 The date of issuing the invoice.

6 Terms of payment and delivery:
   a Carriage fwd means that the buyer is responsible for paying the delivery charges.
   b Payment one month after receipt of statement means that the amount due is payable (without any further discount) not later than 31 August 19–, i.e. one month after receipt of statement (sent 31 July).
7 Order number and date.
8 Quantity, description, catalogue number, price per article and total value.
9 VAT rate – value added tax is a tax on the supply of goods and services in the United Kingdom and European Community. (Certain businesses are required by the government to charge this tax to their customers, i.e. VAT is collected from customers and paid by the firm at regular intervals to the Customs and Excise Department.)
10 Deduction of trade discount at 15 per cent – an allowance made by Outdoor Fabrics plc to P Faulkner & Sons as a concession for trade within the industry. Trade discount might also be allowed for large orders, adjustment of list prices or an agent's profit. It should not be confused with cash discount which is associated with prompt payment.
11 The net value of goods purchased, i.e. the amount recorded in the accounts.
12 An addition of the VAT amount, i.e. 15 per cent for the purpose of this book (but whatever the applicable rate is at the time) of the net value of the goods.
13 An addition for carriage, being the cost of delivering the goods from Bolton to Southampton by Bolton Carriers Ltd.
14 An addition of the VAT amount on carriage.
15 Total amount payable on the invoice, i.e. the net charge of this transaction.
16 Rubber-stamp impression used for checking.

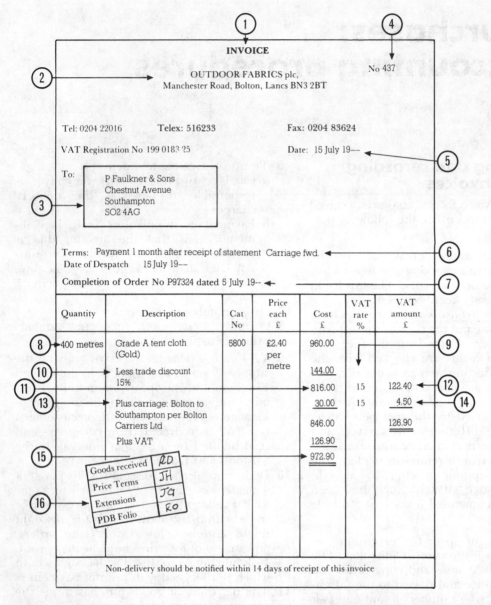

Fig 3.1 A purchases invoice

The purchases invoice received by Faulkner from Outdoor Fabrics in respect of order No P97324 (Fig. 2.5) and goods received note No 7629 (Fig. 2.9).

TASKS

1

Calculate the total cost of the following transactions and add VAT at the current rate:

a 200 reels of sewing thread at £2.99 per reel.
100 metres of nylon cord at 36p per metre.
Less 7½% trade discount.

b 14 blue tarpaulins (4 m × 4 m) at £60 each.
8 green tarpaulins (4 m × 5 m) at £72 each.
6 blue tarpaulins (4 m × 6 m) at £84 each.
Less 12½% trade discount.

c 9 edging shears at £15.99 each.
12 Dutch hoes at £12.36 each.
4 lawn rakes at £14.86 each.
Less 10% trade discount.

2

Check the invoice in Fig 3.2 from the particulars provided, i.e. the extracts from the copies of the order and goods received note. If you discover any discrepancies, attach a note to the invoice with the correct figures. A trade discount of 15 per cent had been agreed.

INVOICE

FETTLENOLD & SONS

No 4926

Birch Lane, Birmingham B29 2BR

Tel: 021 493 6892

Telex: 893462

VAT Registration No 3043739 11

Date: 26 August 19--

To:
P Faulkner & Sons
Chestnut Avenue
Southampton SO2 4AG

Date of
Despatch: 24 August 19--

Terms: Delivered Southampton
Payment 2 months after invoice

Completion of Order No P97429

Quantity	Description	Cat No	Price each £	Cost £	VAT rate %	VAT amount £
320	2 metre 5m/m diam steel rods	SR217	£1.45 per rod	464.00		
	Less trade discount 15%			69.60		
				394.40	15	59.16
	Plus VAT			59.16		
				453.56		

Extract of Goods Received Note No 7726		
Supplier: Fettlenold & Sons Birmingham 15		Date: 24 August 19--
Quantity	Description	Order No
230	2 metre 5 m/m diam steel rods	P97429

Extract of Order No	P97429		
To: Fettlenold & Sons Birmingham 15			Date: 16 August 19--
Quantity	Description	Your Cat No	Price
230	2 metre 5m/m diam steel rods	SR217	£1.54 per rod delivered Southampton

Fig 3.2

3

Check the invoice in Fig 3.3 received from Outdoor Fabrics plc with the documents completed in Unit 2.2 (Task 1) and Unit 2.3 (Task 1). Initial the rubber stamp mark 'extensions' if the invoice is correct, but if you discover any discrepancies attach a note to the invoice with the correct figures. A trade discount of 15 per cent had been agreed. (Continued: Task 10, page 30.)

INVOICE

No 11896

OUTDOOR FABRICS plc
Manchester Road, Bolton, Lancs BN3 2BT

Telephone: 0204 22016   Telex: 516233   Fax: 0204 83624

VAT Registration No 199 018825

To:

| P Faulkner & Sons
Chestnut Avenue
Southampton
SO2 4AG |

Date: 14 January 19—

Terms: Payment 1 month after receipt of statement
Carriage fwd

Goods received RL
Price terms KR
Extensions
PDB Fo.

Date of despatch: 12 January 19—

Completion of Order No P89217   dated 2 January 19—

Quantity	Description	Cat No	Price each £	Cost £	VAT rate %	VAT amount £
100 metres	Grade A2 green tent cloth	S801	2.10 per metre	200.10		
	Less trade discount 15%			30.02		
				170.08	15	25.51
	Plus carriage by Bolton Carriers Ltd			30.00	15	4.50
				200.08		30.01
	Plus VAT			30.01		
				230.09		

Fig 3.3

4

Check the invoice in Fig 3.4 also received from Outdoor Fabrics plc with the documents completed in Unit 2.2 (Task 3) and Unit 2.3 (Task 3). Initial the rubber stamp mark if the invoice is correct, but if you find any errors attach a note to the invoice with the correct figures. (Continued: Task 10, page 30.)

INVOICE

No 11953

OUTDOOR FABRICS plc
Manchester Road, Bolton, Lancs BN3 2BT

Telephone: 0204 22016   Telex: 516233   Fax: 0204 83624

VAT Registration No 199 018825

To: P Faulkner & Sons   Date: 21 January 19—
             Chestnut Avenue
             Southampton
             SO2 4AG

Terms: Payment 1 month after receipt of statement
             Carriage fwd

Date of despatch: 20 January 19—

Completion of Order No P89284   dated 3 January 19—

Quantity	Description	Cat No	Price each £	Cost £	VAT rate %	VAT amount £
ONE	Blue canopy with A1 tent cloth – 2 m × 4 m	S806	240.00	240.00		
	Less trade discount 15%			36.00		
				204.00	15	30.60
	Plus carriage by Bolton Carriers Ltd			30.00	15	4.50
				234.00		35.10
	Plus VAT			35.10		
				269.10		

Goods received RL
Price terms KR
Extensions
PDB Fo.

Fig 3.4

See Fig 3.5.
(*Continued: Task 11, page 30.*)

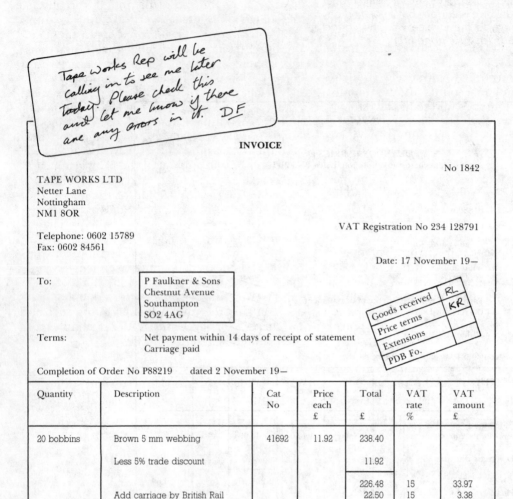

Tape Works Rep will be calling in to see me later today. Please check this and let me know if there are any errors in it. DF

INVOICE

No 1842

TAPE WORKS LTD
Netter Lane
Nottingham
NM1 8OR

VAT Registration No 234 128791

Telephone: 0602 15789
Fax: 0602 84561

Date: 17 November 19—

To:

P Faulkner & Sons
Chestnut Avenue
Southampton
SO2 4AG

Goods received	RL
Price terms	KR
Extensions	
PDB Fo.	

Terms: Net payment within 14 days of receipt of statement
Carriage paid

Completion of Order No P88219   dated 2 November 19—

Quantity	Description	Cat No	Price each £	Total £	VAT rate %	VAT amount £
20 bobbins	Brown 5 mm webbing	41692	11.92	238.40		
	Less 5% trade discount			11.92		
				226.48	15	33.97
	Add carriage by British Rail			22.50	15	3.38
				248.98	15	37.35
	Less VAT			37.35		
				211.63		

Fig 3.5

Purchases day book and ledger

It is standard accounting practice for most businesses to keep at least three ledgers, i.e. systems for recording and filing their accounts on a day-to-day basis. These three ledgers are illustrated in Fig 3.6, together with a description of the information which is entered and filed in them.

This section introduces you to the purchases ledger and related accounts in the nominal ledger for buying goods on credit for resale.

The purchases ledger clerk receives the incoming purchases invoices after they have been checked. Numbers are allocated to them and entered in the space on the box provided by the rubber stamp (see Fig 3.5). The invoices provide the data for entering, either manually, or by computer, in the purchases day book (or other record serving the same purpose).

The purchases day book is a book of *original entry* as it is compiled from the original invoices received and contains a record of all goods bought on credit for resale. It is not used for entering purchases paid for immediately in cash, or for the purchase of goods which are not due to be sold as part of the firm's normal business.

The figures from the purchases day book are transferred to the credit column of the suppliers' personal accounts in the purchases ledger. An account is a record of all the transactions relating to a person with whom business is conducted or to impersonal items affecting the running of a business such as machinery, rent, VAT, etc. At the end of the month the purchases day book is totalled vertically and horizontally, providing a means of cross-casting, i.e. double checking that the individual transactions (horizontal) as well as the totals (vertical) are correct. This is illustrated in the purchases day book (Fig 3.7).

It will be seen that both the invoice numbers and the folio numbers are entered in the book. Folio numbers relate to the pages of the accounts where the entries have been posted (written in). The amount of the invoice appears twice: once as a total, and again analysed according to the net amount of the goods, the carriage and VAT. The total value of the goods is entered in the debit column of the purchases account and the VAT charge appears in the debit column of the VAT account in the Nominal Ledger. The purchases ledger contains the personal accounts of all the firm's suppliers (creditors), whereas the nominal ledger contains the impersonal accounts such as purchases, carriage and VAT. Examples of these accounts are given in Fig 3.7.

Value added tax

Value added tax is a charge on the supply of certain goods and services made in the United

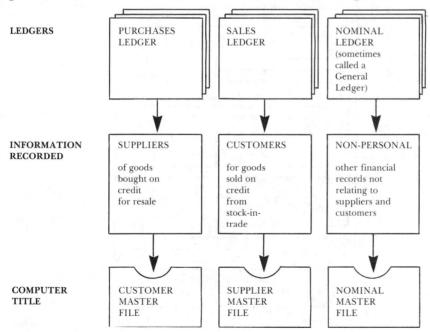

Fig 3.6 Sub-division of the ledger

LEDGERS	PURCHASES LEDGER	SALES LEDGER	NOMINAL LEDGER (sometimes called a General Ledger)
INFORMATION RECORDED	SUPPLIERS of goods bought on credit for resale	CUSTOMERS for goods sold on credit from stock-in-trade	NON-PERSONAL other financial records not relating to suppliers and customers
COMPUTER TITLE	CUSTOMER MASTER FILE	SUPPLIER MASTER FILE	NOMINAL MASTER FILE

Kingdom by a person or firm registered for VAT. Whenever traders buy goods or services to which VAT applies, the supplier gives them a tax invoice indicating the cost of the goods and the VAT charge on these. When, in turn, the traders supply taxable goods and services to their customers they charge them tax at the current rate. Every quarter the traders make a tax return to Customs and Excise, showing the tax charged to them by suppliers (input tax) and the tax they have charged to their customers (output tax) and they pay the difference. If the input is greater than the output tax they are entitled to claim a refund of the difference. It will be seen that in the invoice (Fig 3.1) Faulkner

is being charged £126.90 for VAT, representing 15% of the net invoice price of £972.90. They will add VAT to their invoices when they sell goods (see the sales invoice on page 66). In this capacity Faulkner is serving as a VAT collector on behalf of the government. The principle is illustrated in Fig 3.8 where Faulkner (M) receives materials from a supplier (S), manufactures and sells the finished articles to a retailer (R), who sells them to the consumer (C). Further details concerning the calculation of VAT are given on page 87.

It is impracticable in business to pay for goods as they are received so it is customary for suppliers to give a reasonable time in which to

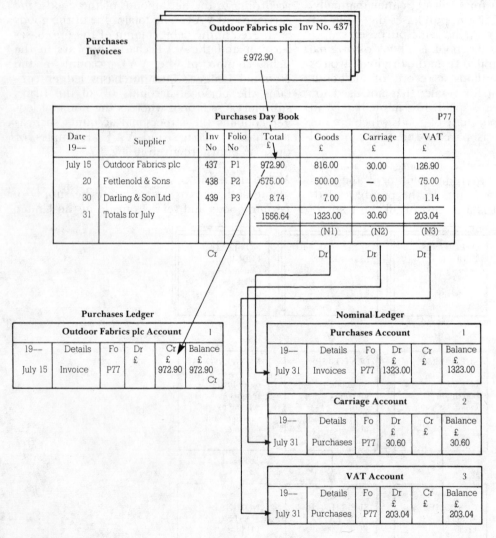

Fig 3.7 Procedure for dealing with purchases invoices

pay, that is they allow credit and are, therefore, known as creditors; in other words they are the people to whom money is owing.

A fundamental rule when entering in the ledger is that the *giver* of either goods or money is *credited* and the *receiver* is *debited*. There are two effects to every transaction – receiving and giving – and for every receiver there must be a giver. In the example (Fig 3.9) the firm *receives* goods which it has purchased and the Purchases Account is debited. The supplier has *given* the

goods to the firm and the supplier's account is, therefore, credited.

Both effects are always recorded in the ledger and this is known as the principle of double entry. It is essential for a business to have a record of its financial position as it affects receiving and giving. For example it wants to know what it owes each creditor as well as the value of the goods received from these creditors.

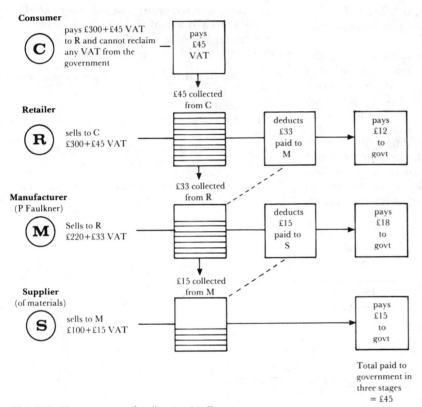

Fig 3.8 The process of collecting VAT

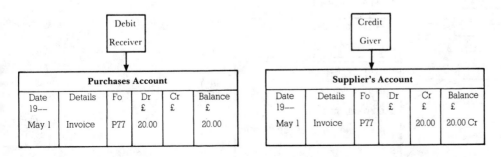

Fig 3.9

Guidelines for entering in ledger accounts

1 Accounts provide a permanent record and all entries should, therefore, be made with a pen.
2 Neatness is essential and lines should be drawn with a ruler.
3 The year must appear at the top of every date column.
4 It is usual to write the month followed by the date, e.g. Sept 19. Dittos can be used for repeating the month, but it is advisable to write the date in every time.
5 The details column contains a brief description of the nature of the transaction, e.g. invoice, payment, etc.
6 The folio column is used for recording the number of the page on which the original entry appears, e.g. P77, providing a quick and easy reference to the full information about the transaction and indicating that it has been entered in both places.
7 The balance column is updated after every entry, e.g. a purchase made on Sept 19 would be indicated as a credit balance, say of £83.05, and a further purchase, say of £50.00, would have the effect of increasing the credit balance to £133.05.

Computerised purchases ledger

Once the computer is set up and disks loaded, a menu appears on the screen. 'Menu' is the name given to the list of operations which may be selected in a computer program. The main menus are divided into sub-menus covering specific tasks, e.g. if a credit note has to be entered in a supplier's account, the main menu 1 (enter transaction) could be selected, followed by the sub-menu 3 (credit note). The menus and sub-menus for transactions involving purchases might include those shown in Fig 3.10.

A computerised purchases ledger holds a record for each supplier and, for example, to enter an invoice for supplying stock items the following would be keyed into a computer:

- account ID number, i.e. supplier's account number
- invoice number
- description of transaction, such as invoice or credit note
- total price (the VAT charge is automatically calculated from this sum)

Note: The current date is automatically inserted.

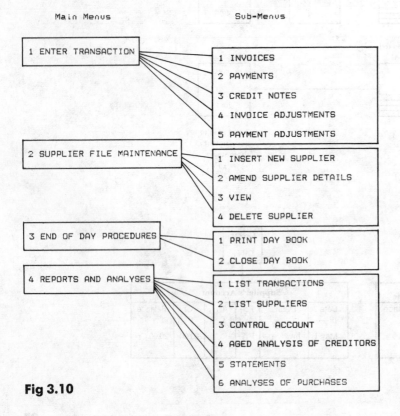

Fig 3.10

A purchases ledger account will normally hold the following data:

- account number
- account name and address
- credit limit
- all transactions in the current year or other period
- cumulative total of purchases made with the supplier

Computerised order procedure

1 The operator keys in catalogue/part numbers of goods ordered to reveal on the screen:

- a description of the item
- the preferred supplier and any other suitable suppliers
- the current price
- discounts allowable
- any charges made for carriage
- normal delivery time

2 The operator keys in details of the order placed to:

- record it in the purchase record file
- print the order at the end of the day
- sort the orders by supplier, to enable all the orders for one supplier to be printed on the same form

3 If terminals are 'on line' to a computer, the following tasks may be carried out automatically:

a When the order clerk keys in details of an order, the computer stores it on the purchase record file.

b When the goods-received clerk keys in details of goods received, the computer checks whether these agree with the data supplied in (a) in the purchase record file.

c When the accounts clerk keys in details from the supplier's invoice, the computer checks these with the data supplied in (a) and (b) in the purchase record file and then enters the transaction.

PERFORMANCE CHECK

When recording purchases invoices in the purchases day book and ledger accounts:

- comply with the guidelines on page 28
- be accurate in transferring the correct amounts and calculating the correct balances
- use the correct books and accounts
- complete entries within the required deadline

TASKS (continued from page 24)

Enter the following invoices in the purchases day book, post them to the appropriate ledger accounts, total the purchases day book at the end of each week and transfer the totals to the appropriate accounts in the nominal ledger.

Note: One set of accounts may be used for tasks 6–8, but if desired they can be treated separately.

Task	Date		Supplier	Invoice No	Total	Goods	Carriage	VAT
					£	£	£	£
6	Sept	19	NKG plc	80	831.45	703.00	20.00	108.45
		19	Tape Works Ltd	81	36.80	30.00	2.00	4.80
		20	Fettlenold & Sons	82	161.00	140.00	—	21.00
		20	CIC plc	83	483.00	400.00	20.00	63.00
		23	Sam Beller & Sons	84	40.25	33.00	2.00	5.25
		24	Outdoor Fabrics plc	85	86.82	68.00	7.50	11.32
		24	Darling & Son Ltd	86	89.70	73.00	5.00	11.70
7	Sept	25	Insulation Supply Co Ltd	87	49.45	43.00	—	6.45
		25	NKG plc	88	595.70	503.00	15.00	77.70
		25	Fettlenold & Sons	89	198.95	173.00	—	25.95
		26	CIC plc	90	368.80	307.20	13.50	48.10
		27	Outdoor Fabrics plc	91	103.50	82.10	7.90	13.50
		30	Darling & Son Ltd	92	82.22	67.00	4.50	10.72
		30	Insulation Supply Co Ltd	93	60.95	53.00	—	7.95
8	Oct	1	NKG plc	94	83.26	69.10	3.30	10.86
		1	CIC plc	95	304.17	253.20	11.30	39.67
		2	Sam Beller & Sons	96	30.26	25.00	1.32	3.94
		3	Outdoor Fabrics plc	97	59.54	47.32	4.45	7.77
		7	Darling & Son Ltd	98	126.20	102.00	7.75	16.45
		7	Insulation Supply Co Ltd	99	45.42	39.50	—	5.92
		7	Tape Works Ltd	100	27.83	23.17	1.03	3.63

(*Continued: Task 4, Unit 3.2.*)

Task	Date		Supplier	Invoice No	Total	Goods	Carriage	VAT
9	Jan	2	B Draper & Sons plc	1	77.28	67.20	—	10.08
		3	Maytree Supply Co	2	489.09	403.10	22.20	63.79
		3	Godfrey & Fry Ltd	3	155.51	127.90	7.33	20.28
		3	Elliot Bros Ltd	4	235.98	193.16	12.04	30.78
		5	Derby Supply plc	5	92.57	76.37	4.13	12.07
		5	C Bond Ltd	6	233.68	203.20	—	30.48
		5	Sam Brown	7	23.17	23.17	—	—

10

Enter the correct amounts for the invoices checked in Tasks 3 and 4 (pages 22 & 23) in a purchases day book. Post them to the Outdoor Fabrics plc account in the purchases ledger, total the purchases day book at the end of the month and transfer the totals to the appropriate accounts in the nominal ledger. (*Continued: Task 2, Unit 3.2.*)

11

Enter the correct amount for the invoice checked in Task 5 (page 24) in a purchases day book and post the entry to Tape Works Ltd's account in the purchases ledger.

12

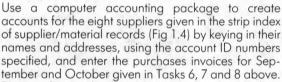

Use a computer accounting package to create accounts for the eight suppliers given in the strip index of supplier/material records (Fig 1.4) by keying in their names and addresses, using the account ID numbers specified, and enter the purchases invoices for September and October given in Tasks 6, 7 and 8 above. Print out the suppliers' accounts at 7 October. (Follow the procedures given in the manual for the accounting package which you are using.) (*Continued: Task 5, Unit 3.2.*)

13

Reply to a telephone request from David Faulkner, who asks you to look at the accounts in your book and let him know the total amount of purchases for July and how much is owing to Outdoor Fabrics.

3.2 Checking and recording credit notes

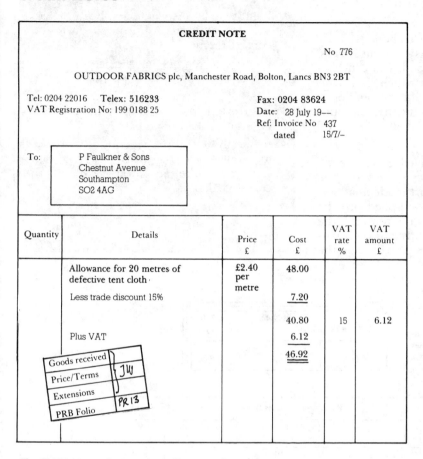

CREDIT NOTE

No 776

OUTDOOR FABRICS plc, Manchester Road, Bolton, Lancs BN3 2BT

Tel: 0204 22016   Telex: 516233
VAT Registration No: 199 0188 25

Fax: 0204 83624
Date: 28 July 19—
Ref: Invoice No 437
        dated   15/7/–

To: P Faulkner & Sons
     Chestnut Avenue
     Southampton
     SO2 4AG

Quantity	Details	Price £	Cost £	VAT rate %	VAT amount £
	Allowance for 20 metres of defective tent cloth	£2.40 per metre	48.00		
	Less trade discount 15%		7.20		
			40.80	15	6.12
	Plus VAT		6.12		
			46.92		

Goods received
Price/Terms   } JW
Extensions   }
PRB Folio   PR 13

Fig 3.11 A credit note (usually printed in red)

The accounts provide a permanent record of transactions and once an entry has been made it can be amended only by making a further entry. An entry must not be crossed out nor, even worse, erased.

A credit note is a document sent by a supplier to a customer when the amount originally charged on an invoice is too much, i.e. it is a reduction of the amount of the invoice, thus making a correction.

Figure 3.11 shows what happened when one of the consignments in the Goods Received Section was reported, at a later stage, to be defective. The defect was reported to the buyer, who contacted the supplier to negotiate an acceptable allowance. The supplier, Outdoor Fabrics plc, agreed to allow the cost of 20 metres of tent cloth and sent this credit note (Fig 3.11) to P Faulkner & Sons.

Trade discount is deducted, as on the original invoice, because the allowance was given off the list price. In addition, the VAT charge must also be added to the amount of the allowance.

The principal reasons for issuing credit notes are to provide for:

a an allowance for goods damaged in transit or found to be defective on arrival
b a return of goods by the customer to the supplier
c an adjustment for short delivery (too few delivered)
d correction of an overcharge arising from an error in the arithmetic, i.e. price, quantity or extensions
e an allowance for returnable cases, jars, etc

All of these allowances are described as purchases returns although some of them do not require the actual returning of goods. Whatever the reason, the procedure is the same, i.e. the supplier issues a credit note which is:

a checked
b entered in a purchases returns book
c posted to the ledger accounts – the customers' accounts are debited because it is a cancellation of part of a purchase which had been credited. The total of the value of the goods is credited to a purchases returns account whilst the VAT is credited to the VAT Account.

When a credit note is received it has to be checked with the discrepancy noted on the goods received note or a report made at a later stage and the information supplied in the invoice. The initials of the checker and the reference numbers of the purchases returns book are inserted in the spaces provided on the rubber-stamp impression on the credit note.

Example

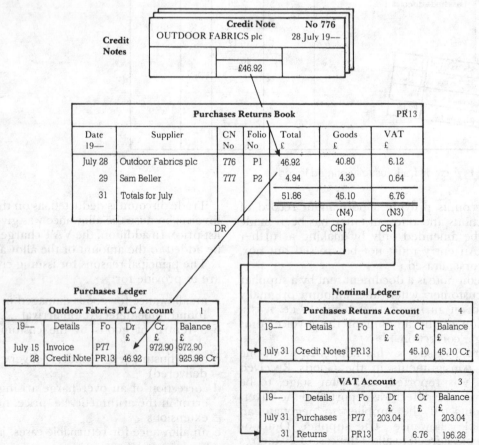

Fig 3.12 Procedure for dealing with suppliers' credit notes

1

Enter the credit notes in Figs 3.13 and 3.14 (page 34) in the purchases returns book, post them to the appropriate ledger accounts, total the purchases returns book at the end of the month and transfer the totals to the appropriate nominal ledger accounts.

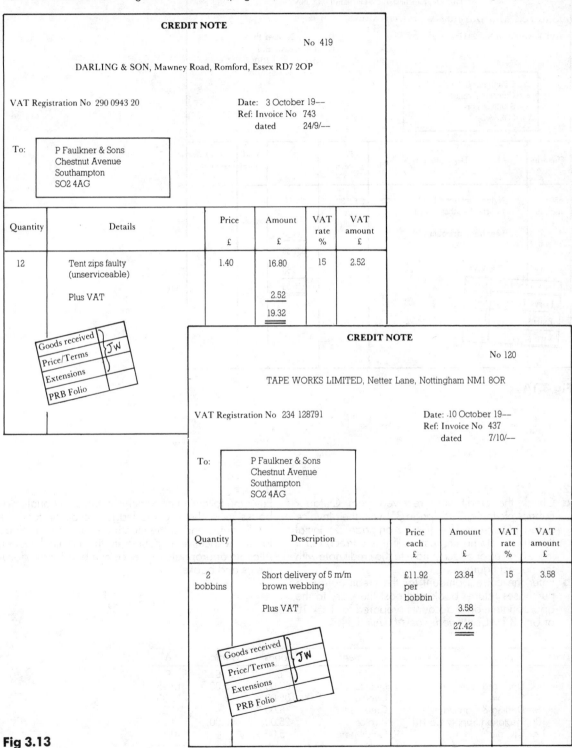

Fig 3.13

CREDIT NOTE

No 473

CIC plc, Lanchester, Co Durham DM4 9SA

VAT Registration No 283 0568 20

Date: 23 October 19--
Ref: Invoice No 274
dated 1/10/--

To:
P Faulkner & Sons
Chestnut Avenue
Southampton
SO2 4AG

Quantity	Description	Price each £	Cost £	VAT rate %	VAT amount £
150 metres	Nylon reinforced PVC returned – substandard	£2.80 per metre	420.00		
	Less trade discount 15%		63.00		
			357.00	15	53.55
	Plus VAT		53.55		
			410.55		

Goods received	
Prices/Terms	JW
Extensions	
PRB Folio	

Fig 3.14

2

a Check the credit note received from Outdoor Fabrics plc in Fig 3.15 (page 35) with their invoice dated 14 January 19— (Fig 3.3 on page 22). Initial the rubber stamp impression if it is correct, but if there is an error attach a note to the credit note with the correct figures.

b Enter the correct amount for the credit note in a purchases returns book and post the entry to the appropriate ledger accounts prepared for Task 10 of Unit 3.1. (*Continued: Task 4, Unit 3.3.*)

3

Enter the following documents in the appropriate day books, post them to the ledger accounts, total the books at the end of the month and transfer the totals to the respective accounts in the nominal ledger. Allocate appropriate reference numbers for the documents and books.

Date	Supplier	Document	Goods	Carriage	VAT
			£	£	£
May 1	Darling & Son Ltd	Invoice	80.00	5.00	12.75
4	CIC plc	Invoice	105.00	8.00	16.95
8	Darling & Son Ltd	Credit note	8.00	—	1.20
10	Insulation Supply Co Ltd	Invoice	25.00	3.00	4.20
12	CIC plc	Credit note	5.00	—	0.75

CREDIT NOTE

No 551

OUTDOOR FABRICS plc, Manchester Road, Bolton, Lancs BN3 2BT

Tel: 0204 22016   Telex: 516233   Fax: 0204 83624

VAT Registration No. 199 0188 25

Date: 19 January 19–

Ref: Invoice No. 11896
dated 14.01.19–

To: P Faulker & Sons
Chestnut Avenue
Southampton
SO2 4AG

Quantity	Details	Price £	Cost £	VAT rate %	VAT amount £
	Allowance for 12 metres of defective A2 tent cloth	2.10 per metre	24.20		
	Less trade discount 15%		3.63		
			20.57	15	3.09
	Plus VAT		3.09		
			23.66		

Fig 3.15

4

For this task use the ledger accounts prepared in Tasks 6–8 of Unit 3.1.

Enter the following credit notes in a purchases returns book, post them to the appropriate ledger accounts, total the purchases returns book at the end of each month and transfer the totals to the relevant accounts in the nominal ledger:

Date	Supplier	Credit Note No	Total £	Goods £	VAT £
Sept 24	CIC plc	56	149.50	130.00	19.50
29	Fettlenold & Sons	57	23.00	20.00	3.00
Oct 3	NKG plc	58	16.10	14.00	2.10
7	CIC plc	59	92.00	80.00	12.00

(*Continued Task 5, Unit 3.4.*)

5

As a continuation of Task 12 in Unit 3.1 use a computer package to enter the credit notes received in September and October for Task 4 above. Print out the suppliers' accounts at 7 October 19–. (*Continued: Task 6, Unit 3.4.*)

You are employed as the buying clerk at P Faulkner & Sons and are required to deal with the following memo received from the works supervisor.

```
MEMORANDUM

From   WORKS SUPERVISOR          Ref  W123
To     BUYING CLERK              Date  29 July 19-

TENT CLOTH

I am not very impressed with the latest consignment of
gold tent cloth which we received on 15 July.  Part of
this consignment was, in any case, defective and we were
given an allowance for it.

Can you please let me know the following:

     a)  name of supplier

     b)  grade of cloth

     c)  price charged

     d)  any trade discount allowed

     e)  Does the firm supply a better quality cloth -

         if so, how much per metre is it and how much
         more would we pay for 200 metres?
```

Fig 3.16

3.3 Reconciling statements with ledger accounts

Once a month suppliers send out statements of account to their credit customers in order to remind them of the amounts due to be paid. A statement of account is a copy of a customer's account in the ledger and customers can check this against the entries made in their own purchases ledger before making payment. The statement acts as a reminder to the customer, as it lists the invoices which they have not yet paid (and any credit notes deducted or payments made during that month).

The statement which Outdoor Fabrics plc would send to Faulkner at the end of July is shown in Fig 3.17. You will see that the statement agrees with the Purchases Ledger Account for Outdoor Fabrics plc shown below but the balance is a *debit*, whereas in Faulkner's accounts it is shown as a *credit*. This transaction in Outdoor Fabrics' accounts is a sale and is debited because Faulkner received the goods. In Faulkner's accounts it is a purchase and Outdoor Fabrics' account is credited to show that they were the sellers. The ledger accounts in the two firms would be as shown below. If the statement is correct, it is initialled and passed to the Cashier's Section for payment.

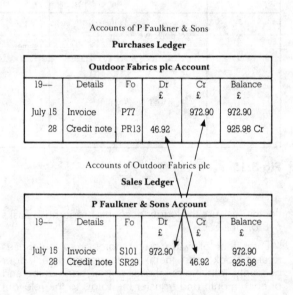

Accounts of P Faulkner & Sons

Purchases Ledger

Outdoor Fabrics plc Account					
19—	Details	Fo	Dr £	Cr £	Balance £
July 15	Invoice	P77		972.90	972.90
28	Credit note	PR13	46.92		925.98 Cr

Accounts of Outdoor Fabrics plc

Sales Ledger

P Faulkner & Sons Account					
19—	Details	Fo	Dr £	Cr £	Balance £
July 15	Invoice	S101	972.90		972.90
28	Credit note	SR29		46.92	925.98

Different descriptions may be used in the details column of accounts and statements, according to the practice of each firm. It does not matter which you use as long as you use them consistently. Alternative descriptions are given below opposite those used by Faulkner:

	Faulkner	*Alternatives*
Purchases on credit	Invoice	Goods/Purchases
Sales on credit	Invoice	Goods/Sales
Purchases returns	Credit note	Returns
Sales returns	Credit note	Returns
Cheque paid	Payment	Bank/Cheque/Cash
Cheque received	Payment	Bank/Cheque/Cash

Example

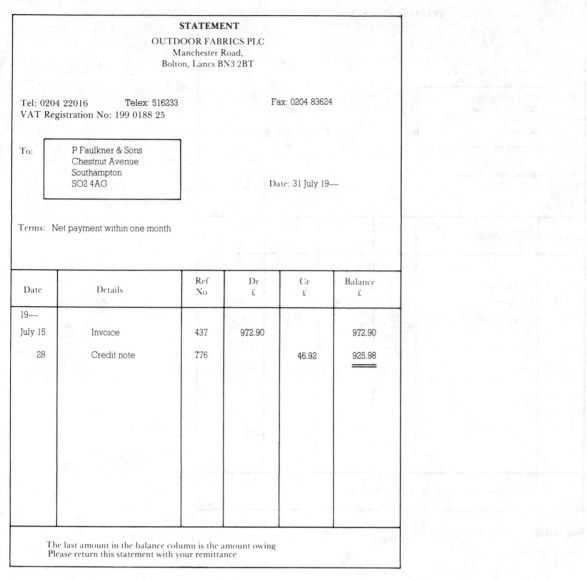

STATEMENT

OUTDOOR FABRICS PLC
Manchester Road,
Bolton, Lancs BN3 2BT

Tel: 0204 22016   Telex: 516233   Fax: 0204 83624
VAT Registration No: 199 0188 25

To: P Faulkner & Sons
     Chestnut Avenue
     Southampton
     SO2 4AG   Date: 31 July 19—

Terms: Net payment within one month

Date	Details	Ref No	Dr £	Cr £	Balance £
19— July 15	Invoice	437	972.90		972.90
28	Credit note	776		46.92	925.98

The last amount in the balance column is the amount owing
Please return this statement with your remittance

Fig 3.17 Statement

On some occasions the statement, at first sight, may not agree with the ledger account. For example, the statement in Fig 3.18 from Fettlenold & Sons (page 38) shows a balance of £670.98 owing by Faulkner, whereas Fettlenold's ledger account (Fig 3.19) shows the balance as £550.00. Each item on the statement has to be checked with the corresponding entry in the ledger and any omissions or errors are entered in a reconciliation statement (see Fig 3.19).

In this case the difference between the statement and the ledger account is made up (or reconciled) by deducting the payment made on 30 July from the statement balance. At the time of despatching the statement Fettlenold & Sons had not received the payment and could not, therefore, include it in the statement. The accounts clerk at Faulkner would have to deduct the payment made on 30 July from the statement before passing it for payment.

STATEMENT

FETTLENOLD & SONS
Birch Lane, Birmingham B29 2BR

Tel: 021 493 6892

To:

P Faulkner & Sons
Chestnut Avenue
Southampton
SO2 4AG

Date: 31 July 19—

Terms: Payment due in 30 days

Date	Details	Ref No	Dr £	Cr £	Balance £
19—					
July 1	Balance				120.98
20	Invoice	321	575.00		695.98
27	Credit note	33		25.00	670.98

Payment of the balance within the time stated will be appreciated

Fig 3.18

Accounts of P Faulkner & Sons
Purchases Ledger

Fettlenold & Sons Account					
19—	Details	Fo	Dr £	Cr £	Balance £
June 20	Invoice	64		120.98	120.98
July 20	Invoice	74		575.00	695.98
27	Credit note	26	25.00		670.98
30	Payment		120.98		550.00 Cr

Fig 3.19

Reconciliation statement
for Fettlenold & Sons' Account

	£
Balance as per statement (31/7/19—)	670.98
Deduct payment made on 30/7/19—	120.98
Balance as per ledger account	550.00

A difference arose in connection with the statement received from Darling & Son Ltd (Fig 3.20).

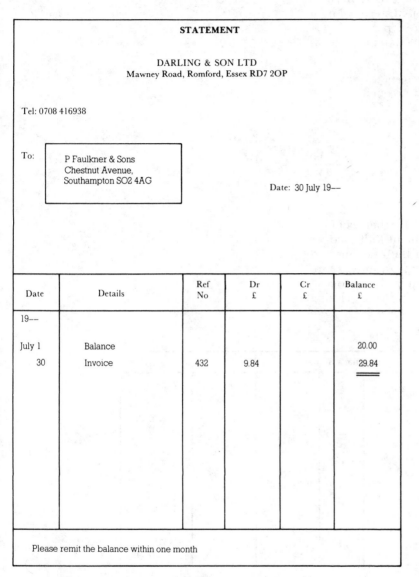

STATEMENT

DARLING & SON LTD
Mawney Road, Romford, Essex RD7 2OP

Tel: 0708 416938

To: P Faulkner & Sons
     Chestnut Avenue,
     Southampton SO2 4AG

Date: 30 July 19—

Date	Details	Ref No	Dr £	Cr £	Balance £
19—					
July 1	Balance				20.00
30	Invoice	432	9.84		29.84

Please remit the balance within one month

Fig 3.20

In the ledger of P Faulkner & Sons, Darling & Son Ltd's Account shows:

19—	Details	Fo	Dr £	Cr £	Balance £
June 28	Invoice	68		25.66	25.66
30	Returns	27	5.66		20.00
30	Invoice	75		8.94	28.94 Cr

It is clear that the 90p difference arises from a transposition of figures (£9.84 on the statement but £8.94 on the account); the amount of £8.94 was found to be correct and the excess of £0.90 was deducted from the statement, reconciling it with the ledger account before passing it for payment. The reconciliation statement is as follows:

Reconciliation Statement
for Darling & Son Ltd Account

	£
Balance as per statement (30/7/19—)	29.84
Deduct amount for incorrect invoice entry on 30 July 19—	0.90
Balance as per ledger account	28.94

Example

Figures 3.21 and 3.22 show a further example of the reconciliation of a statement with a ledger account but in this case both the opening and closing balances are different. Numbers are used to indicate the entries required to reconcile the differences in the opening and closing balances.

Supplier's Account					
19—	Details	Fo	Dr £	Cr £	Balance £
Jan 1	Balance	b/d			600.00 Cr
① 4	Payment		180.00		420.00
4	Discount rec'd		20.00		400.00
② 5	Invoice			500.00	900.00
③ 6	Credit note		40.00		860.00
11	Payment		540.00		320.00
④ 11	Discount rec'd		60.00		260.00
16	Invoice			1240.00	1500.00
⑤ 18	Credit note		40.00		1460.00
28	Payment		414.00		1046.00
⑥ 28	Discount rec'd		46.00		1000.00
29	Invoice			750.00	1750.00
⑦ 30	Credit note		50.00		1700.00 Cr

Fig 3.21

Statement of Account
(received from supplier)

19—	Details	Dr £	Cr £	Balance £
Jan 1				860 Dr
13	Bank		540	320
13	Discount		60	260
14	Sales	1240		1500
20	Returns		40	1460
24	Sales	750		2210
30	Sales	1000		3210
31				3210

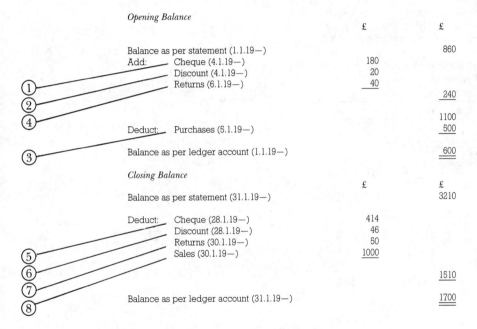

Reconciliation Statement
for Supplier's Account

Opening Balance

		£	£
Balance as per statement (1.1.19—)			860
Add:	Cheque (4.1.19—)	180	
	Discount (4.1.19—)	20	
	Returns (6.1.19—)	40	
			240
			1100
Deduct:	Purchases (5.1.19—)		500
Balance as per ledger account (1.1.19—)			600

Closing Balance

		£	£
Balance as per statement (31.1.19—)			3210
Deduct:	Cheque (28.1.19—)	414	
	Discount (28.1.19—)	46	
	Returns (30.1.19—)	50	
	Sales (30.1.19—)	1000	
			1510
Balance as per ledger account (31.1.19—)			1700

Notes of explanation

Opening Balance

① ② ④ *Add* the cheque paid, discount received and purchases returns because they were debited in the supplier's account *after* the opening balance had been extracted, whereas in the statement they had been credited before calculating the balance on 1 January.

③ *Deduct* purchases because they were credited in the supplier's account on January 5 but in the statement they had been debited *before* calculating the opening balance.

Closing Balance

⑤ ⑥ ⑦ *Deduct* the cheque paid, discount received and purchases returns because they had been debited in the supplier's account but not included in the statement.

⑧ *Deduct* sales (purchases in the buyer's ledger) because they were debited in the statement but not included in the supplier's account.

Fig 3.22

TASKS

1

Study the statement below and state:

a the name of the person supplying the goods

b the significance of the three columns numbered **1, 2** and **3**

c the names of the debtor and creditor and the amount owed on 31 May 19—. (*RSA BK1*)

Statement

In account with

T Wilkinson and Company Ltd
12 Hull Rd
Bridlington B3

31 May 19—

J W Joyce
14 Moor St
Bilston

			1	**2**	**3**
			£	£	£
May	1	Balance			120.98
	7	Invoice 254	120.14		241.12
	8	Cheque		117.37	
		Discount		3.61	120.14
	8	Invoice 297	78.10		198.24
	10	Returns		15.24	183.00
	15	Credit note			
		Overcharge		2.50	180.50
	25	Invoice 509	147.00		327.50

2

Check the statement in Fig 3.23 received from Southampton Welding Co with the account in Faulkner's purchases ledger and prepare a statement to reconcile the balances.

STATEMENT

SOUTHAMPTON WELDING CO
Millbrook Industrial Estate, Southampton SO4 3AL

Tel: 0703 492231

To:

P Faulkner & Sons
Chestnut Avenue
Southampton
SO2 4AG

Date: 15 January 19--

Terms: Payment due in 30 days

Date	Details	Ref No	Dr £	Cr £	Balance £
19-- Jan 1	Balance				53.00
6	Invoice	A1162	37.62		90.62
12	Returns	416		2.33	88.29

The last amount in the balance column is the amount owing

Accounts of P Faulkner & Sons

Purchases Ledger

Southampton Welding Co Account

19--	Details	Fo	Dr £	Cr £	Balance £
Jan 1	Balance				53.00 Cr
6	Invoice	431		27.62	80.62
12	Returns	26	2.33		78.29
30	Payment		53.00		25.29 Cr

Fig 3.23

Fig 3.24

STATEMENT

Electronic Designs plc

108 Charlton Place, Andover, Hants. SP12 3BT

James Blair & Sons
Gosforth
Newcastle upon Tyne
NE5 3SP

Tel: 0264–23461
Terms: Net payment within one month

28 February 19—

			Dr £	Cr £	Balance £
February	1	Balance			3565
	6	Returns		425	3140
	8	Bank		1225	1915
	8	Discount		25	1890
	15	Sales	2110		4000

Fig 3.24

3

Check the statement (Fig 3.24) received from Electronic Designs plc with the account (Fig 3.25) in James Blair & Sons' purchases ledger and prepare a statement to reconcile the balances.

4

Check the statement (Fig 3.26) received from Outdoor Fabrics with the ledger account prepared for Task 2 of Unit 3.2. Say whether you would initial the statement for payment. If there is a discrepancy, prepare a reconciliation statement to identify it. (*Continued: Task 4, Unit 3.4.*)

Purchases Ledger of James Blair & Sons

Electronic Designs plc Account					
19—	Details	Dr £	Cr £	Balance £
Feb 1	Balance b/d			3175 Cr
2	Bank	1500		1675
4	Returns	425		1250
6	Purchases		1890	3140
8	Bank	1225		1915
8	Discount	25		1890
18	Purchases		2110	4000
27	Bank	3675		325
27	Discount	75		250
28	Balance c/d			250

Fig 3.25

STATEMENT

Outdoor Fabrics plc
Manchester Road
Bolton, Lancs BN3 2BT

Tel: 0204 22016   Telex: 516233   Fax: 0204 83624

To: P Faulkner & Sons
       Chestnut Avenue
       Southampton
       SO2 4AG

Date: 31 January 19—

Terms: Net payment within one month

Date	Details	Ref No	Dr £	Cr £	Balance £
19—					
Jan 14	Invoice (amended)	11896	239.78		239.78
21	Invoice	11953	269.10		508.88

Fig 3.26

The last amount in the balance column is the amount owing. Please return this statement with your remittance.

5 🩹

After checking the statement received from Outdoor Fabrics plc in Task 4 you are required to reply to a telephone request from Sarah Faulkner. She asks you to look in the purchases ledger and let her know how much is due to be paid to Outdoor Fabrics at the end of January and when it should be paid to comply with the terms of payment.

3.4 Paying for goods

Once a transaction has been authorised for payment the business must decide which method of payment to use. Cheques and credit transfers are commonly used but the following alternative methods may also be selected:

- Girobank
- Direct debit
- Standing order
- Cash
- Credit card
- Electronic transfer (for retail sales)

Cheques

When preparing cheques:

- Always use a pen for writing cheques.
- After 'Pay' write the correct name of the payee (ie the name of the person to whom the cheque is made payable).
- Insert the amount in words as well as in figures, except for the pence which are shown in figures only.
- Do not leave spaces for other words or figures to be added.
- The day, month and year must be given in the date.
- A record of the date, the payee's name and the amount should be entered on the counterfoil.

- All cheques should be crossed before being sent through the post to ensure that they are paid into a bank account.

The cheque (Fig 3.27) was made out to Outdoor Fabrics plc for the amount outstanding in their account. Cheques are signed by Peter Faulkner, as well as by Sarah Faulkner, the Chief Accountant.

The cheques are entered in a cash payments journal to record the total payments made and, at the same time, to provide a copy from which the purchases ledger entries may be made. The cash payments journal for 10 August is shown in Fig 3.28. Alternatively, the cheques may be entered individually into a columnar cash book and the ledger entries made from the cash book. (The cash book is dealt with in detail in Unit 9.1.)

The cheques are mailed to the creditors with the relevant statements or remittance advice notes which some firms prefer to send. A copy of the cash payments journal is passed on to the purchases ledger section for entries to be made in the purchases ledger and bank account (to be dealt with in a later section). The ledger entries to record the payment made to Outdoor Fabrics plc are given in the procedure for dealing with cheques paid (Fig 3.28 on page 46).

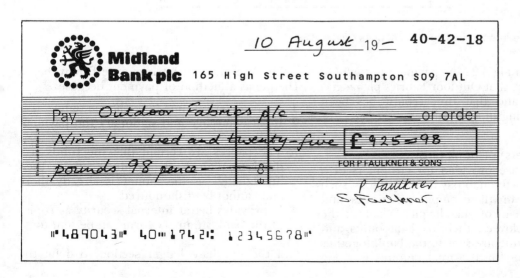

Midland Bank plc 165 High Street Southampton S09 7AL

10 August 19— 40-42-18

Pay Outdoor Fabrics plc ———————— or order

Nine hundred and twenty-five pounds 98 pence ——

£ 925=98

FOR P FAULKNER & SONS

P Faulkner
S Faulkner.

⑆489043⑆ 40⑈1742⑈ 12345678⑆

Fig 3.27

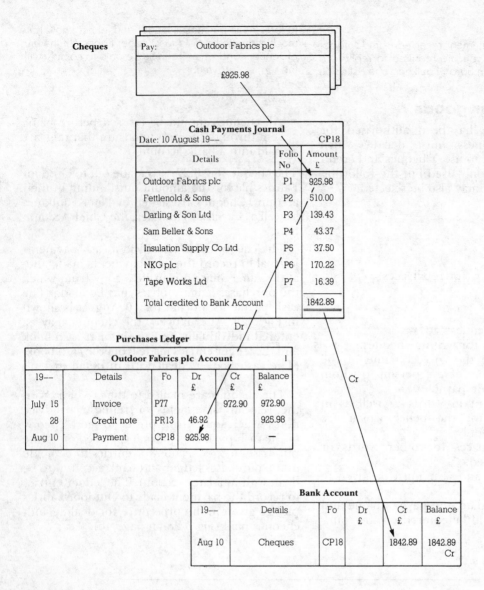

Cheques

Pay: Outdoor Fabrics plc

£925.98

Cash Payments Journal
Date: 10 August 19—   CP18

Details	Folio No	Amount £
Outdoor Fabrics plc	P1	925.98
Fettlenold & Sons	P2	510.00
Darling & Son Ltd	P3	139.43
Sam Beller & Sons	P4	43.37
Insulation Supply Co Ltd	P5	37.50
NKG plc	P6	170.22
Tape Works Ltd	P7	16.39
Total credited to Bank Account		1842.89

Dr

Purchases Ledger

Outdoor Fabrics plc Account   1

19—	Details	Fo	Dr £	Cr £	Balance £
July 15	Invoice	P77		972.90	972.90
28	Credit note	PR13	46.92		925.98
Aug 10	Payment	CP18	925.98		—

Cr

Bank Account

19—	Details	Fo	Dr £	Cr £	Balance £
Aug 10	Cheques	CP18		1842.89	1842.89 Cr

Fig 3.28 Procedure for dealing with cheques paid

Note that in Fig 3.28 the payment is *debited* to record the fact that Outdoor Fabrics plc *receives* the amount and that the account has been settled, resulting in a nil balance.

Credit transfers (or bank giro)

This is a service provided for customers of a bank to enable them to pay their creditors, such as suppliers, or their employees' wages and salaries by means of one cheque. Details of the suppliers/employees, their bank accounts and the amounts due are sent to the bank together with a cheque for the total amount (see Fig 3.29). A credit transfer is more efficient than a cheque as a method of payment because:

1 It saves clerical time (one cheque only)
2 It saves postage and stationery (no payment advices)
3 The payees are certain that the funds credited to their bank accounts can be used immediately as the money is already there and cannot be dishonoured
4 It provides better internal security as copies of the bank summary form can be sent to:

a the purchase ledger section to debit the

TO	**Midland Bank plc**				bank giro credit summary form		

Branch _____ Southampton _____ Date ___ 25.2.19-- ___

Please distribute the bank giro credits attached as arranged with the recipients.

Our cheque for £ ___ 613.34 ___ is enclosed.

Number of Items
7

Customer _____ P FAULKNER & SONS _____

Address _____ Chestnut Avenue _____
Southampton SO2 4AG

Signature/s _____ S Faulkner _____

Bank sorting code number	For account of and account number		Amount		Total amount for each bank	
30.00.09	NKG Limited	23451834	28	14		
30-19-62	Tape Works Limited	81093263	119	00		
30-84-31	Fettlenold & Sons	62345582	18	60		
					165	74
40-17-38	CIC plc	34649810	104	23		
40-23-61	Sam Beller & Sons	23418776	52	00		
					156	23
20-14-32	Outdoor Fabrics plc	12300987	231	15		
20-89-66	Darling & Son Ltd	78452960	60	22		
					291	37
	Totals carried forward £		613	34	613	34

Fig 3.29 Bank Giro credits

suppliers' accounts individually;
b the accounts section (nominal ledger) to debit the purchases ledger control account (see Unit 7.3);
c the cashier's section to credit the bank account with one figure.

The Bankers Automated Clearing Service (BACs) is a fully computerised credit transfer system in which the funds are paid into the payee's account the same day that the bank's account is debited. This provides an even faster means of transferring credit from one account to another.

Customers who do not have a bank account can use the credit transfer service to pay gas, electricity, telephone, insurance and mail order companies. Ready-printed slips are supplied with these bills so that customers can pay their accounts at the bank, but in this case cash has to be paid to the bank at the time of using the service.

Girobank

Girobank plc offers a range of payment services which are conducted through the Post Office with the Girobank Centre at Bootle.

Direct debit

This is an arrangement made with a creditor (the payee) and both the debtor's and creditor's banks, to allow the creditor to claim amounts due directly from the debtor (the drawer). The payee must have written authority from the drawer in order to arrange for direct debiting to take place. This method can be used for fixed amounts at fixed dates or for varying amounts at irregular intervals. Drawers are able to check the amount which will be taken from their account by receiving an invoice several days before the transfer takes place.

The accounting procedure for the direct debit payment (i.e. credit the bank account, debit the supplier's account) cannot be completed until notification has been received from the drawer's bank either by means of an advice or from the bank statement (see Unit 9.2). When there are many direct debits they are sometimes difficult to identify because neither the amount nor the date of payment is fixed. Therefore care must be taken in assigning the payments, i.e. allocating them to the appropriate authorised accounts.

Standing orders

A standing order is an instruction to a bank, given by the drawer, to pay a fixed sum of money regularly on given dates. The drawer does not then have the trouble of remembering the dates of payment and writing and posting cheques. Direct debits are preferable for most business purposes, but standing orders are commonly used by individuals for their private financial commitments such as monthly mortgage repayments, annual subscriptions, insurance premiums, etc. This is because a direct debit may be altered by the payee whereas only the payer can alter a standing order payment.

Cash

Cash is used for small amounts only and the records are kept in a petty cash account (see Unit 9.3).

Credit cards

These provide the means of obtaining goods or services on credit. A business can control the expenses of its executive staff for the payment of travel, entertainment and other incidental costs by providing them with credit cards up to an agreed credit limit. This removes the risk and inconvenience of advancing a cash float or of expecting the staff to pay for business expenses out of their own money and having them reimbursed at a later date.

Electronic funds transfer at point of sale (EFTPOS)

This is a new development for the payment of purchases. The payer presents a card to the retailer who passes it through a computerised terminal which sends the data electronically to the banks concerned and when the transaction is 'approved' the money is automatically debited from the payer's bank account and credited to the retailer's bank account, i.e. buy now: pay now.

PERFORMANCE CHECK

When preparing payments and entering them in the accounts:

- maintain legible and accurate ledger accounts and journals
- follow security procedures for handling money
- complete bank forms, cheques and schedules correctly and legibly
- use the correct books and accounts
- complete tasks within the required deadlines

TASKS

1

a Prepare the personal accounts in the purchases ledger of P Faulkner & Sons as you would expect them to appear from the information supplied in the statements sent by the suppliers listed in Fig 3.30.

b Prepare cheques dated 10 November to settle the accounts for these suppliers, list the items in a cash payments journal and post them to the personal accounts in the purchases ledger.

2

Your cheque book counterfoil for 1 April 19—indicates that you have £268.50 in your bank account. On 2 April you receive an account from Darling & Son Ltd for goods supplied to the value of £160.80.

You are required to complete a cheque on 3 April to settle Darling's account after deducting 2½ per cent cash discount. Record the usual details on the cheque counterfoil, including the balance at bank after payment for this transaction.

3

Enter the following list of documents in the appropriate day books, post them to the ledger accounts, total the books at the end of the month and transfer the totals to the respective accounts in the nominal ledger and the bank account. Allocate appropriate reference numbers for the documents and books.

Darling & Son Ltd

Date 19—	Details	Ref No	Dr £	Cr £	Balance £
Oct 7	Invoice	174	123.74		123.74
14	Invoice	203	203.13		326.87
16	Credit note	43		23.10	303.77

Insulation Supply Co Ltd

Date 19—	Details	Ref No	Dr £	Cr £	Balance £
Oct 7	Invoice	1329	43.00		43.00
23	Invoice	1374	110.23		153.23
30	Credit note	76		17.10	136.13

C I C plc

Date 19—	Details	Ref No	Dr £	Cr £	Balance £
Oct 1	Brought forward				76.92*
10	Payment			76.92	–
11	Invoice	7624X	137.23		137.23
16	Credit note	431		137.23	–
18	Invoice	7726X	116.27		116.27
23	Invoice	7829X			256.52
27	Credit note	434		14.03	242.49

* Note this is the amount which was due for a transaction in September.

Fig 3.30

Date	Supplier	Document	Goods	Carriage	VAT
			£	£	£
Nov 1	Fettlenold & Sons	Invoice	105.00	15.00	18.00
5	Sam Beller & Sons	Invoice	14.00	1.00	2.25
8	Tape Works Ltd	Invoice	240.00	–	36.00
12	Sam Beller & Sons	Credit note	4.00	–	0.60
26	Fettlenold & Sons	Invoice	84.00	6.00	13.50
30	Fettlenold & Sons } Sam Beller & Sons } Tape Works Ltd }	Cheques sent to settle their accounts			

4

Complete a cheque on 7 February to settle Outdoor Fabrics plc's account for January, as dealt with in Task 4 of Unit 3.3. Enter the cheque in a cash payments journal and post it to the supplier's account in the purchases ledger.

5

For this task use the ledger accounts prepared in Tasks 6–8 of Unit 3.1 and continued in Task 4 of Unit 3.2. Enter the following cheques (dated 8 October) in a cash payments journal, post them to the appropriate ledger accounts, total the cash payments journal on 31 October and transfer the total to the bank account:

Supplier	Amount £
NKG plc	1427.15
Tape Works Ltd	36.80
Fettlenold & Sons	336.95
CIC plc	702.30
Sam Beller & Sons	40.25
Outdoor Fabrics plc	190.32
Darling & Son Ltd	171.92
Insulation Supply Co Ltd	110.40

6 As a continuation of Task 5 in Unit 3.2, use a computer package to enter the cheques paid on 8 October in Task 5 above. Print out the suppliers' accounts at 8 October 19—.

7

a Using a bank giro credit summary form, or five bank giro credit slips, enter the following payments relating to the payroll on page 148. It is to be paid in today by you with a cheque.

Account name and number:		P Faulkner & Sons			
		60232785			
Employee	Account No	Sorting Code No	Bank		Amount £
S T Pratt	77733609	20 19 39	Barclays		121.21
T Rawlings	77733555	20 19 39	Barclays		143.77
L O Watson	23451834	40 00 09	Midland		106.92
S Watson	81098263	40 19 82	Midland		82.52
J Wyatt	62345582	30 84 31	Lloyds		128.86
					583.28

b State the benefits to employees of having their wages paid in this manner.

8

a You are employed by P Faulkner & Sons and are required to complete a direct debit mandate sent to you by The Regal Machine Co Ltd relating to a hire purchase agreement for machinery. It should be sent to your bank, Midland Bank plc at 165 High Street, Southampton SO9 7AL.

Account Name: P Faulkner & Sons
Account No: 60232785
Date: 1st day of every month for a period of 2 years
Amount: £1200
Payee: The Regal Machine Co Ltd, Cumberland Place, Southampton SO9 3ZU
Reference No: A23689

b State how P Faulkner & Sons would know that the instruction was carried out and what accounting procedure would then follow.

9

On 31 August Mr John Billingham of Fettlenold & Sons telephones to say that he has not received payment for the amount owing on their July statement (see records on page 38). When was the cheque sent? Assuming that it was sent, what action would you take to trace it?

Assignment – Unit 3

You are employed in the Accounts Department of P Faulkner & Sons and are required to undertake the following tasks:

1 Compare the prices and terms of payment offered by Quality Products plc in their quotation (Fig 3.31) with those offered by Outdoor Fabrics plc for supplying tarpaulins. Write a memo to David Faulkner advising him of the results of your enquiry and any other course of action which you consider should be taken before a decision is made to place an order with the new firm.

2 Assume that a decision is made to place a trial order with Quality Products plc:

a Complete the necessary document on 4 March to instruct Quality Products plc to supply two grey tarpaulins 4 m × 4 m.

b Use the information in the delivery note (Fig 3.32) to inform the relevant departments of the safe arrival of the goods.

c Check the invoice (Fig 3.33). If it is correct, initial the rubber stamp impression on the invoice and enter the invoice details in the appropriate day book and purchases ledger account. If there is an error, write a letter to Quality Products Ltd pointing it out and requesting an amendment.

d After examining the tarpaulins in the stores, one of them is found to have a flaw in the material. Telephone Quality Products Ltd to explain the defect and ask them to send you a credit note to cover the cost of the item. A telephone answering machine is in use at the time of your call. (Record your message on a tape recorder.)

e Check the credit note received for the faulty item (Fig 3.34). If it is correct, initial the rubber stamp impression and enter it in the appropriate day book and account in the purchases ledger. If there is an error, write a letter to the firm pointing it out and requesting an amended credit note.

f Check the statement of account (Fig 3.35) with Quality Products plc's account in your ledger. If it is correct, prepare a cheque to settle the account and enter it in the appropriate journal and purchases ledger account.
Note: These records may be completed on a computer-based system for the purchases ledger instead of a manual system.

3 Write a memo to David Faulkner informing him of the outcome of the trial order with Quality Products plc and say whether you consider future orders for tarpaulins should be placed with this new firm or with Outdoor Fabrics plc, your normal supplier of these goods.

Quality Products plc
224 Hill Park Avenue
Derby
DE8 4SG

Tel: 0322 64312
Fax: 0322 21489

Our Ref:

Your Ref:

28 February 19-

P Faulkner & Sons
Chestnut Avenue
Southampton
SO2 4AG

Dear Sirs

With reference to your telephone enquiry today, I have pleasure in enclosing our illustrated catalogue and quoting you for supplying tarpaulins made to the very best standards and quality. We supply tarpaulins in grey, blue, green and yellow colours in four sizes, as follows:

Cat No		Price £
100	4 metres x 3 metres	110.00
101	4 metres x 4 metres	130.00
102	4 metres x 5 metres	150.00
103	4 metres x 6 metres	170.00

The price includes delivery costs but excludes VAT and I am pleased to offer you favourable terms of a 5% trade discount and the payment of net cash within one month after delivery. Delivery can be arranged within 21 days of receipt of order.

I shall be pleased to supply any further information you may require and in the meantime I look forward to receiving an order from you which will receive our prompt attention.

Yours faithfully
QUALITY PRODUCTS plc

J Black
Marketing Manager

enc

Registered in England (No. 14386) at 224 Hill Park Avenue, Derby DE8 4SG , Derby DE8 4SG

Fig 3.31

DELIVERY NOTE

Quality Products plc
224 Hill Park Avenue
Derby
DE8 4SG

Delivered to:

P Faulkner & Sons
Chestnut Avenue
SOUTHAMPTON

Date of despatch: 18 March 19—

Number of packages	Description	Order No
TWO	Grey Tarpaulins	xxx dated 4.3.19—

Received in good order and condition

Customer's signature ....Jones........

Fig 3.32

INVOICE

No. 8923

QUALITY PRODUCTS plc
224 Hill Park Avenue
Derby
DE8 4SG

Tel: 0322 64312
Fax: 0322 21489

VAT Registration No: 234 012236

Date: 18 March 19—

Goods received	RD / JH
Price terms	
Extensions	
PDB folio	

To:

P Faulkner & Sons
Chestnut Avenue
Southampton
SO2 4AG

Terms: Net cash within one month after delivery
           Carriage paid

Date of despatch: 18 March 19—

Order No: xxx dated 4 March 19—

Quantity	Description	Cat No	Price each £	Cost £	VAT rate %	VAT amount £
2	Grey tarpaulins 4m × 4m	101	130.00	260.00		
	Less 5% trade discount			13.00		
				247.00	15	37.05
	Add VAT			37.05		
				284.05		

Fig 3.33

CREDIT NOTE

No. C316

QUALITY PRODUCTS plc
224 Hill Park Avenue
Derby
DE8 4SG

Tel: 0322 64312
Fax: 0322 21489

VAT Registration No: 234 012236

Date: 21 March 19–

To: ┌─────────────────────┐
       │ P Faulkner & Sons   │
       │ Chestnut Avenue   │
       │ Southampton   │
       │ SO2 4AG   │
       └─────────────────────┘

Order No: dated 4 March 19–

Quantity	Description	Cat No	Price each £	Cost £	VAT rate %	VAT amount £
1	Returned defective grey tarpaulin 4m × 4m	101	130.00	130.00	15	19.50
	Add VAT			19.50		
				149.50		

Fig 3.34

STATEMENT

QUALITY PRODUCTS plc
224 Hill Park Avenue
Derby
DE8 4SG

Tel: 0322 64312
Fax: 0322 21489

To: ┌─────────────────────┐
       │ P Faulkner & Sons   │
       │ Chestnut Avenue   │
       │ Southampton   │
       │ SO2 4AG   │
       └─────────────────────┘

Date: 31 March 19–

Terms: Net cash within one month after delivery

Date 19–	Details	Ref No	Dr £	Cr £	Balance £
March 18	Invoice	8923	284.05		284.05
21	Credit note (amended)	C316		142.02	142.03

The last amount in the balance column is the amount owing.

Fig 3.35

Document	Issued by	Issued to	Day book/ Journal	Ledger Account
1 Stores requisition	Department requesting goods	Stores		
2 Purchases requisition	Stores	Buyer		
3 Price list/Quotation	Supplier	Buyer		
4 Order	Buyer	Supplier copies to: Accounts Goods received Stores		
5 Delivery note	Supplier	Goods received		
6 Goods received note	Goods received	Accounts Buyer		
7 Invoice	Supplier	Accounts	Purchases	Cr Supplier Dr Purchases
8 Credit note	Supplier	Accounts	Purchases returns	Dr Supplier Cr Purchases returns
9 Statement of account	Supplier	Accounts		For checking
10 Payment	Accounts	Supplier	Cash payments	Dr Supplier Cr Bank

4 Sales: order and delivery procedures

Introduction

No matter how efficient a business is in purchasing its materials and manufacturing its products, no profit is made until a sale is satisfactorily negotiated and concluded. It is, therefore, vitally important that the business sells effectively and that the business markets the goods which the consumer needs and is prepared to pay for.

The process of selling goods on credit may involve the following stages:

	Document
1 Promotion of sales by supplying potential customers with details of goods offered for sale	*Catalogue/price list* *Quotation* *Estimate*
2 Purchaser asks for goods to be supplied	*Order*
3 Order confirmed	*Acknowledgement of order*
4 Advice of delivery/despatch	*Advice/despatch note*
5 Purchaser notified of the cost of goods sold – for entry in accounts	*Invoice*
6 If goods are returned or an allowance is made, purchaser is informed of credit given – for entry in accounts	*Credit note*
7 Purchaser notified of the total amount due to be paid and payment requested	*Statement*
8 Purchaser pays seller the amount owing	*Cheque or alternative method of payment*
9 Payment acknowledged, i.e. if cash is paid or payer requests a receipt for payment by cheque	*Receipt*
10 Remittance paid into the bank account	*Bank paying-in slip*

Recall: The reasons why these documents are necessary – see page 9.

4.1 Promoting sales

Faulkner's sales promotion campaign involves exhibitions, press advertising and the mailing of sales literature and catalogues. They show their range of products at exhibitions in various parts of the country and sometimes abroad. The Advertising Section of the Sales Department regularly advertises in *Camping and Caravanning* and other journals for retailers in the trade; the national newspapers also carry the firm's advertisements for mail-order business. Sales representatives are employed in different parts of the country to call on established distributors to stimulate an interest in the firm's products. Catalogues and price lists are prepared by the Advertising Section for distribution to potential customers. Faulkner issues a separate price list (Fig 1.7) and reference will need to be made to this in some of the transactions which follow.

Any customer requesting goods which require modifications and are not included in the normal range or who request special terms are supplied with *quotations*. A quotation may be sent in a letter or it may be a standard form as in Fig 4.1. Note that the price and terms are offered for a stated period. The quotation is used to specify a price for supplying goods or services and the terms of payment being offered.

An *estimate* differs from a quotation in that the final cost can vary from the 'estimated' price. It is usually supplied when work such as building or repairing has to be undertaken.

When offering to supply goods on credit to a new customer, a credit control clerk will normally obtain trade and bank references, to find out if the firm is creditworthy, i.e. it can be relied upon to pay for goods after delivery (usually once a month). A new customer would be asked to supply the name and address of their bank and possibly another trader to whom reference may be made. When this information is received Faulkner will arrange for its bank to make enquiries from the new customer's bank concerning their client's financial standing. Faulkner may also write direct to the trader for a trade reference. Further information concerning credit control is given on page 60.

Example

Prepare a quotation to Brentfords plc (one of Faulkner's regular customers) for supplying 60 Faulkner Major frame tents in orange and gold colours to a modified size given in a drawing submitted by the company.

QUOTATION   No PC123

P FAULKNER & SONS
Chestnut Avenue, Southampton   SO2 4AG

Telephone: 0703 7654321   Telex: 51 7812

Bankers: Midland Bank plc, Southampton

Date 1 May 19--

To: Brentfords plc
     Weston House
     Piccadilly
     London W1V 9PA

In reply to your enquiry dated 28 April 19- we have pleasure in quoting you for the following

60 'Faulkner Major' frame tents in orange and gold supplied to a modified size
as per your drawing @ £260.00 each
(offer valid for 3 months from this date)

Terms: Net cash within one month after delivery
          Price includes delivery costs but excludes VAT
          Trade discount: 15%
          Delivery: 2 months on receipt of order.

We look forward to receiving your instructions which will receive our prompt attention.

D Faulkner

Sales Manager

Fig 4.1 A quotation

TASKS

1

P Faulkner & Sons has received an enquiry from R Barber & Son, Tower House, Sale, Manchester M24 12S, for supplying 20 Mount Farley rucksacks in orange (not offered from stock). These can be supplied at the special price of £23 each, excluding VAT, and with 10 per cent trade discount. Free delivery in one month. Terms of payment as given in the standard price list. Quotation valid for 2 months.

Prepare the quotation which Faulkner would send to R Barber & Son in answer to this enquiry. (*Continued: Task 3, Unit 4.2.*)

2

Design an illustrated catalogue for the Faulkner range of caravans.

3

You are employed at P Faulkner & Sons and are required to undertake the following tasks in connection with the letter received from Leisure Products Ltd (Fig 4.2):

a Write a letter to Faulkner's bank requesting a bank reference for Leisure Products Ltd.

b Prepare a quotation to Leisure Products Ltd for David Faulkner's signature and include the following:

> quote the list price
> price includes delivery but excludes VAT
> trade discount of 12½%
> net cash within one month after delivery (subject to satisfactory bank reference)
> delivery: 6 weeks on receipt of order
> offer valid for 3 months from date of quotation
> (*Continued: Task 4, Unit 4.2.*)

LEISURE PRODUCTS LTD

49 Upper Mill Street

Stockport

SK7 6DR

Tel: 061–326 0142   Telex: 362189   Fax: 061–326 9816

Our Ref: JLT/RN

1 January 19–

P Faulkner & Sons
Chestnut Avenue
Southampton
SO2 4AG

Dear Sirs

Will you please quote us your most favourable terms for supplying ten of your Faulkner Ace range of caravans. If you are able to supply these promptly to our satisfaction and you can give us acceptable discount and credit facilities, we would expect to place further orders with you on a regular basis.

Our bank, Lloyds Bank plc at 18 Market Square, Stockport, may be approached concerning our financial standing.

We look forward to receiving your quotation as soon as possible.

Yours faithfully
LEISURE PRODUCTS LTD

John Turner

John L Turner
Purchasing Manager

Fig 4.2

4 (telephone icon)

Telephone the information requested by Edna Davies in the message form, using your training office telephone.

```
┌────────────────────────────────────────────┐
│              MESSAGE FOR                    │
│                                             │
│  M   SALES OFFICE                           │
│                                             │
│           WHILE YOU WERE OUT                │
│                                             │
│  M   EDNA DAVIES                            │
│                                             │
│  OF  2347 High Street, Swansea, SA6 1H      │
│                                             │
│  TELEPHONE NO.  0792-487632                 │
│                                             │
│  ┌──────────────────┬───┬──────────────┬──┐│
│  │ TELEPHONED       │ ✓ │ PLEASE RING  │ ✓││
│  ├──────────────────┼───┼──────────────┼──┤│
│  │ CALLED TO SEE YOU│   │ WILL CALL    │  ││
│  │                  │   │ AGAIN        │  ││
│  ├──────────────────┼───┼──────────────┼──┤│
│  │ WANTS TO SEE YOU │   │ URGENT       │ ✓││
│  └──────────────────┴───┴──────────────┴──┘│
│                                             │
│  MESSAGE:                                   │
│    Please supply the current price of the   │
│    Faulkner Ranger                          │
│    Ridge Tents.   Is there a delivery       │
│    charge and do you                        │
│    allow a trade discount if she orders     │
│    six tents? She would                     │
│    also like to know the terms of payment.  │
│                                             │
│                                             │
│  DATE  15 February 19—    TIME  0930        │
│  RECEIVED BY   T. Brown                     │
└────────────────────────────────────────────┘
```

Fig 4.3

4.2 Receiving orders

When orders are received from customers they are stamped with a rubber stamp to ensure that a set procedure is followed. You will see the rubber-stamp impression on the order form (Fig 4.4) which was received from Brentfords plc in response to the quotation sent to them.

The procedure for handling incoming orders, controlled by the rubber-stamped impression, is as follows.

```
┌──────────────────────────────────────────────┐
│        Order                      No 1089     │
│ ┌──────────────────────┬─────────────────────┐│
│ │ From: Brentfords plc │ To:  P Faulkner &   ││
│ │   Weston House,      │      Sons           ││
│ │   Piccadilly,        │      Chestnut Avenue││
│ │   London W1V 9PA     │      Southampton    ││
│ │                      │      SO2 4AG        ││
│ │  Telephone:          │                     ││
│ │  071-432 5819        │                     ││
│ └──────────────────────┴─────────────────────┘│
│                   Date: 8 May 19—             │
│                                               │
│ Please supply:                                │
│                                               │
│ Sixty (60) 'Faulkner Major' frame tents       │
│ as per your quotation Ref PC123 dated         │
│ 1 May 19—   @ £260 each                       │
│                                               │
│ Deliver to: Our store at 149 High Street,     │
│             Woking, Surrey                    │
│                                               │
│ ┌─────────────────────────┬──────┐            │
│ │ Credit approval         │  mw  │  R Roberts │
│ │ Order checked           │  TB  │            │
│ │ Confirmation of order   │  TB  │   Buyer    │
│ │ Order entered           │  JR  │            │
│ └─────────────────────────┴──────┘            │
└──────────────────────────────────────────────┘
```

Fig 4.4 An incoming order

1 Credit approval

When an order is received a check is carried out, to be reasonably sure that the customer will pay for the goods on the due date. If a customer fails to pay, this can result in a bad debt, which is a serious matter as the firm not only loses the profit but also the cost of the goods and the VAT charged. The first step to be taken when an order is received is to refer to the records of customers to see if the firm has dealt with the customer before. An extract from these (A to D section), provided in a strip indexing system, is given in Fig 1.5. If the firm has traded with the customer before, as in the case of Brentfords plc, the sales ledger will reveal if they were a satisfactory payer; if not, then payment before despatch of the order would probably be insisted upon. Where a new customer is involved and the order is above a predetermined amount (in Faulkner's case this is £500), a check is made on the customer's creditworthiness. The procedure is to ask the customer to supply references as referred to on page 55. It may be established that a customer is 'good for

£500' but not for £2000, in which case the credit is granted at the lower figure. If all is in order, the credit approval box on the order is initialled and a new index strip is prepared for the records of customers.

2 Order checked

When initialled, this box indicates that the details on the order have been checked to make sure that they agree with the current price list and terms or with a special quotation.

3 Confirmation of order

All orders are confirmed and acknowledged as soon as possible after receipt. An internal number is allocated to the order which is used for identification purposes on all documents relating to it. Five copies of the confirmation order (Fig 4.5) – or works order – are prepared

for the following distribution:

1 Customer (in this case Brentfords plc)
2 Sales Department for entering in the order book and file
3 Works Department for manufacturing the goods; or Stores Section if delivery is from stock
4 Despatch Section to prepare for delivery
5 Costing Section for checking the costs

The order from the customer is stapled behind the Sales Department's copy of the confirmation of order.

4 Order entered

An initial in this box on the order signifies that the order has been entered in the order book (Fig 4.6) so that its progress can be checked and to ensure that delivery is made on time.

Confirmation of Order

P FAULKNER & SONS
Chestnut Avenue
Southampton
SO2 4AG

Order No S63729
(Please quote in all correspondence)

Telephone: 0703 – 7654321
Telex: 517812

To: Brentfords plc
    Weston House,
    Piccadilly,
    London W1V 9PA

Date: 10 May 19—

We wish to confirm your order No 1089 Dated 8 May 19—
      ~~Telephoned~~

Quantity	Description	Cat No	Price
60	'Faulkner Major' frame tents as per our quotation PC123	734T	£260 each excluding VAT Delivered Woking

Terms: Net cash within one month after delivery
       15% trade discount

Delivery: 8 July 19—
     to your order at 149 High Street, Woking, Surrey

For P FAULKNER & SONS
Signed ...*D Faulkner*......
        Sales Manager

Fig 4.5 Confirmation of order form received from Brentfords plc

Order Book						
Date: 10 May 19--						
Order No	Customer	Quantity	Cat No	Delivery	Comments	Delivered
S63720	Arnold & Baker	10	79C	8/7/19---	Send by BR	
S63721	Attwood Camping Distributors plc	6	754T	9/7/19--		
		6	774T	9/7/19--		
S63722	Bell & Sons	50	523T	10/7/19--	Send by van	
		40	553T	10/7/19--	Send by van	
S63723	Brown & Co Ltd	10	27R	8/7/19--		
S63724	Hugh Charles	8	79C	9/7/19--		
S63725	David Coleman (Sports Equipment) Ltd	10	523T)	8/7/19--		
		10	553T)			
S63726	Carters Sports	20	754T	7/7/19--		
S63727	Chudleigh & Sons	3	13SB	8/7/19--	To be collected	
S63728	I N Credit & Co	6	523T	10/7/19--		
S63729	Brentfords plc	60	734T	8/7/19--		

Fig 4.6 An order book showing entry of Brentfords plc's order

Credit control

A sale is not complete until the transaction is finally paid for. The delivery of the goods and despatch of the invoice, still less the receipt of an order, does not constitute a completed sale. It is vital that everything is done to ensure that payment is received and bad debts avoided; in a bad debt not only is the profit lost but the VAT may have to be paid by the seller to Customs and Excise. Furthermore, as the cost of the goods may be 10 times the profit, e.g. cost £100 + profit £10 = selling price £110, 10 sales of the same value would be needed simply to recover the cost from one bad debt. Credit control is, therefore, essential and this entails:

1 Obtaining trade and bank references to discover if customers are creditworthy – further details of credit approval were given on page 55.

2 Drawing up a schedule of customers with the amounts owing for each transaction at the end of the month.
3 Marking the items off when paid.
4 Transferring the amounts in 'arrears' columns when necessary, i.e. one month overdue, etc.
5 Sending additional reminders to the customers.
6 When an account is three months overdue, sending a memorandum to Sarah Faulkner, advising her of the situation.

An extract from the schedule of customers at 30 June is given in Fig 4.7. Several items are deleted to indicate that cheques have been received at 14 July 19–, but I N Credit & Co has not paid the £34 which was owing by them as long ago as 1 January (although it still appears in the 3 months' overdue column).

Schedule of Customers A to D				30 June 19--
Customer	3 months overdue	2 months overdue	1 month overdue	Current
	£	£	£	£
N K Aldous & Sons			67.00	73.00 47.00
J G Andrews			54.00	120.00
Bailey Bros			63.00	225.00 76.00
I N Credit & Co	34.00			

Fig 4.7 Schedule of customers

Several statements and reminders have been sent to them. Sarah Faulkner has telephoned and written to them and in spite of promises by the firm to pay, no payment has been made. At this stage Sarah might decide to consult the firm's solicitors with a view to legal proceedings being taken to recover the debt due.

TASKS

1

Prepare confirmations of orders for the following orders received today, using your own reference numbers (the addresses are given in the records of customers (Fig 1.5) and the prices and terms are given in the price list (Fig 1.7). (*Continued: Task 1, Unit 4.3.*)

N K Aldous & Sons
30 'Arctic 44' sleeping bags
20 'Temperate 38' sleeping bags
Prompt delivery (delivered two days after receipt of order)

Baldwin Stores Ltd
10 'Faulkner Expedition' ridge tents
15 'Faulkner Ranger' ridge tents
Delivery in one month

David Coleman (Sports Equipment) Ltd
30 'Mount Farley' rucksacks
20 'Rover' rucksacks
30 'Guider' rucksacks
40 'Faulkner Major' frame tents
30 'Faulkner Minor' frame tents
Delivery: rucksacks in one month
frame tents in two months

2

Enter the orders received in task 1 into an order book. (*Continued: Task 1, Unit 4.3.*)

3

An order (No 19867) dated 1 March 19— is received from R Barber & Son for the goods quoted in Task 1, Unit 4.1 (page 57). You are required to complete a confirmation of order for distribution at P Faulkner & Son. (*Continued: Task 2, Unit 4.3.*)

4

The order given in Fig 4.8 (see page 62) has been received from Leisure Products Ltd as a result of the quotation prepared in Task 3 of Unit 4.1. A satisfactory bank reference was received for this company. You are required to check the order and, if correct, prepare the confirmation of order for this transaction. (*Continued: Task 3, Unit 4.3.*)

5

Every business which sells goods on credit wishes to avoid bad debts. Describe the steps which may be taken before a new customer is allowed credit.

How may the customer be treated if his creditworthiness is a matter of doubt? (*RSA BK1*)

6

a Copy out the credit control schedule of debtors as at 31 July 19— illustrated (Fig 4.9). Then deal with the cheques received 7 August 19—, by deleting the appropriate amounts on your schedule.

Cheques received on 7 August 19—

	£
N K Aldous & Sons	47.00
J G Andrews	120.00
Bailey Bros	76.00 (Current)
I N Credit	10.00
Dreamland Ltd	196.00

b Rewrite the schedule for 31 August by moving the remaining figures back one month (except for the three months overdue) and adding into the current column:

	£
N K Aldous & Sons	120.00
J G Andrews	150.00
Dreamland Ltd	130.00

Check your figures by adding the schedule vertically (down) and horizontally (across) and double check the total by adding the new current items to the total for 31 July and subtracting the cheques received.

ORDER

No 843

Leisure Products Ltd
49 Upper Mill Street, Stockport, SK7 6DR

Tel: 061-326 0142   Telex: 362189   Fax: 061-326 9816

Date: 10 January 19—

To: P Faulkner & Sons
       Chestnut Avenue
       Southampton
       SO2 4AG

Quantity	Description	Cat No	Price each
10	Faulkner Ace Caravans Carriage paid	FA15	£ 5000.00

Deliver by Road to the above address not later than 24 February 19—.

For LEISURE PRODUCTS LTD

JKTurner

Purchasing Manager

Fig 4.8

Schedule of debtors   A to D   as at 31 July 19—

Customer	3 months overdue	2 months overdue	1 month overdue	Current	Totals
	£	£	£	£	£
N K Aldous & Sons			47.00	102.00	149.00
J G Andrews			120.00	76.70	196.70
Bailey Bros			76.00	76.00	152.00
I N Credit	34.00				34.00
Donald Dentford		127.60		79.00	206.60
Dreamland Ltd	120.00	76.00	54.00		250.00
	154.00	203.60	297.00	333.70	988.30

Fig 4.9

7  **Priority**

Deal with the urgent note left on your desk by
Sarah Faulkner.

URGENT

Please give me a note
of any customers who
are 3 months overdue
in paying their accounts
and the amounts involved.

SF

31.8.19—

4.3 Advising despatch of goods

When the order is made up it is transferred from the Works or Stores to the Despatch Section who have already received notification of it by the copy of the confirmation of order. At this stage the despatch clerk prepares an advice/despatch note (Fig 4.10) to inform the customer that the order has been despatched or is ready for despatch. A copy of the advice/despatch note is passed to the sales ledger section of the Accounts Department so that they can prepare the invoice set (as explained in Unit 5.1) and record the delivery in the order book.

Advice/Despatch Note

P FAULKNER & SONS, Chestnut Avenue, Southampton SO2 4AG
Telephone: 0703 7654321   Telex: 517812

To: Brentfords plc   Reference: Order S63729
     Weston House
     Piccadilly   Date: 6 July 19–
     London W1V 9PA

We wish to advise you that your order dated 8 May 19– has been/~~is ready to be~~ despatched

Quantity	Description	Cat No
60	'Faulkner Major' frame tents	734T

For P FAULKNER & SONS

.... J Jones ....

Order Book

Date: 10 May 19–

Order No	Customer	Quantity	Cat No	Delivery	Comments	Delivered
S63720	Arnold & Baker	10	79C	8/7/19–	Send by BR	7/7/19–
S63721	Attwood Camping Distributors plc	6	754T	9/7/19–		9/7/19–
		6	774T	9/7/19–		9/7/19–
S63722	Bell & Sons	50	523T	10/7/19–	Send by van	9/7/19–
		40	553T	10/7/19–	Send by van	9/7/19–
S63723	Brown & Co Ltd	10	27R	8/7/19–		7/7/19–
S63724	Hugh Charles	8	79C	9/7/19–		9/7/19–
S63725	David Coleman (Sports Equipment) Ltd	10	523T	8/7/19–		6/7/19–
		10	553T	8/7/19–		6/7/19–
S63726	Carters Sports	20	754T	7/7/19–		6/7/19–
S63727	Chudleigh & Sons	3	13SB	8/7/19–	To be collected	
S63728	I N Credit & Co	6	523T	10/7/19–		
S63729	Brentfords plc	60	734T	8/7/19–		6/7/19–

Fig 4.10 Despatch of tents to Brentfords plc

TASKS

1

Prepare advice notes for the goods ordered by N K Aldous & Sons, Baldwin Stores Ltd and David Coleman (Sports Equipment) Ltd in Task 1 of Unit 4.2 and enter the date of delivery (3 weeks after receipt of orders) in the order book prepared for Task 2 of Unit 4.2. (*Continued: Task 1, Unit 5.1.*)

2

Prepare an advice note for the goods ordered by R Barber & Son in Task 3 of Unit 4.2 and delivered by van on 28 March 19—. (*Continued: Task 3, Unit 5.1.*)

3

The caravans ordered by Leisure Products Ltd in Task 4 of Unit 4.2 were despatched on 20 February 19—. Complete an advice note on this date and make the entry for this transaction in an order book. (*Continued: Task 4, Unit 5.1.*)

4

Reply to the following message left on the telephone answering machine:

Message from: Mr R Roberts, Buyer of Brentfords plc.

'*Please telephone as soon as possible to give me the date when the sixty Faulkner Major frame tents are to be despatched.*'

5 Sales: accounting procedures

5.1 Preparing and recording sales invoices

Sales invoices are prepared by the sales invoice clerk in the sales ledger section. This section is much larger than the purchases ledger section because the firm has to deal with about 3000 orders annually and prepare the same number of sales invoices (10 times as many as the purchases ledger section). Although most of these are 'repeat orders' from the same customers, there are often as many as 200 accounts open at one time in the busy season from March to August. In order to spread the work out the sales ledger is divided into three sections, i.e. for customers A–D, E–L and M–Z. An extract of the customers' records at 1 January for the A–D section is given in Fig 1.5.

The sales invoices are prepared in 'sets' in one typing; alternatively, they can be prepared by a computer. The diagram (Fig 5.1) shows how the 'set' is distributed.

The following procedure is adopted for preparing the sales invoice set:

1 The advice/despatch note is received from the stores section.
2 The copy order is extracted from the sales order file to obtain the prices and terms.
3 The sales invoice clerk calculates the prices on the invoice in readiness for typing.
4 Trade discount (referred to in the quotation and also in the price list) is deducted from the list price *before* VAT is calculated.

   The amount of VAT is calculated on the discounted value of the goods, including cash discount where appropriate. (The discounted value is the price as given in the price list less any discounts.)

   The rate and amount of VAT are shown in separate columns against the items to which they refer(see Fig 5.2).

   VAT is added to the net value of the goods to arrive at the net value of the invoice.
5 The quantities, terms and extensions are checked by another member of staff in the invoice section. A print calculator is useful for doing this.
6 The invoice set is typed using carbon paper or NCR (no carbon required) paper to reproduce the copies.

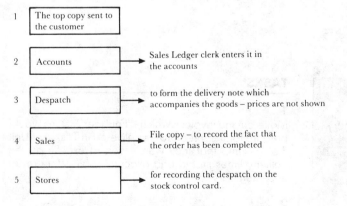

1 | The top copy sent to the customer

2 | Accounts → Sales Ledger clerk enters it in the accounts

3 | Despatch → to form the delivery note which accompanies the goods – prices are not shown

4 | Sales → File copy – to record the fact that the order has been completed

5 | Stores → for recording the despatch on the stock control card.

Additional copies may be required for representatives, statistics and market research.

Fig 5.1

INVOICE

No 1624

From: P FAULKNER & SONS, Chestnut Avenue, Southampton SO2 4AG

Tel: 0703 7654321

Telex: 517812

VAT Registration No 304 3739 11

Date: 8 July 19—

To:

Brentfords plc
Weston House
Piccadilly
London W1V 9PA

Terms: Net cash within one month after delivery
Delivered Woking

Completion of Order No 1089 dated 8 May 19—

Quantity	Description	Cat No	Price each £	Cost £	VAT rate %	VAT amount £
60	'Faulkner Major' frame tents	734T	260.00	15600.00		
	Less trade discount 15%			2340.00		
				13260.00	15	1989.00
	Plus VAT			1989.00		
				15249.00		
	Delivered 6/7/19— by our van to your order at 149 High Street, Woking					

Fig 5.2 Example – the sales invoice prepared for Brentfords' order

---

TASKS

1

Make out the invoices which P Faulkner & Sons would prepare for the three orders delivered in Task 1 of Unit 4.3. Assume that they were invoiced exactly on the delivery times stated and allocate appropriate reference numbers.

2

Prepare invoices dated 10 July 19— for the following customers (see page 67). Refer to the price list (Fig 1.7), the customer records on Fig 1.5 and the order book on page 63 for relevant data.

Customer	Order No	Quantity	Cat No	Invoice No
Arnold & Baker	S63720	10	79C	1629
Attwood Camping Distributors plc	S63721	6	754T ⎱	1630
		6	774T ⎰	
Bell & Sons	S63722	50	523T ⎱	1631
		40	553T ⎰	
Brown & Co Ltd	S63723	10	27R	1632
Hugh Charles	S63724	8	79C	1633
David Coleman (Sports Equipment) Ltd	S63725	10	523T ⎱	1634
		10	553T ⎰	

(*Continued: Task 7 (page 70.*)

3

Prepare an invoice dated 28 March 19— to R Barber & Son in respect of the rucksacks delivered in Task 2 of Unit 4.3. (*Continued: Task 13.*)

4

Complete an invoice on 21 February 19— to Leisure Products Ltd for the caravans despatched in Task 3 of Unit 4.3. (*Continued: Task 14.*)

5

Use a computer accounting package to set up the customer records of P Faulkner & Sons (Fig 1.5) and key in the data given in Task 2 above to produce printouts for the invoices. (*Continued: Task 15.*)

6  **Priority**

(*Continued: Task 6, Unit 5.2*)

Please check my calculations in this invoice before I type it. Joan

INVOICE

..., Southampton SO2 4AG

No 1985

...e: 0703 7654321

Telex: 517812

VAT Registration No 304 373911

Date: 1 July 19—

To:

> Edna Davies
> 2347 High Street
> Swansea
> S. Wales
> SA6 JH

Terms: *Net cash within one month after delivery*
Delivered Swansea

Completion of Order No 416 dated 20 June 19—

Quantity	Description	Cat No	Price each £	Cost £	VAT rate %	VAT amount £
12	Arctic 44 Sleeping Bags	135B	16·50	198·00		
6	Temperate 38 Sleeping Bags	145B	14·25	85·50		
3	Junior 36 Sleeping Bags	155B	13·10	39·30		
				328·80		
	Less trade discount 5%			16·44		
				312·36	15	46·85
	Plus VAT			46·85		
				359·21		
	Delivered by van on 30 June 19—					

Fig 5.3

Sales day book and ledger

The sales ledger contains the personal accounts of all the firm's customers (debtors). Only goods sold on credit are entered in the sales day book; cash sales are entered in the bank account, and the sale on credit of assets, such as surplus furniture or equipment, would be entered in a separate journal. The procedure involved in entering sales on credit in the day book and ledger accounts is as follows:

1 Enter the copy sales invoice in the sales day book as in the example given.
2 Transfer the total value of the invoice to the debit column of Brentfords' account in the sales ledger as they *received* the goods and are, therefore, *debtors*, i.e. customers who owe the firm for goods supplied.

3 At the end of the month the three columns of the sales day book are totalled. The total for the net value of the goods is credited to the sales account and the total of the VAT output tax is credited to the VAT account in the nominal ledger. The VAT account will have both debit and credit entries and may have a debit balance or, as would be expected in the case of P Faulkner & Sons, a credit balance because the value of their sales would normally exceed the value of their purchases and expenses.

Recall: Guidelines for entering in ledger accounts – see page 28.

An example of the procedure involved in entering the invoice to Brentfords' account is given in Fig 5.4.

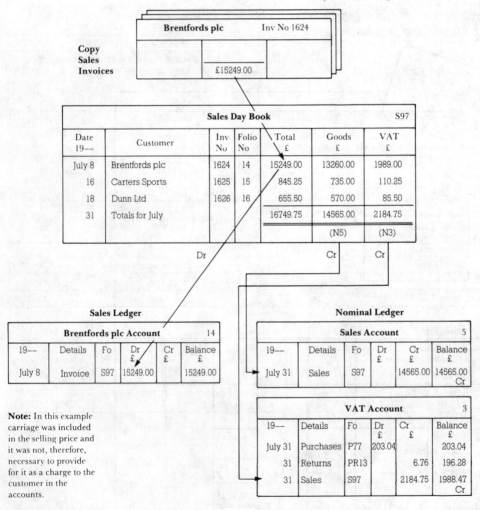

Note: In this example carriage was included in the selling price and it was not, therefore, necessary to provide for it as a charge to the customer in the accounts.

Fig 5.4 Procedure for dealing with sales invoices

Example

Question

On 1 September 19— Faulkner's debtors included Baldwin Stores Ltd £80.40, Hugh Charles £214.00 and Dreamland Ltd £105.08. During September the credit transactions with these customers were as follows:

Date	Customer	Inv No	Amount £
Sept 3	Hugh Charles	50	105.00
21	Baldwin Stores Ltd	51	62.80
29	Dreamland Ltd	52	400.20

These transactions are subject to VAT at the standard rate.

You are required to enter these transactions in the sales day book and post them to the customers' personal accounts in the sales ledger and the relevant accounts in the nominal ledger.

Answer

Sales Day Book							S100
Date 19–	Customer	Inv No	Fo No	Total £	Goods £	VAT £	
Sept 3	Hugh Charles	50	2	120.75	105.00	15.75	
21	Baldwin Stores Ltd	51	1	72.22	62.80	9.42	
28	Dreamland Ltd	52	3	460.23	400.20	60.03	
30	Totals for September			653.20	568.00	85.20	
					(21)	(22)	

Sales Ledger

19–	Details	Fo	Dr	Cr	Balance
		Baldwin Stores Ltd Account			1
			£	£	£
Sept 1	Balance	b/d			80.40
21	Invoice	S100	72.22		152.62
		Hugh Charles Account			2
			£	£	£
Sept 1	Balance	b/d			214.00
3	Invoice	S100	120.75		334.75
		Dreamland Ltd Account			3
			£	£	£
Sept 1	Balance	b/d			105.08
28	Invoice	S100	460.23		565.31

Nominal Ledger

19–	Details	Fo	Dr	Cr	Balance
		Sales Account			21
			£	£	£
Sept 1	Balance	b/d			347.37 Cr
30	Invoices	S100		568.00	915.37 Cr
		VAT Account			22
			£	£	£
Sept 1	Balance	b/d			52.11 Cr
30	Sales	S100		85.20	137.31 Cr

Computerised sales records

A computerised sales ledger holds a record for each customer. To issue an invoice and enter it in the customer's account the following would be keyed into a computer:

- account ID number, i.e. customer's account number
- description of transaction, such as invoice or payment
- order number – to recall details of the goods ordered and cost

The current date is automatically inserted and trade discount and VAT amounts are calculated from the sum given with the order.

When an invoice is entered, the stock position is checked and updated, and if the goods are available immediately, an invoice is produced.

The sales ledger account is updated at the same time as the invoice or credit note is prepared. Up-to-date statements can be printed out, therefore, at any time during the financial period.

When all the invoices for a day have been completed, the computer can be instructed to print out:

- the daily total of sales and, if necessary, the total sales for each country, region or division
- the totals of each product sold
- the totals of each product remaining in stock after the day's sales.

A sales ledger account will normally hold the following data:

- account number
- account name and address
- credit limit
- payment history to bring to light any outstanding debts
- special delivery instructions
- all transactions in the current year or other period
- cumulative total of orders placed by the customer

The sales ledger sub-menus will normally contain:

- preparation of invoices and their entry in customers' accounts
- preparation of credit notes and their entry in customers' accounts
- entry of receipts in customers' accounts
- printing statements
- printing sales day books and sales returns day books
- printing cash and VAT accounts
- sales analysis

PERFORMANCE CHECK

When recording invoices in the sales day book and ledger accounts:
- comply with the guidelines given on page 28
- be accurate in transferring the correct amounts and calculating the correct balances
- use the correct books and accounts
- complete entries within the required deadlines

TASKS (continued from page 67)

7

Prepare sales ledger accounts for the six customers named in Task 2 of this unit. Assume that they all had nil opening balances. Enter the invoices into a sales day book and post to the customers' accounts in the sales ledger, total the sales day book and post the total of the net amount of the goods to the sales account and the VAT output charges to the VAT account in the nominal ledger.

Note: Tasks 8, 9, 10 and 11 (see page 71) are intended as a continuation of this task, using the accounts already opened together with a further eight personal accounts, but if preferred each task can be treated separately.

Enter the following sales invoices into a sales day book and post to the appropriate ledger accounts.

Date 19—	Customer	Invoice No	Total £	Goods £	VAT £
8 Week ending 5 August 19—					
Aug 1	N K Aldous & Sons	1701	454.69	395.38	59.31
1	J G Andrews	1702	39.73	34.55	5.18
2	Bailey Bros	1703	253.84	220.73	33.11
2	Bostock (DIY)	1704	132.43	115.16	17.27
3	Carters Sports	1705	397.30	345.48	51.82
4	Chudleigh & Sons	1706	129.13	112.29	16.84
5	Dreamland Ltd	1707	226.25	196.74	29.51
9 Week ending 12 August 19—					
Aug 8	J G Andrews	1708	25.39	22.08	3.31
8	Arnold & Baker	1709	84.98	73.90	11.08
9	Bailey Bros	1710	233.97	203.45	30.52
9	Carters Sports	1711	49.67	43.19	6.48
9	Chudleigh & Sons	1712	797.92	693.84	104.08
12	David Coleman (Sports Equipment) Ltd	1713	481.18	418.42	62.76
10 Week ending 19 August 19—					
Aug 15	N K Aldous & Sons	1714	16.56	14.40	2.16
16	Bailey Bros	1715	588.45	511.70	76.75
16	Bostock (DIY)	1716	879.81	765.05	114.76
16	Carters Sports	1717	123.61	107.49	16.12
16	David Coleman (Sports Equipment) Ltd	1718	51.88	45.11	6.77
17	Dreamland Ltd	1719	633.04	550.47	82.57
18	Dunn (Sports Outfitters) Ltd	1720	476.77	414.58	62.19
11 Week ending 26 August 19—					
Aug 22	Arnold & Baker	1721	1663.15	1446.22	216.93
22	Bailey Bros	1722	254.94	221.69	33.25
22	Bostock (DIY)	1723	55.19	47.99	7.20
24	Carters Sports	1724	840.96	731.27	109.69
25	Chudleigh & Sons	1725	1232.74	1071.95	160.79
25	Dreamland Ltd	1726	4422.17	3845.37	576.80
25	Dunn (Sports Outfitters) Ltd	1727	764.81	665.05	99.76

(*Continued: Task 1, Unit 5.2.*)

12

Using the same sales ledger and nominal ledger accounts as in the example on page 69, enter the opening balances for 1 October 19—. During October Faulkner's credit transactions with these customers were as follows:

Date	Customer	Inv No	Goods amount £
October 5	Dreamland Ltd	53	129.70
6	Hugh Charles	54	22.00
19	Baldwin Stores Ltd	55	1100.00
26	Hugh Charles	56	240.40

These transactions were subject to VAT at the standard rate.

Enter them in the sales day book and post them to the customers' personal accounts and the sales and VAT accounts.

13

Enter the invoice sent to R Barber & Son (in Task 3 on page 67 of this unit) in a sales day book and post it to Barber's account in the sales ledger. (*Continued: Task 5, Unit 5.4.*)

14

Enter the invoice sent to Leisure Products Ltd in Task 4 of this unit in a sales day book and post it to the Leisure Products Ltd account in the sales ledger. (*Continued: Task 3, Unit 5.2.*)

15

As a continuation of Task 5 of this unit, use a computer package to enter the sales invoices in Tasks 7, 8, 9, 10 and 11 for July and August and print out the customers' accounts at the end of August. (*Continued: Task 5, Unit 5.2.*)

16

Reply to a telephone request from David Faulkner, who asks you to look at the accounts in your book and let him know how much Brentfords owe the firm and when they can be expected to pay it.

5.2 Preparing and recording credit notes

The Purchases Department occasionally has to deal with returns in respect of goods sent back to suppliers or for claims on them for complaints such as short delivery, i.e. below the invoiced quantity, inferior quality, damaged goods and invoice errors (see page 31). Whatever the reason for the 'return', the supplier has to provide a credit note and the transaction is called a *purchases return*.

P Faulkner & Sons was itself also required to supply a credit note when a claim for an allowance was agreed with a customer. Because the firm takes pride in its workmanship and goods are inspected before despatch, together with the system of checking invoices before sending them out, the need to issue credit notes is rare.

One such occasion did, however, arise in connection with the delivery of the 60 'Faulkner Major' frame tents to Brentfords plc on 8 July 19—. When Brentfords opened the packages it was discovered that some of the metal poles were bent and the stitching had split in a few places. Faulkner was not sure whether it was the fault of their driver who had helped to load them on the delivery van or whether the damage was due to careless handling by Brentfords. In any event, as Brentfords was a good regular customer and Faulkner was anxious to retain their goodwill, it was decided to agree to the return of the two damaged tents and to issue Brentfords with a credit note (Fig 5.5). Note that this document would be printed in red to draw attention to the credit effect.

Although sales returns are rare, David Faulkner insists that they are to be recorded separately and each item, even if it is only an arithmetical error, has to be brought to his attention as he is very keen to preserve the good reputation of the firm. The procedure for recording sales returns is illustrated in Fig 5.6.

CREDIT NOTE

No 12

From: P FAULKNER & SONS, Chestnut Avenue, Southampton SO2 4AG

Tel: 0703 7654321

VAT Registration No 3043739 11

Telex: 517812

Date: 28 July 19—

Ref: Invoice No 1624

dated   8/7/19—

To:
> Brentfords plc
> Weston House,
> Piccadilly,
> London W1V 9PA

Quantity	Details	Price each £	Amount £	VAT rate %	VAT amount £
2	'Faulkner Major' frame tents returned damaged	260.00 each	520.00		
	Less trade discount 15%		78.00		
			442.00	15	66.30
	Plus VAT		66.30		
			508.30		
	Received via British Rail 27 July 19—				

Fig 5.5 Credit note issued to Brentfords plc for damaged goods

The credit note is typed and checked with the original sales invoice, particular attention being paid to any trade discount which is deducted, as shown on page 66.

Four copies of the credit note are prepared, for the following reasons:

1 **Customer** receives the top copy.
2 **Accounts** (sales ledger section) copy for entry into the customer's account.
3 **Sales** copy for filing and linking with the order and invoice.
4 **Sales** copy for Sales Manager's personal attention.

The sales ledger clerk enters the copy of the credit note in the sales returns book, as in the example given in Fig 5.6. Because the goods are 'given back' by the customer their personal account is *credited* in the sales ledger, which has the effect of cancelling part of the sale and reducing the amount owing by the customer. At the end of the month the sales returns book is totalled and cross-balanced, the total value of the goods is *debited* to a sales returns account (the firm's 'receiving' account) and the total value of VAT is *debited* to a VAT account in the nominal ledger.

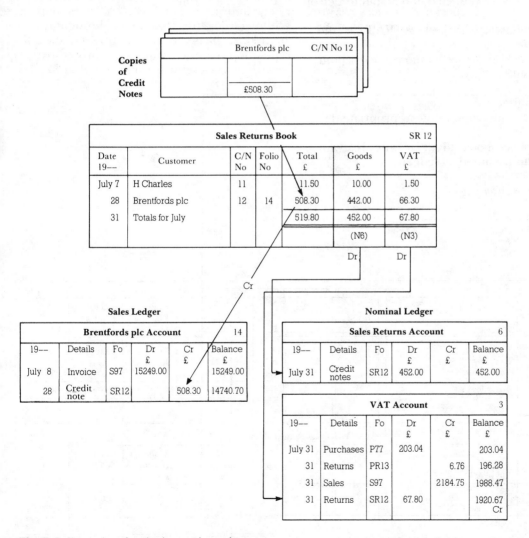

Fig 5.6 Procedure for dealing with credit notes issued to customers

Example

Question

P Faulkner & Sons arranged the following credit transactions during May 19—:

		Catalogue prices £
May 1	Purchased goods from Tape Works Ltd	1000
4	Sold goods to Arnold & Baker	2800
6	Purchased goods from Sam Beller & Sons	1600
10	Returned goods to Tape Works Ltd	400
12	Sold goods to E Davies	1500
17	Arnold & Baker returned goods sold to them on 4 May	360
19	Returned goods to Sam Beller & Sons	200
22	Purchased goods from Tape Works Ltd	1400
29	E Davies returned goods sold to her on 12 May	120

All transactions are subject to VAT at the standard rate. Trade discount of 10 per cent is allowable on all purchases but no trade discount is given on sales.

You are required to:

a enter each transaction in the appropriate day book;

b post the day book totals to the relevant accounts in the nominal ledger.

Answer (continues on page 75)

Purchases Book									P20
Date 19—	Supplier	Inv No	Fo No	Total £	Goods (gross) £	Trade Discount £	Goods (– TD) £	VAT £	
May 1	Tape Works Ltd	1	100	1035	1000	100	900	135	
6	Sam Beller & Sons	2	101	1656	1600	160	1440	216	
22	Tape Works Ltd	3	100	1449	1400	140	1260	189	
31	Totals for May			4140	4000	400	3600	540	
							(400)	(404)	

Purchases Returns Book									PR20
Date 19—	Supplier	CN No	Fo No	Total £	Goods (gross) £	Trade Discount £	Goods (– TD) £	VAT £	
May 10	Tape Works Ltd	50	100	414	400	40	360	54	
19	Sam Beller & Sons	51	101	207	200	20	180	27	
31	Totals for May			621	600	60	540	81	
							(401)	(404)	

Sales Book							S20
Date 19–	Customer	Inv No	Fo No	Total £	Goods £	VAT £	
May 4	Arnold & Baker	200	300	3220	2800	420	
12	E Davies	201	301	1725	1500	225	
31	Totals for May			4945	4300	645	
					(402)	(404)	

Sales Returns Book							SR20
Date 19–	Customer	CN No	Fo No	Total £	Goods £	VAT £	
May 17	Arnold & Baker	400	300	414	360	54	
29	E Davies	401	301	138	120	18	
31	Totals for May			552	480	72	
					(403)	(404)	

Nominal Ledger

19–	Details	Fo	Dr £	Cr £	Balance £
	Purchases Account				400
May 31	Invoices	P20	3600		3600
	Purchases Returns Account				401
May 31	Credit Notes	PR20		540	540 Cr
	Sales Account				402
May 31	Invoices	S20		4300	4300 Cr
	Sales Returns Account				403
May 31	Credit Notes	SR20	480		480
	VAT Account				404
May 31	Purchases	P20	540		540
31	Purchases Returns	PR20		81	459
31	Sales	S20		645	186 Cr
31	Sales Returns	SR20	72		114 Cr

PERFORMANCE CHECK

When preparing and recording credit notes:

- complete all essential information legibly
- record correct information from related sales invoices
- calculate extensions, discounts, etc, correctly
- be accurate in transferring the correct amounts in the sales returns book and ledger accounts and in calculating the correct balances
- use the correct books and accounts
- complete tasks within the required dead-lines

TASKS

1

This task is a continuation of Tasks 7–11 in Unit 5.1 using the same customers' accounts.

a Prepare credit notes for the customers listed below with the information supplied.

b Enter the credit notes in a sales returns book and post to the appropriate ledger accounts.

Date 19—	Customer	Credit note No	Credit note total £	Net value of goods £	VAT £	Original No	Invoice date	Reason for credit
Sept 7	Arnold & Baker	13	8.05	7.00	1.05	1709	8.8.19—	1 rucksack returned – buckles missing
14	Chudleigh & Sons	14	57.50	50.00	7.50	1712	9.8.19—	1 tent returned damaged
20	N K Aldous & Sons	15	1.15	1.00	0.15	1714	15.8.19—	Error in calculation of invoice

(*Continued: Task 2, Unit 5.4.*)

2

Enter the following documents in the appropriate day books, post to the ledger accounts, total the books at the end of the month and transfer the totals to the respective accounts in the nominal ledger. Allocate appropriate reference numbers for the documents and books.

Date	Customer	Document	Goods £	VAT £
Mar 1	Bailey Bros	Invoice	105.00	15.75
2	Brown & Co Ltd	Invoice	29.50	4.42
4	Dreamland Ltd	Invoice	64.80	9.72
8	Brown & Co Ltd	Credit note	8.00	1.20
11	Dreamland Ltd	Credit note	30.00	4.50

3

a The Accountant of Leisure Products Ltd telephones to say that his Showroom Supervisor has drawn his attention to a deep scratch on the side of one of the caravans and that it will cost £80 + VAT for the defect to be remedied. Sarah Faulkner agrees to make Leisure Products an allowance for this work to be done. Using the information recorded in the invoice in Task 4 of Unit 5.1, prepare the credit note on 28 February 19— for the necessary allowance to be made.

b Enter the credit note prepared in (*a*) in a sales returns book and post the entry to the personal ledger account prepared for Task 14 of Unit 5.1. (*Continued: Task 4, Unit 5.4.*)

4

R Hamilton is in business as a distributor of catering equipment and his credit transactions for the month of November 19— were as follows:

			£
November	1	Sold goods to R Harvey-Smith	1400
	2	Purchased goods from Vendepac plc	1250
	2	Purchased goods from Mayfair plc	2000
	5	Sold goods to Unique Traders Ltd	3800
	8	Returned goods to Vendepac plc	150
	15	Sold goods to R Harvey-Smith	840
	16	Unique Traders Ltd returned goods	60
	23	Purchased goods from Mayfair plc	1000
	25	R Harvey-Smith returned goods	140
	29	Returned goods to Mayfair plc	100

All transactions are subject to VAT at the standard rate. Trade discount of 20 per cent is allowable on all purchases but no trade discount is given on sales.

You are required to:

a enter each transaction in the appropriate day book;

b post the day book totals to the relevant accounts in the nominal ledger.

5

As a continuation of Task 15 of Unit 5.1, use a computer package to enter the credit notes in Task 1

above and print out the customers' accounts at the end of September. (*Continued: Task 5, Unit 6.1.*)

6 📞

a What would you say to Edna Davies who telephones you on 4 July 19— concerning the sleeping bags supplied on 30 June 19—. (The invoice you checked in Task 6 of Unit 5.1 refers to this consignment.)
  '*Some of the stitching on two of the Arctic 44 sleeping bags has come undone. I could have them restitched here at a cost of £5 each (plus VAT) or I could return them to you, but in either case I would expect you to make a reduction in my bill. What do you want me to do with them?*'

b Prepare the necessary paperwork to implement the decision made in (*a*).

5.3 Analysing day books

It is important for any business to know how its profit is made up. Consequently it is necessary to analyse the sales, purchases and costs into such categories as areas, countries, products, sales personnel, etc. This helps the management to be more efficient as they will be able to see those aspects of the business which make most profit or loss.

Although Sarah Faulkner could ascertain the profit from the trading and profit and loss account, she would have had little idea which products were bringing in the most profit if she had not analysed the sales of the different products. In order to see at a glance the proportion of sales for each group of products, the sales day book is analysed by using additional columns for tents, sleeping bags, rucksacks and camp beds. The example in Fig 5.7 of a columnar sales day book, based on Task 8 of Unit 5.1, shows the breakdown of the sales of £1420.33 into:

	£
Tents	820.86
Sleeping bags	375.47
Rucksacks	100.00
Camp beds	124.00
	£1420.33

The analysis takes place at the time the sales invoice is entered into the sales day book, i.e. the total value is entered twice – once in the total column and again under the product heading(s) and VAT.

A columnar purchases day book can be used to apportion costs to the different departments of a firm, as in the example given in Fig 5.8, or it may be used to analyse the cost of materials used in the manufacture of different products. The analysis totals can be posted to a total purchases account or, if required, to separate departmental or product purchases accounts.

Columnar books with analysis columns may also be used for the cash book, to provide a breakdown of receipts and payments for ledger sections, eg A–D, and the petty cash book, for analysing expenses, as explained in Unit 9.3.

Columnar Sales Day Book									
Date 19--	Customer	Inv No	Folio	Total £	Tents £	Sleeping bags £	Rucksacks £	Camp beds £	VAT £
August 1	N K Aldous & Sons	1701		454.69	395.38				59.31
1	J G Andrews	1702		39.73		34.55			5.18
2	Bailey Bros	1703		253.84	100.00	120.73			33.11
2	Bostock (DIY)	1704		132.43	80.00	35.16			17.27
3	Carters Sports	1705		397.30	245.48		100.00		51.82
4	Chudleigh & Sons	1706		129.13		88.29		24.00	16.84
5	Dreamland Ltd	1707		226.25		96.74		100.00	29.51
				£1633.37	820.86	375.47	100.00	124.00	213.04

Debit each customer

Credit Sales Account

Credit VAT Account

Total of debits = £1633.37 = £1420.33 + £213.04

Fig 5.7 Columnar sales day book

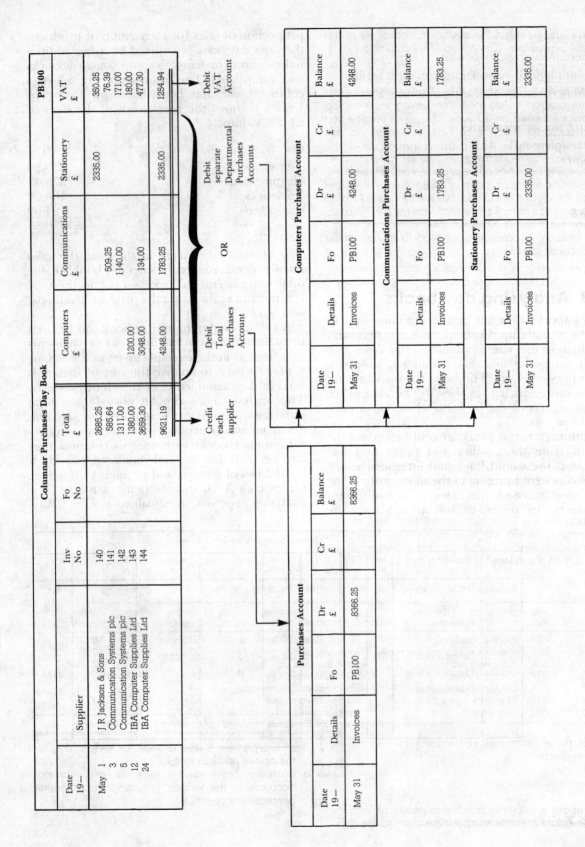

Fig 5.8 Columnar purchases day book

TASKS

1

Using the same rulings as on page 77 enter the invoices listed in Task 9 of Unit 5.1 into an analysed sales day book and cross balance. The products on the invoices were:

Invoice No	Product
1708	Sleeping bags
1709	Tents
1710	Tents
1711	Rucksacks
1712	£400 sleeping bags and £293.84 camp beds
1713	Rucksacks

2

Enter the invoices prepared in Task 2 of Unit 5.1 into an analysed sales day book, using appropriate analysis columns for the products invoiced.

3

Topshop plc is a large department store with major departments selling electrical appliances; television and radio; household products and stationery supplies. Credit purchases for the month of January 19— were:

Date	Inv No	Product	Supplier	Quantity	Price each	Trade discount
Jan 2	834	Electric supply sockets	Skylark Electrical Services	100 packs	5.00	15%
4	835	Portable colour television sets	Johnsons plc	20	300.00	10%
5	836	Stationery packs	Avon Supplies Ltd	50	2.75	12½%
10	837	Kitchen scales	P J Housewares Ltd	20	8.00	20%
17	838	Electric soldering tools	Skylark Electrical Services	40	16.00	15%
24	839	Non-stick frying pans	P J Housewares Ltd	10	18.00	20%
25	840	Staplers	Avon Supplies Ltd	60	9.50	12½%

All of these purchases are subject to VAT at the standard rate.

You are required to:

a prepare a columnar purchases day book with the necessary columns to apportion costs to the different departments and provide for VAT, and enter the above invoices in it;

b post the items to the personal and nominal accounts in the ledger, providing departmental purchases accounts.

4

Data Supplies Limited distributes three principal products: computers, computer furniture and computer consumables. Invoices for the purchase of stock are analysed in the purchases day book with analysis columns for the three products. Credit purchases for the month of December 19— were:

Date	Inv No.	Product	Supplier	Quantity	Price each £
Dec 5	116	Computer tables	Avon Computer Accessories Ltd	10	125
6	117	Floppy disks (10 per box)	Office International Ltd	200 boxes	30 per box
12	118	Microcomputers	ATR Computing Ltd	6	1400
13	119	Listing paper (1000 sheets per box)	Office International Ltd	20 boxes	35
20	120	Film ribbon cartridges for computer printers	Office International Ltd	400	6
21	121	Daisy wheel printers	ATR Computing Ltd	4	450
29	122	Swivel chairs	Avon Computer Accessories Ltd	12	90

All of these transactions are subject to VAT at the standard rate.

You are required to:
a rule up a suitable purchases day book with appropriate columns and enter the above invoices in it;
b post the entries from the day book to the personal accounts in the purchases ledger and to the purchases and VAT accounts in the nominal ledger.

Note: Separate product accounts are not required.

5

Use a computer spreadsheet package to enter the invoices listed in Tasks 10 and 11 of Unit 5.1 and calculate and print out a product analysis of sales for the period 15 August to 25 August 19—. The products on the invoices were:

Invoice No	Caravans £	Tents £	Sleeping bags £	Camp beds £	Rucksacks £
1714				14.40	
1715		511.70			
1716		600.10			164.95
1717			107.49		
1718				45.11	
1719			230.18	320.29	
1720		414.58			
1721		1246.11			200.11
1722			221.69		
1723				47.99	
1724		731.27			
1725		723.18	213.26		135.51
1726	3845.37				
1727		665.05			

Details of the entries and formulae are given on page 81.

Entries and formulae for Task 5
Enter the following headings across the top:

A INVOICE NO	B CARAVAN SALES £	C TENT SALES £	D S/BAGS SALES £	E C/BEDS SALES £	F R/SACKS SALES £	G INVOICE TOTALS £

Enter the invoice numbers as row titles followed by 'Totals' for the final row

Enter the following formulae: (as required for Lotus 1-2-3)

Invoice totals: Cell G6: @ SUM (B6..F6)
               and copy for all invoice totals
Product totals: Cell B20: @ SUM (B6..B19)
               and copy for all product totals
Note: Show all amounts with two decimal places.

6  Priority

Deal with the memo (Fig 5.9) left on your desk by Peter Faulkner's secretary.

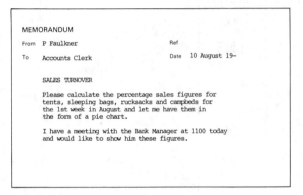

MEMORANDUM

From P Faulkner   Ref

To   Accounts Clerk   Date 10 August 19-

SALES TURNOVER

Please calculate the percentage sales figures for tents, sleeping bags, rucksacks and campbeds for the 1st week in August and let me have them in the form of a pie chart.

I have a meeting with the Bank Manager at 1100 today and would like to show him these figures.

Fig 5.9

5.4 Preparing statements

It is a curious concept of accounting that the figure of sales is used to calculate the profit, even if the money for those sales has not been received. Although a business may be making profits, unless these are translated into money the firm cannot pay its way for long and would soon be made bankrupt. This aspect of a firm's operations is, therefore, most important; no matter how many sales there are and whatever the stated profit, if the sales are not paid for there will soon be no business.

A statement of account is used to inform the customer of the total amount owing and to request payment. It is a copy of the customer's account in the sales ledger, containing a record of all transactions for a given period, usually a month.

The statement may begin with a balance brought forward from the previous period, followed by the net amount of each transaction carried out in the current period. These transactions are entered as follows:

- Invoices for sales are entered in the 'Dr' column and added to the balance.
- Credit notes for sales returns, cheques received and any cash discount allowed are entered in the 'Cr' column and deducted from the balance (see Unit 6.1 for further details of recording remittances and discount).
- The balance column is updated after every entry, the last amount in the balance column being the amount owing at the end of the period covered by the statement.

Example

The sale to Brentfords plc was due for payment on 8 August 19— but, as a credit note had been issued by P Faulkner & Sons, Brentfords was only required to pay £14 740.70 (i.e. sales £15 249.00 − £508.30 sales returns). The statement of account shown in Fig 5.10 is used to remind Brentfords plc of the net amount due for payment.

The statement, a copy of the debtor's account in the sales ledger, is not entered in any accountancy record as it is merely a reminder to the debtor to pay the amount outstanding.

A remittance advice, as shown with the statement in Fig 5.10, should be completed by the remitter, Brentfords, detached and sent to the payee, Faulkner, with the remittance. This form helps to identify the payment with the statement or invoice to which it relates, thus giving greater security when making payment and saving time for Faulkner's staff in recording the payment.

STATEMENT

From: P FAULKNER & SONS, Chestnut Avenue, Southampton SO2 4AG

Telephone: 0703 7654321   Telex: 517812

To: Brentfords plc
     Weston House
     Piccadilly
     London W1V 9PA   Date: 31 July 19—

Terms: Net cash within one month after delivery

Date	Details	Ref No	Dr £	Cr £	Balance £
19— July 8	Invoice	1624	15249.00		15249.00
28	Credit note	12		508.30	14740.70

The last amount in the balance column is the amount owing

- -

Remittance Advice

Please detach and return this remittance advice when making payment

To: P FAULKNER & SONS, CHESTNUT AVENUE,
    SOUTHAMPTON SO2 4AG

Cheque/cash for
in payment of statement dated

From:

Date:

If you require a receipt please insert 'R' here ☐

Fig 5.10

TASKS

1

Prepare statements for Chudleigh & Sons and Dream-land Ltd as at 31 August 19— from the information given in Tasks 8–11 of Unit 5.1.

2

Given that Chudleigh & Sons paid £129.13 on 3 September 19— and £740.42 on 17 September, and that there were no other transactions in September except the return covered by the credit note No 14 in Task 1 of Unit 5.2, make out a statement as at 30 September 19—.

3

a Is the ledger account in Fig 5.11 that of a customer or a supplier?

b For what purpose would a remittance advice be used?

c How would a statement of account differ from Fig 5.11?

d What is usually done before a firm will grant a prospective customer a credit account?

e Copy the ledger account in Fig 5.11 and complete any unfinished details.

4

Using the data recorded in Leisure Products Ltd's Account in Task 4 of Unit 5.1 and Task 3 of Unit 5.2 prepare a statement of account as at 1 March 19—. (*Continued: Task 2, Unit 6.1.*)

5

Prepare a statement of account to be sent to R Barber & Son as at 1 April 19— using the data recorded in their account for Task 13 of Unit 5.1. (*Continued: Task 3, Unit 6.1.*)

Ledger Account

Everyman Bargains Ltd
123 High Street,
Whitley Bay, Northumberland

Account No:

Credit £

Terms – 5% monthly

Date	Details	Debit £	p	Credit £	p	Balance £	p	Old Balance £	p
19—— April 30	A/c rendered					25	00		
May 1	Goods	31	60					25	00
8	Goods	27	25						
15	Goods	5	00						
17	Cheque			23	75				
17	Discount			1	25				
23	Returns			4	10				
30	Goods	12	50						

Fig 5.11

STATEMENT

From: P FAULKNER & SONS, Chestnut Avenue, Southampton SO2 4AG

Telephone: 0705 7654321   Telex: 517812

To:
| Bailey Bros |
| School Lane |
| Littlemelton |
| Norwich |
| Norfolk |
| NH8 1AD |

Date: 2 October 19—

Terms: Net cash within one month after delivery

Date	Details	Ref No	Dr £	Cr £	Balance £
19—					
Sept 1	Balance	b/f			129.00
5	Invoice	136	236.14		365.14
10	Payment	49		129.00	236.14
12	Credit note	87		62.18	298.32

The last amount in the balance column is the amount owing

- -

REMITTANCE ADVICE

Please detach and return this remittance advice when making payment

To: P FAULKNER & SONS, CHESTNUT AVENUE, SOUTHAMPTON SO2 4AG

tement dated

insert 'R' here ☐

Please check and, if necessary amend this statement
Joan

Fig 5.12

6 Sales: payment procedures

6.1 Checking and recording remittances

The first job of the day in any business is to open and sort the mail and at Faulkner a special procedure is adopted for dealing with any payments received in the post. These are recorded in a remittances book and signed for as they are handed over to the cashier. The cashier lists them in a cash receipts journal, making absolutely sure that the cheques are in order. The following points are checked:

- the cheques all have current dates
- the amounts in words and figures are the same
- the cheques are signed
- the payee's name (i.e. P Faulkner & Sons) is correct
- any alterations on the cheques are clear and are signed

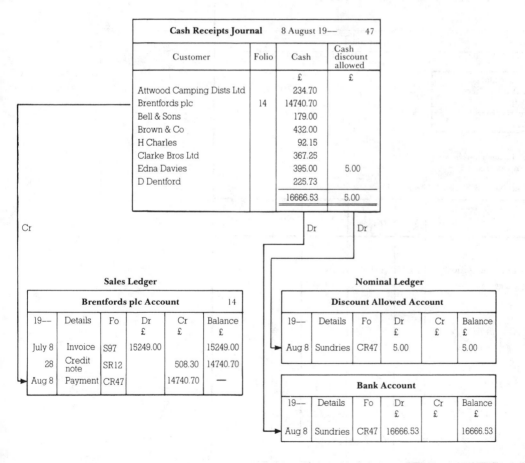

Fig 6.1 Cash receipts journal and posting procedure

The following procedure is used for recording remittances:

1 All cheques received are entered in a cash receipts journal by the cashier. Copies of the cash receipts journal, together with any returned statements or remittance advices, are passed to the sales ledger section for each day's transactions to be entered in the ledger accounts.
2 The customers' accounts in the sales ledger are credited.
3 The total of the remittances received is transferred from the cash receipts journal to the Dr column of the bank account.

4 The total of cash discount allowed is transferred from the cash receipts journal to the Dr column of the discounts allowed account.
5 The receipts are marked off on the schedule of customers (see Fig 4.7 on page 60).

Example
An example of the cash receipts journal for 8 August 19—, together with the posting procedure is given in Fig 6.1 (on the previous page). Note the receipt of a cheque from Brentfords plc in respect of the transaction which we have been following.

INVOICE

No 1813

P FAULKNER & SONS, Chestnut Avenue, Southampton SO2 4AG

Tel: 0703 7654321   Telex: 517812

VAT Registration No 3043739 11   Date: 7 September 19—

To:
Donald Dentford Ltd
1 High Road
Wormley
Broxbourne, Herts
BE3 8AS

Terms: 5% cash discount for payment within 7 days
Delivery Broxbourne

Completion of Order No S93421 dated 14 August 19—

Quantity	Description	Cat No	Price each £	Cost £	VAT rate %	VAT amount £
10	'Faulkner Ranger' tents Plus VAT	553T	130.00	1300.00 185.25 1485.25	15	185.25

Fig 6.2 An invoice

Cash discount

As already discussed in Unit 2, cash discount is an allowance made as a consideration for the prompt settlement of an account within a stated period; it is deducted at the time when payment is made. It should not be confused with trade discount, which is described on page 19.

An agreement to allow cash discount must be made before the invoice is prepared because it affects the value of the VAT charged. (This is still the case even if the customer does not pay promptly and take advantage of the discount offered.) Cash discount cannot be allowed on VAT and therefore, it would not, be permissible to deduct it from the net amount of an invoice or statement which included a VAT charge.

Figure 6.2 (on page 86) is an example of an invoice on which cash discount is allowed. The calculation of the invoice price is as follows:

	£
10 'Faulkner Ranger' tents @ £130.00 each=	1300.00

Cash discount of 5% on the value of the goods

$$\frac{5}{100} \times \frac{1300}{1} = \frac{65}{1} \qquad = \qquad 65.00$$

Value of goods for VAT purposes = £1300 − £65	= 1235.00
VAT at 15% on £1235	= 185.25
Net value of invoice = £1300 + £185.25	= 1485.25
Net amount payable if cash discount is taken = £1485.25 − £65.00	= 1420.25

You will see, therefore, that not only does Donald Dentford Ltd save £65 on the goods by paying early but also another £9.75 on the VAT charged. Without cash discount the invoice would be £1300 + VAT @ 15% (£195) = £1495.00. Where trade discount is deducted, the value which remains is used in calculating any cash discount.

Discount allowed to customers is credited in the customer's account to reduce the amount due, and debited in a discount allowed account, because the amount allowed to the customer is an expense to the firm. Cash discount allowed by suppliers would be called discount received and the entries in the accounts would be reversed.

TASKS

1

This task can be used with the sales ledger accounts already opened for Tasks 7–11 of Unit 5.1 and continued in Task 1 of Unit 5.2, or it may be worked separately. Enter the following cheques which were received by P Faulkner & Sons into a cash receipts journal, total the journal after each day's cheques have been entered and post them to the customers' accounts in the sales ledger and to the bank account.

Date	Customer	£
Sept 3	N K Aldous & Sons	454.69
	Bailey Bros	253.84
	Bostock (DIY)	132.43
	Chudleigh & Sons	129.13
	Dreamland Ltd	226.25
Sept 10	J G Andrews	65.12
	Carters Sports	446.97
	David Coleman (Sports Equipment) Ltd	3781.68
Sept 17	Arnold & Baker	266.10
	Bailey Bros	822.42
	Chudleigh & Sons	740.42
	Dreamland Ltd	633.04
	Dunn (Sports Outfitters) Ltd	476.77
Sept 24	N K Aldous & Sons	15.41
	Bostock (DIY)	879.81
	Carters Sports	964.57
	Dreamland Ltd	4422.17
	Dunn (Sports Outfitters) Ltd	764.81

(Continued: Tasks 1 and 2, Unit 6.2.)

2

Enter a cheque for £50 220.50 received from Leisure Products Ltd on 14 March 19— in a cash receipts journal and in the sales ledger account prepared in Task 14 of Unit 5.1 and continued in Task 3 of Unit 5.2. (*Continued: Task 2, Unit 6.3.*)

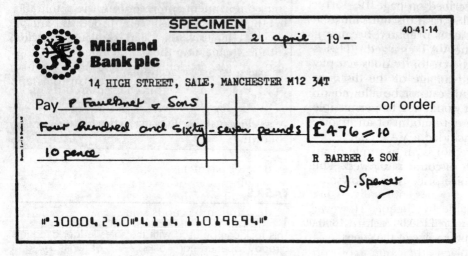

SPECIMEN _____ 21 april ____ 19 —

40-41-14

Midland Bank plc

14 HIGH STREET, SALE, MANCHESTER M12 34T

Pay P Faulkner & Sons _____ or order

Four hundred and sixty-seven pounds £476=10

10 pence

R BARBER & SON

J. Spencer

⑈3000424011114 1101969411⑈

Fig 6.3

3

Examine the cheque received from R Barber & Son in Fig 6.3 and, if it is correct, enter it in a cash receipts journal and in the sales ledger account prepared in Task 13 of Unit 5.1. If the cheque is not acceptable, return it to the cashier with a note of explanation.

4

On 1 September 19— M Lewis owed Harbour Engineering Ltd £200 and Harbour Engineering Ltd owed D Hammond £380. During September the following transactions took place with Harbour Engineering Ltd:

Sept 1 M Lewis paid the balance outstanding on his account by cheque and was allowed a cash discount of 4%.
  3 Harbour Engineering returned goods to D Hammond value £80.
  9 Goods for £500 were purchased on credit from D Hammond.
  10 Goods to the value of £816 were sold on credit to M Lewis.
  15 M Lewis returned goods to Harbour Engineering value £96.
  24 M Lewis paid a cheque for £500 on account.
  30 D Hammond was paid a cheque for the balance outstanding on his account after deducting a cash discount of 2½%.

Enter the above transactions in the accounts of M Lewis and D Hammond as they would appear in the ledgers of Harbour Engineering Ltd.

5

As a continuation of Task 5 of Unit 5.2 use a computer package to enter the cheques in Task 1 on page 87 and print out the weekly cash receipts journal and customers' accounts at the end of September 19—.

6

Telephone the information requested by John Perkins which you have received on your telephone answering machine:

'John Perkins of Clarke Bros Ltd here. I have mislaid your statement for March. I think the amount we owe you is £2850 but please telephone me and let me know if this is correct. If it is not correct, please explain what I owe and the reason for the discrepancy. I have assumed that I will be allowed a cash discount of 5%.'

The account in your sales ledger is given below:

Clarke Bros Ltd Account				
19—	Details	Dr £	Cr £	Balance £
March 1	Balance			1 200.00
1	Payment		1 140.00	60.00
1	Discount allowed		60.00	
9	Invoice	2 340.00		2 340.00
17	Invoice	660.00		3 000.00
23	Credit note		120.00	2 880.00

6.2 Handling cash payments and issuing receipts

Strict security procedures should be observed with the handling of money. It is most important that cash is always correctly and carefully counted and that, when required, the correct amount of change is given. When change is required from a note or coin presented by a customer, remember to be careful not to place it in the cash till until the customer has accepted the amount of change given, as then there can be no dispute about the amount of the note or coin paid.

Receipts

As we have already seen, a cheque passing through a bank is sufficient evidence of payment and receipts are not normally issued where payment is made by cheque. However, the receipt or payment of cash requires some form of documentary evidence. Where cash transactions are involved, the issuing of consecutively numbered receipts and remittance advices should be under the control of a senior member of staff to avoid duplicate (false) figures being used.

The payer (or remitter) requires a receipt (and may complete a remittance advice) to provide written evidence of the payment for their purchase. In addition to providing evidence of the payment of cash, a receipt provides information on any VAT which may have been charged, so that this can be claimed back from Customs and Excise.

The payee when receiving the cash issues a receipt and keeps a copy of the receipt as a source document for recording the remittance in their books. Cash sale proceeds can be checked by totalling cash takings (reconciled with payments into the bank). The receipt copy also provides evidence of any VAT for which the payee may be accountable to Customs and Excise.

A receipt, as in Fig 6.4, should record the following:

- date of payment
- serial number of receipt
- name of remitter
- description of goods sold
- amount paid, including the portion relating to VAT
- recipient's signature

A retail trade desk at Faulkner's Stores caters for members of the public who call at the factory to make cash purchases. Payment may be made by cash, cheque or credit card.

Cheque cards

Customers paying by cheque are expected to produce a cheque card (see Fig 6.5) as this is a

CASH RECEIPT	P FAULKNER & SONS Chestnut Avenue, Southampton, SO2 4AG		NO 120	
Date:	1 March 19—			
Description		£	p	
One Resteasy Camp Bed VAT @ 15%		15 2	75 36	
TOTAL		18	11	
RECEIVED WITH THANKS from: Mr Hugh Charles Cashier M Brown				
	VAT Registration No 304 3739 11			

Fig 6.4 A receipt form

guarantee that sums up to the value of £50/£100 will be honoured by the banks issuing the cards. The following steps should be taken when accepting a cheque with a cheque card:

- check that the card has the same account name and code number as on the cheque
- check that the date on the card has not expired
- check that the signature on the card is the same as the one on the cheque
- ensure that the cheque has been fully and correctly completed with:
  current date
  correct name of payee
  correct amount in both words and figures
  drawer's signature
- enter the card number on the back of the cheque

The card illustrated in Fig 6.5 is a multi-purpose card as, in addition to providing a guarantee for cheques, it may be used to:

- withdraw cash at a bank counter
- withdraw cash from an autobank or cash dispenser
- pay for goods or services without using a cheque at places where the 'Switch' sign is displayed – in this service, known as EFTPOS (electronic funds transfer at point of sale), the sales assistant passes the card through a point of sale electronic device which produces a receipt, the purchaser signs it to authorise payment and the amount of the purchase is automatically debited to the customer's bank account and credited to the seller's bank account.

Fig 6.5 A cheque card

Credit cards

Faulkner accepts Access credit cards (see Fig 6.6). A credit card, such as Access and Barclaycard, can be used to purchase goods up to an approved credit limit without paying a cheque or cash at the time. People are notified of their credit limit, which is the maximum amount that they can owe to the bank at any time. The credit card centre issues each card holder with a monthly statement of the amount owing and, provided the card holder makes a payment not later than twenty-five days after the date on the statement, no charge is incurred.

Fig 6.6 A credit card

The procedure for accepting payment by credit card is as follows:

- insert the customer's credit card into an embossing machine to reproduce the holder's name and account number on a multi-part sales voucher using NCR forms – in this process the seller's name, address and account number are also automatically embossed on the forms
- write the date and amount of the purchase on the forms
- ask the customer to sign the forms
- check that the signature on the forms is the same as the one on the card
- give the customer a copy of the sales voucher with their credit card

The seller deposits the sales vouchers at their bank and is credited with these amounts, less a charge for the service.

TASKS

1

Issue a receipt for cash paid on 30 September 19—by Bostock (DIY) for the amount outstanding in their account (as completed in Task 1 of Unit 6.1). Enter this payment in Bostock's account in the sales ledger.

2

N K Aldous requested a receipt for the cheque paid on 24 September 19— (Task 1 of Unit 6.1). Prepare a receipt form ready for the cashier's signature.

3

Prepare receipts for the cash items given in the remittances book in Fig 6.7 below. (*Continued: Task 5, Unit 6.3.*)

4

What course of action would you take when a customer presents you with this card (Fig 6.8) and a cheque for the purchase of goods? How would you know that the card had not been stolen?

Fig 6.8

5

Irene Digwell, PO Box 100, Spalding, Lincs PE8 2RA, is in the nursery business selling fruit trees, shrubs and spring bulbs by mail order and at garden centres. Many of her customers pay in cash, for which she issues receipts and retains carbon copies for her own records.

a For what purposes will Irene Digwell use the carbon copies of receipts issued?

b Why do you think her customers will require receipts for their cash payments?

c If customers pay by cheque should they ask for a receipt?

d In this morning's post Irene Digwell receives an

Remittances Book					
Date	Remitter	Cat No	Method of payment	Amount	Signature
19—				£	
June 1	J G Andrews	553T	Chq	260.00	
1	Carters Sports	774T	Chq	476.00	
1	Lake Park Sports Centre	31R	Cash	30.20	
1	Bailey Bros	583T	Chq	112.00	M Brown
1	Dreamland Ltd	734T	Chq	894.00	
1	Barton Youth Club	79C	Chq	15.75	
1	J R Green	13SB	Cash	16.50	
1	Dunn (Sports Outfitters) Ltd	754T	Chq	268.00	

Fig 6.7

order accompanied by cash for six Victoria Plum Trees @ £8.95 each from Mr R H Lane, 2 The Precinct, Eccles, Manchester, M21 6PR. Mr Lane has deducted 2½ per cent cash discount for an order in excess of £50, which was allowable. Prepare the receipt you would issue to Mr Lane acknowledging
receipt of his cash payment.

6  Priority

You are working in the stores at P Faulkner & Sons when Mrs Jill Barber calls in to buy two sleeping bags (Junior 36) and pays cash for them. Prepare the receipt you would give her for this cash sale.

6.3 Paying money into the bank

It is advisable for money to be paid into the bank as soon as possible after receipt to avoid the security risk of holding large sums of money on the premises. Until such time as it is taken to the bank, the money should be supervised carefully and locked in a safe. If large sums of money have to be transported to and from the bank, security agency staff will normally be engaged, but if the office staff have to undertake this task, two people should go, using specially designed cash-carrying cases.

A paying-in slip is used for paying cheques and cash into the firm's bank account. The remittances listed on the paying-in slip should be checked carefully with the cash receipts journal. The use of a print calculator simplifies this work as a tally roll is supplied and the total calculated automatically. Fig 6.9 is an illustration of the paying-in slip for the cheques received on 8 August, i.e. a total of £16 666.53, as listed in the cash receipts journal in Fig 6.1. As Faulkner often has as many as forty cheques in one day, a copy of the cash receipts journal is supplied to the bank to save having to repeat the names of the customers on the paying-in slip.

When there are only four or five cheques these are listed in the column headed 'cheques, etc' on the reverse of the paying-in slip. On occasions cash and postal orders are received for sales and, as with cheques, these must be banked on the same day as they are received. An example of a paying-in slip with cheques and cash is given in Fig 6.10. It was compiled from the following remittances received by P Faulkner & Sons on 9 August 19—:

Coins: 57 @ 1p; 20 @ 2p; 17 @ 5p; 7 @ 10p; 23 @ 50p; 37 @ £1.

Notes: 20 @ £5; 3 @ £10; 1 @ £20.

Cheques: £7.90 (J Andrews); £21.79 (Bailey Bros); £436.23 (Carters Sports); £43.10 (Dunn Ltd).

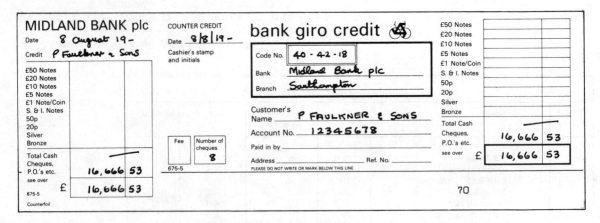

Fig 6.9 Paying-in slip

Fig 6.10 Paying-in slip listing cheques and cash

TASKS

1

Enter the cheques recorded in the cash receipts journal for September 3 (Task 1 of Unit 6.1) on a paying-in slip ready for payment into the bank.

2

Pay the cheque received from Leisure Products Ltd (Task 2 of Unit 6.1) into the bank.

3

You are working in the general office of a small firm called Easiglide Ltd.

a This morning you opened the mail and among the correspondence were the following payments:
  1 Cheque for £75.32 sent by Dickenson & Brown;
  2 Crossed postal order for £6.50 from Miss L Waters;
  3 Registered packet from Joe Twining containing: 1 × £10 note, 3 × £5 notes, 2 × £1 coins.
  Enter these in a remittance book.

b During the lunch hour you were looking after the reception desk and Mrs L M Oldenbourg from Central Cleaners called with a £16 cash refund (3 × £5 notes, 2 × 50p coins) on a cleaning bill for office curtains. Make out a receipt for Mrs Oldenbourg.

c You are asked to take the payments received in the morning mail to the bank, together with the amount from Central Cleaners. Complete the paying-in book to cover the total. Your company's bank account number is 50347479.

d Explain why Joe Twining sent his payment in a registered packet.

e Give the reason why Miss Walters crossed the £6.50 postal order.

f Explain in detail why a written record is kept of cash receipts and payments. (RSA OP1)

4

a The morning post contains the following remittances:

Sender	Method of payment	Amount £
J Smith Ltd	Cheque	4.63
R Peters	Cheque	6.50
P South & Co	Cheque	5.60
M Rayner	PO	1.50
R Jones	Registered mail (five £1 coins)	5.00
The Albright Co Ltd	Cheque	41.31
R Smith	Cheque	4.48

In addition, the following payments are made in cash at the main office:

Paid by:	Money paid:
J Brown	Three £1 coins, two 10p coins and one 5p coin
R Smith	One £5 note, two £1 coins, one 50p coin, two 5p coins and four 1p coins
S Wilson	One £5 note, and four 10p coins.

Prepare a paying-in slip for all the above receipts to be paid into the bank. The company for whom you work is Western Designs Ltd. Their account number is 1093706. (*RSA OPII*)

5

Pay the items recorded in the remittances book for Task 3 of Unit 6.2 into the bank. The cash items consisted of the following notes and coins:

Lake Park	1 £20 note
Sports Centre	1 £10 note
	1 20p coin

J R Green	1 £10 note
	1 £5 note
	1 £1 coin
	1 50p coin

6 **Priority**

Deal with the letter (Fig 6.11) given to you by the Cashier.

Midland College of Further Education

STUDENTS UNION
14 Marchwood Place
Aston
Birmingham B4 C16

Tel: 021–234789

4 October 19–

P Faulkner & Sons
Chestnut Avenue
Southampton
SO2 4AG

Dear Sirs

Will you please supply TWO of your Arctic 44 Sleeping Bags as soon as possible.

I enclose cash for £40 to cover the cost.

Yours faithfully

R. A. Smith

R A Smith (Miss)
Treasurer

Note that they have sent too much.
① Pl. write a letter saying that the sleeping bags are being sent by parcel post, enclose a remittance for the amount in excess of the list price, and a receipt.

② Pay the money into the bank today. M.B.

2 × £20 notes

Fig 6.11

Assignment – Unit 6

Situation: The sales ledger section of P Faulkner & Sons' Accounts Department.
Reference sources:
Customer records: Fig 1.5
Price list: Fig 1.7
Blank forms: *Lecturer's Manual*

Deal with the following items of business as they affect three customers' ledger accounts during the course of July. You are expected to make all the necessary entries in the documents, day books and ledger accounts; to check incoming documents for discrepancies and omissions; and, where necessary, take appropriate action to communicate with the customers to rectify any inaccuracies. Any letters required are prepared for Sarah Faulkner's approval and signature.

The records in this assignment may be completed either on a computer-based system for the sales ledger or a manual system.

July	1	Balances brought forward in customers' accounts: Attwood Camping Distributors plc £2056.20 Dr Carters Sports £248.50 Dr Donald Dentford £52.16 Dr
	3	Order received from Carters Sports (Fig 6.12) – the goods can be delivered in 10 days.
	4	Letter received from Attwood Camping Distributors plc (Fig 6.13) for your attention.
	11	Telephone message from Malcolm Wright of Attwood Camping Distributors (Fig 6.14) for you to deal with. Record your reply on a tape recorder.
	13	Goods despatched to Carters Sports for order received on 3 July. Send the invoice. You agreed to allow them a 5 per cent trade discount.
	15	Donald Dentford telephones to order two Rover Rucksacks, urgently required by a customer going abroad at the end of the month. They can be despatched tomorrow by parcel post. Invoice them at the time of despatch.
	20	Pay the cheques received (Fig 6.15) into the bank.
	31	Prepare statements for the three customers.

ORDER

No 12896

From: CARTERS SPORTS
57 Victoria Street
Wolverhampton
WN7 1DE

Tel: 0902-1223384

Date: 1 July 19—

To: P Faulkner & Sons
Chestnut Avenue
Southampton
SO2 4AG

Please supply:

TWENTY Rover Rucksacks (Cat No 29R) @ £15.10

Deliver to our branch at 120 Cathedral Place, Coventry, within 2 weeks

J McDonald
Buyer

Fig 6.12

ATTWOOD CAMPING DISTRIBUTORS PLC

48 Desborough Road
Eastleigh, Hants SO4 4AG

Telephone: 0703–3891423   Telex: 238963

3 July 19–

This is correct. Please write to Attwoods and apologise. Joan misread the quantity figure. Can you suggest how such errors can be avoided in future?
SF

P Faulkner & Sons
Chestnut Avenue
Southampton
SO2 4AG

Dear Sirs

INVOICE NO 8163 DATED 27 JUNE 19–

I am concerned that the invoice you sent to me on
27 June 19– was made out for six Faulkner Major Tents,
whereas only five were ordered and received.

Please confirm that the amount charged to my account
will be reduced by the cost of one tent.

Yours faithfully
ATTWOOD CAMPING DISTRIBUTORS PLC

Malcolm Wright

Malcolm Wright
Buyer

Registered in England No 346781 at 48 Desborough Road, Eastleigh, Hants.

Fig 6.13

```
┌─────────────────────────────────────────────────────┐
│              MESSAGE FOR        Please telephone     │
│  M   S Faulkner                  for me              │
│            WHILE YOU WERE OUT                         │
│  M  r Malcolm Wright                    SF           │
│                                                      │
│  OF   Attwood Camping Distributors plc               │
│                                                      │
│  TELEPHONE NO.  0703–3891423                         │
│                                                      │
│  ┌──────────────────┬───┬──────────────────┬───┐    │
│  │ TELEPHONED       │ ✓ │ PLEASE RING      │ ✓ │    │
│  ├──────────────────┼───┼──────────────────┼───┤    │
│  │ CALLED TO SEE YOU│   │ WILL CALL AGAIN  │   │    │
│  ├──────────────────┼───┼──────────────────┼───┤    │
│  │ WANTS TO SEE YOU │   │ URGENT           │   │    │
│  └──────────────────┴───┴──────────────────┴───┘    │
│                                                      │
│  MESSAGE: .........................................  │
│     Mr Wright has received your credit note to reduce the amount │
│     charged  in Invoice No. 8163 dated 27 June and he thinks you │
│     must have made   a mistake as you have added 15% VAT to     │
│     the list price of the tent.  Can you please explain the reason for │
│     adding VAT to the return.                        │
│                                                      │
│  DATE  11 July 19—          TIME   1500              │
│  RECEIVED BY  W.Cox                                  │
└─────────────────────────────────────────────────────┘
```

Fig 6.14

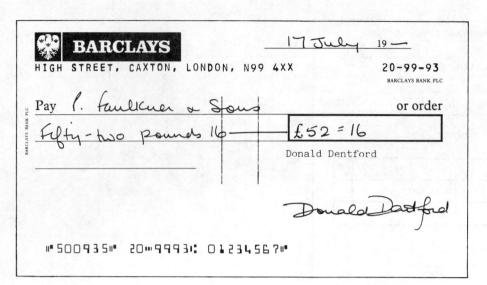

BARCLAYS

HIGH STREET, CAXTON, LONDON, N99 4XX

17 July 19—

20-99-93
BARCLAYS BANK PLC

Pay P. Faulkner & Sons   or order

Fifty-two pounds 16 ————   £52 = 16

Donald Dentford

Donald Dentford

⑈500935⑈ 20⑈9993⑈ 0123456 7⑈

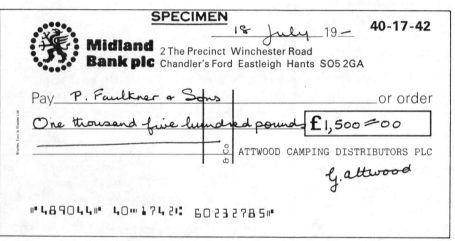

SPECIMEN

Midland Bank plc

2 The Precinct Winchester Road
Chandler's Ford Eastleigh Hants SO5 2GA

18 July 19—   **40-17-42**

Pay P. Faulkner & Sons   or order

One thousand five hundred pounds £1,500 = 00

ATTWOOD CAMPING DISTRIBUTORS PLC

G. attwood

⑈489044⑈ 40⑈1742⑈ 60232785⑈

1

National Westminster Bank PLC

Canterbury City Centre Branch
7 St George's Street, Canterbury, Kent CT1 2JU

60-64-27
15 July 19—

Pay P. Faulkner & sons   or order

Two hundred and forty-eight   £248 - 50
pounds 50 ————

CARTERS SPORTS

J Carter

⑈000725⑈ 60⑈0427⑈ 935046⑈

Fig 6.15

Document	Issued by	Issued to	Day book/Journal	Ledger Account
1 Catalogue/price list Quotation Estimate	Sales	Customer		
2 Order	Customer	Sales		
3 Confirmation order	Sales	Customer Works Despatch Costing		
4 Advice/Despatch note	Despatch	Customer Accounts		
5 Invoice	Accounts	Customer Despatch Sales Stores	Sales	Dr Customer Cr Sales
6 Credit note	Accounts	Customer Sales	Sales returns	Dr Sales returns Cr Customer
7 Statement of account	Accounts	Customer		
8 Payment	Customer	Accounts	Cash receipts	Dr Bank Cr Customer
9 Receipt (normally for cash)	Cashier	Customer		
10 Bank paying-in slip	Cashier	Bank		

7 Controlling accuracy

If financial records are to be of any use to a business, they must be reliable and periodic checks must be made to control their accuracy. The two principal ways of doing this are:

- by constructing a **trial balance** – which can reveal errors made in the accounts from various ledgers
- by preparing a **control account** – which is a means of checking the posting of entries to a particular ledger, such as the purchases ledger

7.1 Trial balance

At the end of every month it is the normal practice for a business to test the accuracy of its accounts by constructing a trial balance. A trial balance is a list of balances extracted from all the ledger accounts on a certain date to see if the total of the debit entries is equal to the total of the credit entries. Ledger account debit balances are entered in the Dr column of a trial balance and the credit balances in the Cr column. For every debit entry there must be a corresponding credit entry and vice versa and it follows that if the entries have been recorded correctly the totals of the trial balance should be the same.

If the totals of the trial balance do not agree, you should check the following points:

- the balances are entered in the correct columns of the trial balance (see page 104)
- there are no errors in the addition of the trial balance
- the entries in the accounts are in the correct columns
- the balances in the accounts are calculated correctly
- the totals in the day books are correct
- all accounts with balances have been entered in the trial balance (note that where there is a nil balance in an account it is not included in the trial balance)

Accounts will normally be entered in the trial balance in the following columns:

Suppliers (i.e. creditors)	Cr
Customers (i.e. debtors)	Dr
Bank (assuming a balance in hand)	Dr
Purchases	Dr
Purchases returns	Cr
Sales	Cr
Sales returns	Dr
VAT (assuming a balance due to be paid)	Cr

The accounts of other assets, liabilities and capital are dealt with later in Unit 11.

The purposes of the trial balance are:

- to check the arithmetical accuracy of the entries in the accounts (this does not, however, guarantee the total accuracy of the accounts as some errors are not revealed by arithmetical means, e.g. the incorrect posting to Arnold & Baker's account of goods sold to J G Andrews)
- to provide a basis for calculating the profit and preparing the balance sheet, dealt with in Unit 11

Example
Open ledger accounts and enter the following balances as at 21 January 19—.

	A/c No	£	
Purchases ledger:			
Tape Works Ltd	PL1	142.00	Cr
Fettlenold & Sons	PL2	95.64	Cr
Outdoor Fabrics plc	PL3	800.00	Cr
Sales ledger:			
J G Andrews	SL1	583.32	Dr
Baldwin Stores Ltd	SL2	284.33	Dr
Dreamland Ltd	SL3	1800.00	Dr
Nominal ledger:			
Bank	N1	406.99	Dr
Purchases	N2	1243.60	Dr
Purchases returns	N3	150.00	Cr
Sales	N4	2914.90	Cr
Sales returns	N5	50.00	Dr
VAT	N6	265.70	Cr

Enter the following transactions in the appropriate day books, post the entries to the ledger accounts and extract a trial balance as at 31 January 19—.

Date 19—	Transaction	Name	Voucher No	Total £	Goods £	VAT £
Jan 22	Sold goods on credit	Dreamland Ltd	200	598.00	520.00	78.00
22	Goods returned	Tape Works Ltd	300	36.80	32.00	4.80
23	Paid cheque	Fettlenold & Sons		95.64		
23	Paid cheque	Tape Works Ltd		105.20		
24	Purchased goods on credit	Outdoor Fabrics plc	100	287.91	250.36	37.55
24	Received cheque	J G Andrews		583.32		
24	Received cheque	Dreamland Ltd		1800.00		
25	Goods returned	Baldwin Stores Ltd	400	138.00	120.00	18.00
28	Purchased goods on credit	Fettlenold & Sons	101	474.37	412.50	61.87
28	Sold goods on credit	J G Andrews	201	269.10	234.00	35.10
29	Goods returned	Outdoor Fabrics plc	301	345.00	300.00	45.00
31	Goods returned	J G Andrews	401	39.10	34.00	5.10

Answer

Purchases Book PB1

Date 19–	Supplier	Inv No	Fo No	Total £	Goods £	VAT £
Jan 24	Outdoor Fabrics plc	100	PL3	287.91	250.36	37.55
28	Fettlenold & Sons	101	PL2	474.37	412.50	61.87
31	Totals for January			762.28	662.86	99.42
					(N2)	(N6)

Purchases Returns Book PRB1

Date 19–	Supplier	CN No	Fo No	Total £	Goods £	VAT £
Jan 22	Tape Works Ltd	300	PL1	36.80	32.00	4.80
29	Outdoor Fabrics plc	301	PL3	345.00	300.00	45.00
31	Totals for January			381.80	332.00	49.80
					(N3)	(N6)

Sales Book SB1

Date 19–	Customer	Inv No	Fo No	Total £	Goods £	VAT £
Jan 22	Dreamland Ltd	200	SL3	598.00	520.00	78.00
28	J G Andrews	201	SL1	269.10	234.00	35.10
31	Totals for January			867.10	754.00	113.10
					(N4)	(N6)

Sales Returns Book

Date 19–	Customer	CN No	Fo No	Total £	Goods £	VAT £	SRB1
Jan 22	Baldwin Stores Ltd	400	SL2	138.00	120.00	18.00	
31	J G Andrews	401	SL1	39.10	34.00	5.10	
31	Totals for January			177.10	154.00	23.10	
					(N5)	(N6)	

Cash Payments Journal   CP1

Date 19–	Details	Fo No	Amount £
Jan 23	Fettlenold & Sons	PL2	95.64
23	Tape Works Ltd	PL1	105.20
23	Total credited to Bank A/c	N1	200.84

Cash Receipts Journal   CR1

Date 19–	Details	Fo No	Amount £
Jan 24	J G Andrews	SL1	583.32
24	Dreamland Ltd	SL3	1800.00
24	Total debited to Bank A/c	N1	2383.32

Purchases Ledger

Date 19–	Details	Fo No	Dr £	Cr £	Balance £	
	Tape Works Ltd Account					PL1
Jan 21	Balance	b/d			142.00 Cr	
22	Credit note	PRB1	36.80		105.20 Cr	
23	Payment	CP1	105.20		–	
	Fettlenold & Sons Account					PL2
Jan 21	Balance	b/d			95.64 Cr	
23	Payment	CP1	95.64		–	
28	Invoice	PB1		474.37	474.37 Cr	
	Outdoor Fabrics Plc Account					PL3
Jan 21	Balance	b/d			800.00 Cr	
24	Invoice	PB1		287.91	1087.91 Cr	
29	Credit note	PRB1	345.00		742.91 Cr	

Sales Ledger					
Date 19–	Details	Fo No	Dr £	Cr £	Balance £
J G Andrews Account					SL1
Jan 21	Balance	b/d			583.32
24	Payment	CR1		583.32	–
28	Invoice	SB1	269.10		269.10
31	Credit note	SRB1		39.10	230.00
Baldwin Stores Ltd Account					SL2
Jan 21	Balance	b/d			284.33
22	Credit note	SRB1		138.00	146.33
Dreamland Ltd Account					SL3
Jan 21	Balance	b/d			1800.00
22	Invoice	SB1	598.00		2398.00
24	Payment	CR1		1800.00	598.00

Nominal Ledger					
19–	Details	Fo No	Dr £	Cr £	Balance £
Bank Account					N1
Jan 21	Balance	b/d			406.99
23	Cheques	CP1		200.84	206.15
24	Cheques	CR1	2 383.32		2 589.47
Purchases Account					N2
Jan 21	Balance	b/d			1 243.60
31	Invoices	PB1	662.86		1 906.46
Purchases Returns Account					N3
Jan 21	Balance	b/d			150.00 Cr
31	Credit Notes	PRB1		332.00	482.00 Cr
Sales Account					N4
Jan 21	Balance	b/d			2 914.90 Cr
31	Invoices	SB1		754.00	3 668.90 Cr
Sales Returns Account					N5
Jan 21	Balance	b/d			50.00
31	Credit Notes	SRB1	154.00		204.00
VAT Account					N6
Jan 21	Balance	b/d			265.70 Cr
31	Purchases	PB1	99.42		166.28 Cr
31	Purchases Returns	PRB1		49.80	216.08 Cr
31	Sales	SB1		113.10	329.18 Cr
31	Sales Returns	SRB1	23.10		306.08 Cr

Trial Balance of P Faulkner & Sons
as at 31 January 19—

Accounts	Fo No	Dr £	Cr £
Fettlenold & Sons	PL2		474.37
Outdoor Fabrics plc	PL3		742.91
J G Andrews	SL1	230.00	
Baldwin Stores Ltd	SL2	146.33	
Dreamland Ltd	SL3	598.00	
Bank	N1	2589.47	
Purchases	N2	1906.46	
Purchases returns	N3		482.00
Sales	N4		3668.90
Sales returns	N5	204.00	
VAT	N6		306.08
		5674.26	5674.26

TASKS

1

Prepare a trial balance for P Faulkner & Sons from the following balances extracted from the ledger accounts on 31 December 19—:

	£
Suppliers (amounts due to be paid):	
CIC plc	238.23
Insulation Supply Co Ltd	1812.41
Darling & Son Ltd	1950.66
Customers (amounts due to be received):	
Brown & Co Ltd	650.03
Donald Dentford	1463.21
Dunn (Sports Outfitters) Ltd	2236.50
Cash at bank (balance in hand)	2419.60
Purchases	3461.29
Purchases returns	482.13
Sales	4863.20
Sales returns	502.00
VAT (due to be paid)	1386.00

2

The balances in the accounts of P Fry on 1 May 19— were as follows:

	£	
Cash at bank	510.00	Dr
Debtors	1100.00	Dr
Creditors	800.00	Cr
Purchases	2000.00	Dr
Sales	2710.00	Cr
VAT	100.00	Cr

Open accounts and enter the balances.

Enter the following transactions into the accounts and take out a trial balance on 31 May 19—:

			£
May	6	Received by cheques from debtors	750.00
	10	Paid creditors by cheque	800.00
	13	Sales returns (including £6 VAT)	46.00
	20	Sales on credit (including £60 VAT)	460.00
	27	Purchases on credit (including £45 VAT)	345.00

3

E Parsons is in business as a dealer in musical instruments. On 1 April 19— he had the following balances in his accounts:

	£	
Cash at bank	4000.00	Dr
Creditors	2500.00	Cr
Debtors	2000.00	Dr
VAT	500.00	Cr
Sales	5000.00	Cr
Purchases	2000.00	Dr

Open accounts and enter the balances.

Record the following transactions for April in the accounts and take out a trial balance on 30 April 19—:

			£
April	4	Bought new instruments on credit (i.e. purchases) including £450 VAT	3450.00
	8	Sales on credit including £75 VAT	575.00
	15	Sales on credit including £240 VAT	1840.00
	24	Paid creditors by cheques	2000.00
	30	Received cheques from debtors	500.00

4

Using the figures shown in P Faulkner & Sons' trial balance on 31 January 19— (page 104), open accounts and enter the balances at 1 February 19—.

Enter the following transactions in the appropriate day books, post the entries to the ledger accounts and extract a trial balance at 28 February 19—:

Date		Transaction	Name	V/N	Total £	Goods £	VAT £
Feb	1	Purchased goods on credit	Tape Works Ltd	102	294.40	256.00	38.40
	2	Sold goods on credit	Dreamland Ltd	202	649.75	565.00	84.75
	8	Paid cheque	Fettlenold & Sons		474.37		
	8	Paid cheque	Outdoor Fabrics plc		742.91		
	9	Sold goods on credit	Baldwin Stores Ltd	203	1725.00	1500.00	225.00
	10	Goods returned	Tape Works Ltd	302	74.75	65.00	9.75
	12	Purchased goods on credit	Fettlenold & Sons	103	526.70	458.00	68.70
	15	Received cheque	J G Andrews		230.00		
	15	Received cheque	Dreamland Ltd		598.00		
	16	Goods returned	Baldwin Stores Ltd	402	402.50	350.00	52.50
	22	Sold goods on credit	J G Andrews	204	66.70	58.00	8.70
	26	Purchased goods on credit	Outdoor Fabrics plc	104	477.25	415.00	62.25

(Continued: Task 1, Unit 7.3.)

5 **Priority**

A trainee accounts clerk asks for your help with the following trial balance. She cannot see why the totals do not balance. Rewrite the trial balance correctly and explain the reasons for the errors.

Trial Balance of P Faulkner & Sons
as at 30 June 19—

Accounts	Dr £	Cr £
Customers:		
Bailey Bros		192.00
Hugh Charles		1183.49
Donald Dentford		621.11
Suppliers:		
Sam Beller & Sons	426.10	
Insulation Supply Co Ltd	1009.49	
Purchases	1048.34	
Sales		3500.17
VAT (due to be paid)		367.78
Sales returns		236.00
Purchases returns	200.00	
Cash at bank	2222.60	
	4906.53	6100.55

7.2 Control of computerised data

Accuracy of data

It is important to make sure that data entered into a computer is accurate (or validated) and the following are some of the checks which can be made:

- **Input validation:** checks automatically made when keying in data, as the computer will only accept certain terms and formats, such as 'invoice', 'credit note', for transactions.
- **Range check**: checks that numerical data lies between two extremes, for example if the quantity of nuts normally supplied is between 100 and 1000, any amounts appearing outside this range are rejected.
- **Reference sources**: the use of reference sources built into the computer memory, such as income tax and national insurance tables, to provide automatic access to the accurate data contained in them.
- **Data completeness**: the software program ensures that items are not overlooked, as all entries are automatically completed in a data transaction entry, and that the correct number of characters are present in a 'field'.

Security of data

Precautions must be taken to safeguard computerised data against loss or corruption and this can be done by:

- keeping back-up duplicate copies of disks in a secure place
- arranging for personal passwords to be used by the staff authorised to have access to the computer, the passwords being changed at regular intervals
- using codes, known only to the users, for document files
- using write-protect tags on system disks to prevent data from being altered or added to them

7.3 Control accounts

Control accounts relate to particular ledgers and provide a means of tracing errors and calculating the total amount of creditors (purchases ledger control account) and the total amount of debtors (sales ledger control account).

Purchases ledger control accounts

The purchases ledger control account is kept in the nominal ledger and contains a summary of all the items which have been posted to the accounts in a purchases ledger, such as purchases, purchases returns, payments and discounts received.

The procedure for opening and keeping a purchases ledger control account is as follows:

1 **Credit** the total of the creditors' balances at the beginning of the month, e.g. £70 + £120 + £400 = £590 (see example below).
2 **Credit** the totals of the net value of the invoices including VAT in the purchases book, i.e. £4502.82 for week ending 7 January.
3 **Debit** the total of the credit notes as entered in the purchases returns book, i.e. £40.25.
4 **Debit** the total of the cheques paid for purchases as listed in the cash payments journal, i.e. £9370.50.
5 **Debit** the total of cash discount received as listed in the cash payments journal, i.e. £119.50.
6 The final **credit** balance, resulting from the above entries, should equal the total of all the balances in the creditors' accounts at the end of the month, i.e. £5075.73, thus providing a check on the arithmetical accuracy of the ledger postings.

Purchases Ledger Control Account				
Date 19–	Details	Dr £	Cr £	Balance £
January 1	Balance			590.00 Cr
7	Purchases		4 502.82	5 092.82
14	Purchases		3 355.72	8 448.54
21	Purchases		2 805.19	11 253.73
28	Purchases		3 352.25	14 605.98
31	Purchases Returns	40.25		14 565.73
31	Payments	9 370.50		5 195.23
31	Discount Received	119.50		5 075.73 Cr

Sales ledger control accounts

The sales ledger control account is used for controlling the accuracy of the sales ledger and contains summaries of sales, sales returns, payments received, discounts allowed and bad debts incurred.

The procedure for this account is as follows:

1 **Debit** the total of the debtors' balances at the beginning of the month, e.g. £1234.50 + £69.45 + £3208.70 = £4512.65.
2 **Debit** the totals of the net value of the invoices including VAT (taken from the pre-lists) in the sales book, i.e. £5536.40 for the month. Note that cash sales are not included.
3 **Credit** the total of the credit notes as entered in the sales returns book, i.e. £123.20.
4 **Credit** the total of the cheques received for sales as listed in the cash receipts journal, i.e. £3712.10.
5 **Credit** the total of cash discount allowed as listed in the cash receipts journal, i.e. £84.70.
6 **Credit** the total of bad debts (irrecoverable amounts in debtors accounts), i.e. £101.50.
7 The final **debit** balance, resulting from the above entries, should equal the total of all the balances in the debtors accounts at the end of the month, i.e. £6027.55.

Example

Sales Ledger Control Account				
Date 19–	Details	Dr £	Cr £	Balance £
January 1	Balance			4 512.65
31	Sales	5 536.40		10 049.05
31	Sales Returns		123.20	9 925.85
31	Payments Received		3 712.10	6 213.75
31	Discount Allowed		84.70	6 129.05
31	Bad Debts		101.50	6 027.55

TASKS

1

Prepare a purchases ledger control account and a sales ledger control account from the accounts and books completed in Task 4 of Unit 7.1.

2

The following transactions took place during the month of May. Construct a purchases ledger control account given that on 1 May the balances in the suppliers' accounts = £4593 credit:

Purchases invoices received £	Credit notes received £	Cheques paid £
437.00	47.00	372.00
234.00	23.00	134.00
112.00	9.00	461.00
472.00		231.00
57.00		666.00
93.00		
12.00		
116.00		

3

The following figures were extracted from the books of Pevatec & Co for April 19—:

	£
Sales ledger balances 1 April	4842
Purchase ledger balances 1 April	2182
Receipts from customers	84 804
Payments to suppliers	63 294
Sales	86 402
Purchases	64 823
Returns inwards	1420
Returns outwards	1210
Bad debts written-off	496
Discounts allowed	1902
Discounts received	1048
Sales ledger balances 30 April	2622
Purchase ledger balances 30 April	1453

Prepare a sales ledger control account and a purchases ledger control account for the month of April from the above information. (*RSA BKI*)

4

Your purchase ledger control account had an opening balance of £4243 at 1 June.

During June the business received invoices for £2333, £1669 and £2000 on 10 June; a credit note for £205 on 14 June; invoices for £2000, £559 and £1263 on 23 June.

The business paid the following cheques and claimed the discount shown on 30 June:

Amount of cheque £	Discount received £
817.00	43.00
952.85	50.15
2261.00	119.00

Prepare the purchases ledger control account for June.

5

On 31 March 19— the following balances appeared in John Richard's sales ledger (W section):

	£
W Wilkins	1200 Dr
T Wright	750 Dr
L Williams	325 Dr

During April 19— the following transactions took place:

Credit sales		£
April 3	W Wilkins	1370
13	T Wright	600
23	W Wilkins	450

Sales returns		£
April 15	L Williams	200
24	T Wright	30

Payments received and cash discounts allowed		£	£
April 10	W Wilkins	1170	30
10	T Wright	740	10

You are to:

a write up the personal accounts of the three customers in John Richard's sales ledger (W section)

b write up the sales ledger (W section) control account for the month of April 19—

c reconcile the control account balance with the personal account balances (*RSA BKI*)

6  Priority

Using the accounts and books completed in the example on pages 101–103, reply to the note (Fig 7.1) from Sarah Faulkner.

Please supply me with control accounts so that I can see our position with debtors and creditors at 31 January.

SF

Fig 7.1

TO SUM UP
CONTROLS OF ACCURACY

- Trial balance   for checking ledger accounts
- Control accounts   for checking posting to ledger accounts and totalling debtors and creditors

8 Stock control

All materials used in the manufacture of camping equipment are stored in numbered bays in the stores department. The quantity in stock for each item is recorded on individual stock control cards (Fig 8.1). In this example 350 metres of tent cloth were in stock at 1 July. As you will recall from Unit 2.1, before any materials can be taken from the stores a stores requisition (Fig 2.1) has to be made out as an instruction to the storekeeper to release the items listed. The storekeeper initials the requisition after handing over the stock items and the issue is recorded on the stock control card. This reduces the balance so that it agrees with the quantity remaining in the stores. For example, on 1 July there were 350 metres of Grade A Gold Tent Cloth in stock; 100 metres were taken out of the stores, as required by stores requisition No 811, and the new balance of 250 metres was entered on the stock control card.

The stock control card shows the maximum, minimum and reorder levels of stock. The firm does not wish to hold too much stock because this means that more money than is necessary has to be paid out to buy stock and there is not a great deal of storage space available.

The maximum stock figure is the largest quantity of stock which should be held at any one time, having regard to the efficient use of capital and accommodation and to avoid stock deteriorating and becoming obsolete in the store room.

The minimum stock figure is the smallest quantity which should be maintained to prevent stocks running out. In order to allow time to replenish the stock before it reaches this minimum level, a reorder level is given, to remind the buyer to place a further order.

The reorder level is calculated as follows:

$$\begin{array}{ccc} \text{daily/weekly} & \text{number of} & \text{minimum} \\ \text{usage} \quad \times & \text{days/weeks} \quad + & \text{stock level} \\ & \text{for delivery} & \end{array}$$

For example, in the case of the Grade A Tent

STOCK CONTROL CARD

Description Grade A tent cloth (gold) Bay No 13
Maximum 650 metres
Code No 60 TC A/G Minimum 100 metres
Reorder level 250 metres

| Date | Receipts | | Issues | | Balance in stock | Remarks |
	Goods received note No	Quantity	Reqn No	Quantity		Goods on order and audit check
19— July 1		metres		metres	metres 350	
July 2			811	100	250	5/7 Order No 97324
July 14			823	100	150	
July 15	7 629	400			550	

Fig 2.1 → July 2

Fig 2.9 → July 15

Fig 2.5 → (5/7 Order No 97324)

Fig 8.1 Stock control card

Cloth it is estimated that 50 metres are used weekly, 3 weeks are required for orders to be delivered and the minimum stock level is 100 metres, therefore

$$50 \times 3 + 100 = 250 \text{ reorder level.}$$

When the amount of stock has been reduced to the reorder level, the stock control clerk knows that a further quantity of the item must be ordered. The clerk is guided in the amount of the order, as the total of the balance in stock and the new order must not exceed the maximum stock figure, and an order is prepared for the buyer's approval.

A computer with a record processing package can be used to maintain stock records; the minimum, maximum and reorder levels can then be stored on disk. When stock receipts and issues are entered on the keyboard, the balance of stock left is automatically updated and the screen shows the operator when the stock falls to the reorder level, indicating the need to place an order. Stock valuations can also be seen and/or printed out because stock prices can also be stored.

Stocktaking

Stocktaking has to be carried out regularly by physically counting the stock to check that it agrees with the written records; it is essential that this is done at the end of each year at the time when the trading account is prepared (see Unit 11).

On 31 March 19–1 P Faulkner & Sons had £200 of stock as shown in the stock account in Fig 8.2. This amount (known as *opening stock*), which will be used during the year, is held (shown) in the stock account. When it is required for calculating the profit or loss, the opening stock figure is transferred to the trading account (by a credit entry in the stock account) as part of the cost of sales. At the end of the year also, after stocktaking, the value of the stock remaining (known as *closing stock*) is deducted from the cost of sales in the trading account. It is then transferred to the stock account (Dr column) on the first day of the next trading year – 19–2 in the example – and now becomes opening stock for that year.

At the end of each year stock sheets (as in Fig 8.2) are prepared recording:

1 The description, quantity and any special comments after counting each stock item.
2 The cost price and the expected selling price taken from the records in the accounts department.
3 The extensions, i.e. the quantities multiplied by the prices in the relevant columns.
4 The lower of either the cost value or the expected selling value in the right-hand, final column.
5 The totals of the three columns; cost of value, net realisable value and lower of cost or net realisable value.

The right-hand, final column, i.e. the lower of cost or net realisable value, is the value used for stocktaking purposes and for the closing stock figure.

The stock sheet may also be called a stock inventory. If, as a result of stocktaking, there is a discrepancy between the amount of stock in hand on the inventory and the amount recorded on the stock control card, an adjustment is made to the stock control card figure. For example, if stocktaking on 1 July revealed a stock figure of 340 metres of Grade A Tent Cloth instead of the 350 metres recorded, the balance on the stock control card would be adjusted by the following entry:

July 1   Stock check   Balance: 340

Example

						Net realisable price	Net realisable value	Lower of cost or net realisable value
Stock at 31 March 19–2 (extract)								
Code No	Details	Special comment	Quantity	Cost price	Cost value			
				£	£	£	£	£
523T	Expedition		1	108.00	108.00	157.00	157.00	108.00
583T	Hiker	Old Stock	5	70.00	350.00	34.00	170.00	170.00
79C	Resteasy		1	13.00	13.00	15.75	15.75	13.00
79C	Resteasy	Damaged/ shop soiled	3	13.00	39.00	3.00	9.00	9.00
					510.00		351.75	300.00

Stock Account						**NL1**
19—	Details	Fo	Dr £	Cr £	Balance £	
19—(1) April 1	Balance	b/f			200.00	
19—(2) March 31	Transfer to Trading A/c	J59		200.00	—	
April 1	Transfer from Trading A/c	J59	300.00		300.00	

Fig 8.2

TASKS

1

Enter the stores requisitions prepared in Task 1 of Unit 2.1 and the order from Task 1 of Unit 2.2 (delivered on 14 January 19—, GRN 7723) on a stock control card and calculate the balance after each transaction. The balance of stock on 1 December was 480. The stock levels were: maximum 600, minimum 200 and reorder level 300. The stock is held in bay No 15.

2

Prepare a stock sheet of completed products for P Faulkner & Sons at 31 March 19—:
enter the following items;
extend the cost values;
enter the net realisable prices;
extend the net realisable values;
enter the lower of the cost or net realisable values in the last column;
total the three value columns.
  Refer to the price list in Fig 1.7 for the descriptions.

Code No	Quantity	Cost price £	Net realisable price £
774T	28	180.00	195.00
583T	60	70.00	112.00
13SB	80	13.50	16.50
14SB	40	13.00	13.00
15SB	100	12.00	11.50

3

Mayflower Fashion Boutique has the following goods in stock at 31 December 19—. Enter them on to a stock sheet and work out the stock value for the end of the year.

Commodity	Quantity	Cost price £	Net realisable price £
Jeans	60	24.00	22.00
Track suits	40	30.00	32.00
Sweat shirts	100	18.00	18.00
Trainers	30	35.00	30.00

4

Enter the following items in a stock account, including the entry transferring stock to the trading account at 31 March 19–2:

19–1	1 April	Opening stock	£12 000
19–2	31 March	Closing stock	£15 000

5

Complete a stock control card for terylene filling (stock reference 21 SM) with the following entries:

Max 500 kilos. Min 200 kilos. Reorder level 250 kilos.

December	1	Balance in stock	400 kilos
	7	Requisition No 934	100 kilos
	10	Requisition No 1023	100 kilos
	14	Purchases order No 97394	300 kilos
	28	Goods received note No 7847	300 kilos
	31	Requisition No 1079	50 kilos

6

a From the following information for April 19— relating to component XYZ you are to complete a stock card.

At 1 April the opening stock was 250 units. On 30 April it was discovered that there was a stock loss of 30 units.

Date		Reqn No	Issues	Receipts
April	3	K14	42	
	15	K126	40	
	18			100 Invoice 7321
	20			6 Returns RN176
	21	K176	126	
	28			50 Invoice 7328
	29	K190	80	

b How could you verify that the records were correct on 30 April 19—? (*RSA BK1*)

7

Calculate the reorder levels for the following stock items:

Stock item		Minimum stock figure	Weekly usage	Time required for order to be delivered
Code No	Description			
100	Steel rods	200	30	4 weeks
101	Springs	300	100	2 weeks
102	Hooks	600	200	3 weeks

8

Use a computer accounting package to create stock records for tent zips (Task 1) and terylene filling (Task 5). Print out the stock record sheets for December and January for these items.

9   Priority

Peter Faulkner telephones you:

'I want to know urgently our expected profit for the half-year to 30 September, at the end of the camping season, so that we can have an end-of-season sale to make room for next year's range of new products. Please let me have the stock sheet at 30 September.'

The stock list given in Fig 8.3 was taken out in a hurry and contains a number of errors. Rewrite it for Mr Faulkner, making any necessary corrections.

Stock of completed products at 30 September 19—						
Ref	Quantity	Cost price £	Cost value £	Net realisable price £	Net realisable value £	Lower of cost or net realisable value £
734T	70	170.00	11900.00	298.00	20860.00	11900.00
754T	40	140.00	5600.00	136.00	5440.00	5440.00
553T	30	84.00	2520.00	130.00	390.00	390.00
583T	12	70.00	840.00	60.00	720.00	720.00
13SB	20	13.50	250.00	12.00	240.00	250.00
14SB	15	13.00	195.00	14.00	210.00	159.00
			£21305.00		£27860.00	£18859.00

Fig 8.3

Assignment – Unit 8

Situation: Assume that you are in charge of stationery supplies at P Faulkner & Sons.

Use the stationery stock inventory in Fig 8.4 as the source for your calculations in the following tasks:

1 Calculate and insert the total cost value of each item of paper held in stock at 1 January and the total of all the items for this section of the inventory.

2 Calculate and insert the reorder level for each item on the stock inventory.

3 There is a discrepancy between the stocktaking figure for copying paper (Code No 149) as revealed in the inventory and the balance given in the stock record card (Fig 8.5). Check the entries on the card and, if a mistake has been made, correct it. How would you adjust the figure if an error has not been made?

4 If you consider that any of the items should be reordered:
   a Prepare stock record cards for them and enter the balance(s) at 1 January 19—.
   b Select a suitable local supplier (comparing prices, discounts, etc) and place an order for the item(s) required.
   c Prepare a goods received note when the goods are delivered and record them on the stock records.

5 Peter Faulkner is concerned about the excessive quantities of copying paper being used and asks you to draft a memo which he can send to all staff suggesting ways to economise in the use of the copiers.

6 Use a computer to make the following calculations on the stationery stock inventory:
   a The total cost value of each item held in stock at 1 January 19— for all the items of paper (as in 1 above).
   b The annual consumption rate (based on the weekly usage figures for 50 weeks), the annual cost value of each item and the total of all the items of paper.
   c The effects on (b) of the following projected increase in prices for next year:

	Percentage increase
Printout paper	5
Headed bond paper	10
Plain bond paper	7.5
Bank paper	2.5
Lined paper	5
Memo paper	5
Copying paper	7.5

   d Assuming that a weekly saving of one ream of copying paper could be made, what effect would this have on the annual cost for this item based on (1) the current figures and (2) next year's projected figures?

Stationery Stock Inventory at 1 January 19–						
Code No	Item	Location	Stock balance reams	Max stock reams	Min stock reams	Cost price per ream
PAPER						£
140	A4 printout paper	C2	40	60	20	4.15
141	A4 headed bond paper	C3	48	60	20	5.10
142	A5 headed bond paper	C4	42	60	20	4.10
143	A4 plain bond paper	C5	21	50	15	4.20
144	A5 plain bond paper	C6	28	40	15	3.95
145	A4 bank paper	D8	32	60	20	3.65
146	A5 bank paper	D9	34	40	15	3.25
147	A4 lined paper	E1	18	30	5	3.60
148	A4 memo paper	D6	35	40	10	4.00
149	A4 copying paper	D7	43	50	15	4.20

Item	Weekly usage	Time required for orders to be delivered (weeks)
Printout paper	5	3
Headed bond paper	3	6
Plain bond paper	2	3
Bank paper	4	3
Lined paper	1	3
Memo paper	2	4
Copying paper	3	3

Fig 8.4

STOCK CONTROL CARD

Description ..Copying Paper.................... Location ...D7.....................

Maximum ..50.....................

Code No ......149.................................. Minimum ..15.....................

Reorder level ....24.........................

Date	Receipts		Issues		Balance in stock	Remarks
	Goods received note No	Quantity	Reqn No	Quantity		Goods on order and audit check
19— Dec 1		reams		reams	reams 30	
3			981	6	23	3/12 order 9823
10			990	4	19	
13			996	2	17	
17	7816	25			42	

Fig 8.5

TO SUM UP
STOCK CONTROLS

Stock control records:

1 Stock control card   records movement of individual items of stock

2 Stores requisition   provides authorisation for stock to be issued

3 Order   requests the supplier to supply stock

4 Goods received note   provides confirmation of the receipt of stock

5 Stock inventory sheet   record of stock check showing quantities and values of stock held on a particular date – the stock being valued at cost price or selling price, whichever is lower

6 Stock ledger account   holds the value of stock debited with opening stock at the beginning of the year

An effective stock control system should enable a business to:

• keep an accurate check on the quantities of stock issued and avoid pilferage

• ensure that production is not stopped, which would happen if the stores ran out of stock

• minimise the space occupied by stock

• avoid goods deteriorating or becoming obsolete

• calculate gross profit with accurate opening and closing stock figures

9 Financial data

Introduction

Now we turn our attention to cash transactions and their entry in a columnar cash book and a petty cash book. A cash transaction is one which involves the payment or receipt of money in any form, i.e. cash, cheques, credit transfers, etc.

Every organisation handles cash in one form or another and those responsible for it are conscious of the need to have accurate and up-to-date cash and bank figures. This is necessary so that the organisation knows whether it will be able to meet its current financial demands. Wages, salaries and creditors must be paid on time to avoid serious difficulties; even if profits are being made, unless there is an adequate cash flow or supply of money, the organisation will soon be unable to continue in business.

Computerised aids to financial planning

As explained in Unit 1, a spreadsheet may be used to assist with financial planning and decision-making. Note the example given in that unit for calculating and comparing profits and Task 5 in Unit 5.3 for analysing sales.

9.1 Recording cash transactions

A cash account is used to record cash transactions and a bank account for the receipt and payment of cheques, credit transfers, direct debits and other non-cash payments. So far I have shown a single account in the nominal ledger for bank transactions, but the cash and bank accounts are usually combined for convenience in the form of a columnar cash book. An example of the merging of these two accounts is given in Fig 9.1. In this example the business has £200 in cash and £4000 in its current account at the bank on 1 July. During the first week of July these transactions took place:

July 2 Paid rent in cash £80.

     3 Paid by cheque £500 to settle the amount owing to Electrical Supplies plc, a supplier.

     3 Cashed a cheque for £100 office cash.

     4 Paid £131 in cash for gas to heat storeroom

     5 Received a cheque for £120 from B Reynolds, a customer, in settlement of his account.

     6 Received £61 in cash for sales.

     6 Paid by cheque £2400 to G W Ball & Sons, a supplier, to settle his account.

     6 Paid £50 cash into the bank.

     6 The cash and bank accounts were balanced and the balances carried down in the cash book.

Note that the entries are made in date order on two sides, the left-hand side (Dr) for money coming in – receipts, and the right-hand side (Cr) for money paid out – payments. At the end

Example 1

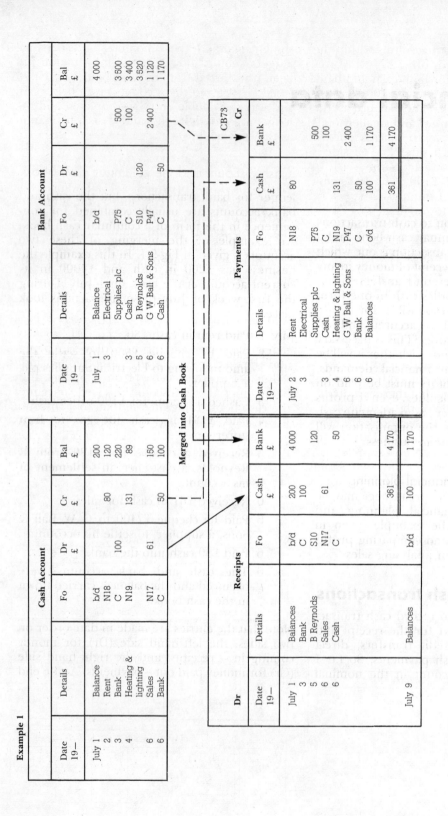

Merged into Cash Book

Fig 9.1

of the week or month both accounts within the cash book are 'balanced off'. This involves making the totals equal for both cash and bank by means of a 'balancing entry', £100 for cash and £1170 for the bank. The balance is the difference between the larger and smaller totals on both sides. For example, the larger amount of cash (£361) is on the Dr side. The Cr side is added up (£261) and subtracted from £361, to arrive at the balance of £100. The balancing entry is then taken out of one period (week or month) and transferred to the next.

When cash in hand is paid into the bank or a cheque is cashed to provide cash in hand, entries are required on both sides of the cash book. For example:

Cash paid into the bank: Dr Side Bank column 'cash'
Cr side Cash column 'bank'
Cashed cheque: Dr side Cash column 'bank'
Cr side Bank column 'cash'

The letter 'C' (an abbreviation for *contra* – meaning opposite) is entered in both columns of the folio (page) to indicate that there is a double entry on the opposite side of the cash book.

The folio numbers in the cash book are cross referenced either to the nominal ledger (for accounts other than customers and suppliers) or to the sales or purchases ledger for the personal accounts of customers and suppliers. In a

similar manner, these nominal and personal ledgers should show that the information has been transferred from the cash book (e.g. CB73 – see Fig 9.1 and the accounts given below). In this way the double entry is completed and the ledger accounts have the same basic information as the cash book.

Cash discount and the columnar cash book

Cash discount provides an allowance for prompt payment to customers (discount allowed) or by suppliers (discount received). The day book details for discount are entered in additional columns in the cash book. Any columns which are incorporated in a cash book to provide such details are known as memorandum columns.

To complete the double entry, discount allowed to customers, after being entered in a discount allowed column of the cash book, is debited in total to a Discount Allowed Account and the customers' accounts are credited individually. Discount received from suppliers, after being entered in a discount received column of the cash book, is credited in total to a Discount Received Account and the suppliers' accounts are debited individually. Figure 9.2 illustrates the use of discount columns in a three-column cash book and posting the entries to ledger accounts.

Nominal Ledger					
Sales Account (17)					
Date 19–	Details	Fo	Dr £	Cr £	Bal £
July 6	Cash payment	CB73		61	61 Cr
Rent Account (18)					
Date 19–	Details	Fo	Dr £	Cr £	Bal £
July 2	Cash payment	CB73	80		80
Heating and Lighting Account (19)					
Date 19–	Details	Fo	Dr £	Cr £	Bal £
July 4	Cash payment	CB73	131		131

Sales Ledger					
B Reynolds Account (10)					
Date 19–	Details	Fo	Dr £	Cr £	Bal £
July 1 5	Balance Payment	b/d CB73		120	120 –

Purchases Ledger					
Electrical Supplies plc Account (75)					
Date 19–	Details	Fo	Dr £	Cr £	Bal £
July 1 3	Balance Payment	b/d CB73	500		500 Cr –

G W Ball & Sons (47)					
Date 19–	Details	Fo	Dr £	Cr £	Bal £
July 1 6	Balance Payment	b/d CB73	2400		2400 Cr –

Fig 9.1 (cont'd)

Example 2

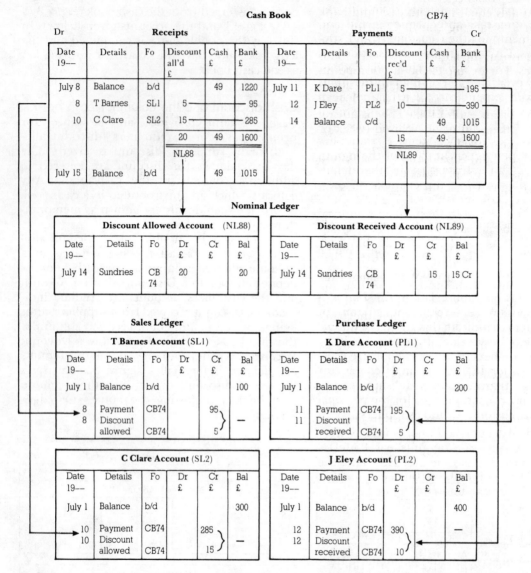

Fig 9.2

Extract of receipts side of an analysed Bank Account

19—	Details	Fo	Discount allowed £	Bank £	Analysis of receipts £
Sept 2	Sales (cash)	NL			47.00
	B Williams	SL			105.00
	P McDonald	SL	5.00		95.00
				247.00	

Fig 9.3

VAT and the cash book

Faulkner uses the system of cash receipts journals and cash payments journals to simplify the task of recording cash and cheque receipts and cheque payments for their customers and suppliers. The VAT in these transactions is recorded in the sales and purchases day books. VAT is, however, charged on many other items of income and expenditure; if it has not been recorded in a day book it will have to be shown in the cash book. Faulkner usually pays the 'expense' invoices for such items as stationery and motor expenses on the 20th of the month and analyses the information in the details column (as illustrated in the example of their analysed bank account/cash book, Fig 9.4). Once the cash receipts and cash payments journal transfers have been made to the Bank Account and the other ledger accounts, the double entry is completed. It only remains for the 'other items' for August to be posted as indicated to the nine accounts. It should be noted that the bank balance at 29 August was £11 938.30 and it was not until 2 September, when the bank statement was received, that the other information was known and entered in the August account.

The analysis column for receipts can be used to give the details of several items contained in a paying-in slip in order to match with the total shown in the bank column (as shown in Fig 9.3). The individual ledger accounts would be credited with their separate amounts, e.g. P McDonald with both the payment of £95 and the discount of £5. The bank account column has been debited with the total paid in of £247.00.

PERFORMANCE CHECK

When recording receipts and payments in the cash book and posting entries to the ledger accounts:

- comply with the guidelines on page 28
- be accurate in transferring the correct amounts and calculating the correct balances
- complete all essential information legibly
- use the correct books and accounts
- complete entries within the required deadline
- follow cash security procedures at all times

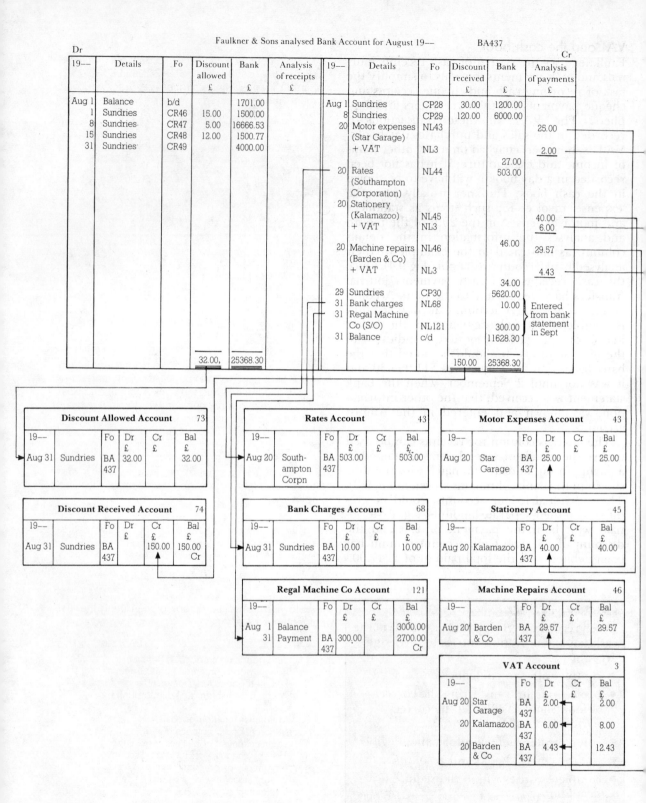

Fig 9.4

120 Finance: first levels of competence

TASKS

1

On 1 January 19— W P Jackson has £250 in cash, £3500 in his current account at the bank, and his sales and purchase ledger accounts include the following balances:

Sales ledger: R A Brown £1000 Dr
                   Broadway Builders Ltd £120 Dr
Purchase ledger: Contract Supplies plc £900 Cr
                 Palmer & O'Neill £2000 Cr

You are required to open the accounts (including a cash book) at 1 January 19— and make the necessary entries in the accounts to record the following transactions for January 19—:

Jan 2 Received a cheque from R A Brown for £840 in part-payment of his debt.
    3 Paid £34 in cash for stationery.
   10 Paid Contract Supplies plc by cheque £900.
   17 Received a cheque from Broadway Builders Ltd for £120.
   23 Paid £20 in cash for petrol.
   24 Paid Palmer & O'Neill by cheque £1560 on account.
   30 Received £192 in cash for sales.
   31 Paid £100 cash into the bank.

2

a Enter the following items in an analysed Bank Account:

19—	Fo	Amount £	Discount £
Jan 1 Balance in Bank Account		1075.00 Dr	
2 Cash Receipts Journal	CR52	149.50	3.70
3 Cash Receipts Journal	CR53	228.41	6.92
4 Cash Receipts Journal	CR54	1052.00	23.50
5 Cash Payments Journal	CP101	341.60	15.07

b Enter the following items in the Bank Account and post them to the relevant accounts in the nominal ledger:

Cheques paid for expenses on 6 January	Total £	VAT included £
British Gas for gas	64.00	Nil
Southern Insurance Co Ltd for insurance	108.00	Nil
E Colley & Sons for building repairs	60.00	7.82
Red Star Garage Ltd for petrol	12.40	1.62
British Telecom for telephone charges	58.00	7.56

c Balance the Bank Account on 6 January and bring down the balance on 7 January. Total the discount columns and post them to the Discount Allowed and Discount Received Accounts in the nominal ledger.

3

On 1 September 19— the Bank Account of P Faulkner & Sons had a debit balance of £11 628.30. During September the following cheques were received and payments made:

Cheques received on 11 September

	£
Arnold & Baker	150.00
Baldwin Stores Ltd	205.05
Brentfords plc	48.10
Donald Dentford	750.00

Cheques paid on 25 September

	£
Insulation Supply Co Ltd	343.00
CIC plc	14.85
Outdoor Fabrics plc	106.50
Darling & Son Ltd	241.30

Cheques paid for expenses on 18 September		VAT included
Southern Electricity for electricity	60.00	Nil
Wessex Insurance Co Ltd for insurance	106.00	Nil
Star Garage Ltd for motor expenses	36.00	4.69
W H Smith & Sons Ltd for stationery	28.40	3.70
Southern Newspapers Ltd for advertising	17.00	Nil

Enter the above transactions in the appropriate cash journals and post to the Bank Account. Enter the expenses and the VAT into the Bank Account and post them to the relevant accounts in the nominal ledger. Balance the Bank Account on 30 September and bring the balance down on 1 October.

4

The accounts which appear on 1 June 19— in the ledger of R Wilson, a stationery wholesaler, include the following:

	£	
M Porcher, a customer, balance	200	debit
S Seaman, a customer, balance	75	debit
L Tidmarsh, a supplier, balance	43	credit
A Waters, a supplier, balance	75	credit
Stock of stationery in hand for own office use valued at	20	

The following transactions took place during the first week of June 19—:

19— June		£
1	Sold goods on credit to M Porcher	270
	Bought goods on credit from L Tidmarsh	75
2	Returned goods to L Tidmarsh	24
	Paid L Tidmarsh amount due to date, by cheque	
3	M Porcher returned goods	48
	M Porcher paid balance due at commencement of business on 1 June 19— by cheque less 3% cash discount	
4	Bought goods on credit from A Waters	125
7	Bought stationery for own office use from L Tidmarsh	120
	Sold goods on credit to S Seaman	150

You are required to write up the personal accounts and the Stationery Account as they would appear in

R Wilson's ledger. Sales, Purchases and Returns Accounts are not needed.

To obtain full marks the personal accounts should be written up in three column form: debit, credit and balance. (*RSA BKI*)

5

The following balances were extracted from the books of P Faulkner & Sons at 1 July 19—:

	£
Purchases	5200
Sales	7500
Purchases returns	58
Creditors:	
CIC plc	1800
Tape Works Ltd	518
Debtors:	
Bailey Bros	240
Donald Dentford	350
Cash at bank	3786
Motor expenses	300

The following transactions took place during the month of July:

	£
Purchases day book (PB1):	
July 3 Tape Works Ltd	383
17 CIC plc	105
Sales day book (SB1):	
July 10 Bailey Bros	1000
24 Donald Dentford	750
Purchases returns book (PRB1):	
July 10 Tape Works Ltd	76
Cash payments journal (CP1):	
July 4 CIC plc	1800
4 Tape Works Ltd	518
Cash receipts journal (CR1):	
July 3 Donald Dentford	350
3 Bailey Bros	100
Cheque paid for petrol:	
July 20	24
Cash sale to R Martin:	
July 26	345

You are required to open the accounts (including the cash book) as they would appear in the books of P Faulkner & Sons, make the necessary entries in the accounts to record the above transactions and extract a trial balance as at 31 July 19—.

6

Use a computer package to enter the cheques received and paid in Task 3 and print out the bank account as at 30 September 19—.

7 Priority

After completing the financial records and entering the receipts and payments for 8 September (Fig 9.5 on page 123) in the cash book given in Fig 9.6, supply Sarah Faulkner with a note stating the following information:

a total receipts paid into the bank on 8 September
b total of cheques paid out on 8 September
c balance of cash at bank on 8 September
(*Continued: Task 7, Unit 9.2.*)

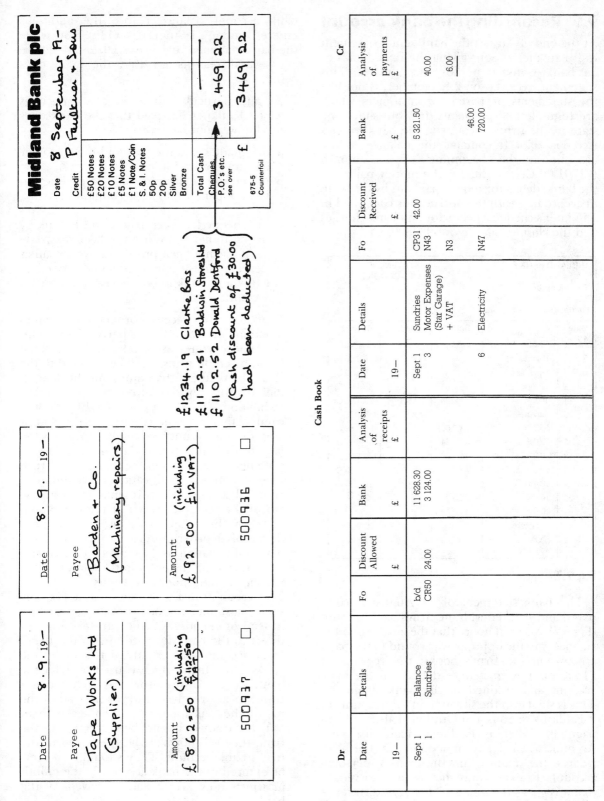

Fig 9.5

Fig 9.6

9.2 Reconciling the bank account

At the end of August the bank sent a statement to P Faulkner & Sons giving the firm details of its bank transactions for one month. This statement, received on 2 September, is not like the statements prepared for customers which are reminders of payments due, but shows the state of the firm's account in the bank's books (see Fig 9.7). It contains the balance of the account at the beginning of the month (£1701.00 Cr); credits for the money paid into the bank; debits for money paid out by the bank in accordance with the instructions contained in Faulkner's cheques; debits for any bank charges and the closing balance of £9328.30 Cr.

MIDLAND BANK PLC Southampton			STATEMENT OF ACCOUNT 31 August 19—	
Name: P Faulkner & Sons				
Date 19—	Details	Debit £	Credit £	Balance £
Aug 1	Balance b/f			1701.00 Cr
1	Sundries		1500.00	3201.00 Cr
3	100746	500.00		2701.00 Cr
4	100747	700.00		2001.00 Cr
8	Sundries		16666.53	18667.53 Cr
11	100749	2377.00		16290.53 Cr
12	100748	1211.34		15079.19 Cr
12	100750	2411.66		12667.53 Cr
15	Sundries		1500.77	14168.30 Cr
25	100751	27.00		14141.30 Cr
25	100752	503.00		13638.30 Cr
31	100755	4000.00		9638.30 Cr
31	Bank charges	10.00		9628.30 Cr
31	S/O	300.00		9328.30 Cr

Fig 9.7

The bank statement of 31 August is compared and checked with the firm's bank account (Fig 9.4). You will notice that the entries and the balances are the opposite way round to the bank account in the firm's books; the receipts of £1500 on 1 August were debited in the bank account and credited in the bank statement. This is similar to the situation in the accounts of P Faulkner & Sons and Outdoor Fabrics plc on page 36. Whereas Faulkner debits its Bank Account when it pays money in, i.e. the bank *receives* the money, in the bank's personal accounts Faulkner must be credited to record that it is *giving* the money. There is a difference in the actual figures of the closing balances; the

bank account balance before the additions entered under 31 August is £11 938.30 while the bank statement balance is £9328.30. There are several reasons for this, the main ones being:

1 At any particular time there are cheques which Faulkner has paid that the bank does not know about because:

   a the cheque is in the post and the customer has not received it, or

   b the customer has received the cheque but has not paid it into his account at his bank, or

   c the cheque has been paid into his bank by the customer but it has not been 'cleared', i.e. it has not been processed by the bank's clearing house and it has not arrived at Faulkner's bank to be entered in the firm's account.

2 Faulkner often receives orders and cheques at exhibitions in different parts of the country. The cheques are paid into the nearest bank, by credit transfer, to be credited to the firm's bank at Southampton, but this takes a day or so; those received at the London Exhibition on 31 August (CR49 = £4000) cannot, therefore, be credited to the South-ampton branch until September, which is too late for the bank to record them in its August statement. On the other hand, the firm receives prompt notification of remittances received, as the sales representatives, with the aid of the secretarial staff at the exhibition, telex to the head office at Southampton details of all orders and remittances received. This information is 'documented' immedi-ately, including the entry in the bank account for the current month of August.

3 The credit transfer system is also used by some customers, who prefer this system instead of cheques. Credit transfers are sent direct to the bank for crediting in the firm's bank account and an advice is sent by the bank to the firm, which is used to debit the bank account in the usual way. When credit transfers are received towards the end of the month they will appear on the bank statement but, as the advice has not been received by the firm, they will not have been entered in the firm's bank account. They should, however, be entered in the bank account in the month in which they are actually received by the bank.

4 Occasionally payments are made by standing orders, i.e. the bank carries out instructions by its customers to pay someone a stated amount on an agreed date. This method of payment is suitable for regular payments of the same amount such as subscriptions or insurance premiums. Faulkner had entered into a hire-purchase agreement with the Regal Machine Company for the purchase of 10 industrial sewing machines involving a payment of £300 at the end of every three months. Holidays or weekends sometimes coincided with the due date and on these occasions the bank made the payment on the first working day in the next month. In any event Faulkner did not know for sure if the payment had been made until the bank statement was received, unless the bank was asked. (*Note* A direct debit has exactly the same effect; the only difference being that the money is paid out on the creditors' instructions.)

5 The bank makes a charge for its services and takes the money out of the firm's account at the end of the month. It debits the amount charged to the firm's account to record the service that the firm has received. As Faulkner does not know what this charge will be, it cannot be entered in the bank account until the statement is received, i.e. the bank account is left open and entered up from the bank statement as at 31 August.

These factors account for the different figures to be found in the bank statement and the firm's bank account. A bank reconciliation statement (see page 126) is drawn up to check the accuracy of the bank statement with the firm's bank account.

Procedure for preparing a bank reconciliation statement

1 Check both opening balances – in this case bank account £1701.00 debit = bank statement £1701.00 credit is correct. If the opening balances are different it will have been 'reconciled' in the previous bank reconciliation statement. It may be necessary, however, to examine the previous statement to check if any differences then are still outstanding.

2 Check the debit column of the bank account with the credit column of the bank statement. In this case all the items appear in both places except the £4000 in the bank account on 31 August which the bank had not received. It is

necessary to make a note of this for inclusion in the bank reconciliation statement as an *addition* to the balance of the bank statement.

3 Check the credit column of the cash book, using the cash payments journal for the cheque numbers, with the debit column of the bank statement. It is seen that:

a Cheques numbered 100746 and 100747 = £1200 paid on 1 August.

b Cheques numbered 100749, 100748 and 100750 = £6000 paid on 8 August.

c Of the £610 paid on 20 August only the £27 and £503 appear on the bank statement; the cheques for Kalamazoo (£46) and Barden & Co (£34) have not been received by the bank. These must be noted as a *deduction* in the bank reconciliation statement under the heading of 'Cheques drawn but not presented'.

d The cash payments journal on 29 August reveals two cheques drawn – 100755 and 100756 for £4000 and £1620 respectively (credited in the bank account as £5620) but only the £4000 cheque appeared on the bank statement. The £1620 cheque must, therefore be noted as a *deduction* in the bank reconciliation statement.

4 Examine the bank statement for any other items which have not been included in the bank account. It is seen that:

a Bank charges of £10 are included on the bank statement but not in the bank account. This item must be entered in the bank account so that the true balance at the bank is recorded at the end of August.

b There is a standing order of £300 payable to the Regal Machine Co which is also not included in the bank account but has been debited in the bank statement. This is treated in the same way as in **a**.

5 Prepare the bank reconciliation statement, as shown on page 126 using the following rules (use the bank statement balance as the starting point):

Add money paid in but not credited
Deduct unpresented cheques
Balance = bank account balance

If the balance on the bank statement has Dr following it this means that the account is overdrawn, that is more money has been spent than there is in the account. Most businesses have permission to overdraw but only up to an agreed amount. An overdraft in a bank statement would be shown as a minus figure in a bank reconciliation statement.

If the final balance of the bank reconciliation statement agrees with the bank account balance, P Faulkner & Sons will be satisfied that both records are correct.

Bank reconciliation statement at 31 August 19—

	£	£
Balance as per bank statement		9 328.30
Add Money paid in but not credited (CR49)		4 000.00
		13 328.30
Deduct Unpresented cheques:		
Kalamazoo cheque No 100753	46.00	
Barden & Co cheque No 100754	34.00	
Supplier cheque No 100756	1620.00	
		1700.00
Balance as per bank account		11 628.30

Amended bank account

	£	£
Balance as at 31 August		11 938.30
Less		
Bank charges — entered 2 September	10.00	
Standing order — but dated 31 August	300.00	
		310.00
		11 628.30

TASKS

1

It is the usual practice for a business to receive a statement from the bank at the end of each month. This statement is then compared with the bank columns of the cash book in order to extract a bank reconciliation statement. Figure 9.8 (page 127) shows a bank statement for the month of June 19— and an extract from the cash book (bank columns only) for the same month.

By comparison of the two records you are asked to bring the bank account up to date and construct a bank reconciliation statement as at 30 June 19—.

2

The bank account of V White and his bank statement received on 31 March 19— are given in Fig 9.9. You are required to:

a Bring the bank account up to date, and state the new balance at 31 March 19—.
b Prepare a statement, under its proper title, to reconcile the difference between the new up-to-date balance in the bank account and the balance in the bank statement on 31 March 19—.

3

On 31 May the debit balance on Carr's bank account as shown in the cash book was £370.41. The bank statement at that date showed a credit balance of £309.10.

On checking the bank statement against the cash book the following differences were found:

a Interest due to be received on a county council loan £36.15 had been collected by the bank but not entered in the cash book.
b A standing order £112.17 payable for fire insurance had been paid by the bank but not entered in the cash book.
c Cheques amounting to £100.41 entered in the cash book had not been presented for payment.
d On 31 May a cheque for £85.70 had been entered in the cash book and paid into the bank after the bank statement had been collected from the bank.

Show your calculation of the balance that should appear in the cash book and then prepare a bank reconciliation statement.

4

From the following draw up a bank reconciliation statement:

	£
Cash at bank as per bank account	678.00
Unpresented cheques	256.00
Cheques received and paid into the bank but not yet entered on the bank statement	115.00
Credit transfers entered as banked on the bank statement but not entered in the cash book	56.00
Cash at bank as per bank statement	875.00

```
MIDWEST BANK LTD                          Account Number    21/368

Mr I N Hand
```

19——		Debit £	Credit £	Balance £	
June 1	Balance b/f			468.90	Cr
5	Sundries		392.83	861.73	Cr
12	129346	129.76		731.97	Cr
14	Sundries		198.83	930.80	Cr
20	129349	63.15 ·		867.65	Cr
27	Credit transfer - Jones		100.00	967.65	Cr
28	Standing order – Subscription	20.00		947.65	Cr
28	Bank charges	15.00		932.65	Cr

Cash Book of I N Hand				
19——		Debit £	Credit £	Balance £
June 1	Balance b/d			468.90 (Dr)
5	Cash	392.83		861.73
6	Farmer		129.76	731.97
10	Butcher		63.15	668.82
14	Cash	198.83		867.65
20	Baker		292.22	575.43
26	Burdon		77.69	497.74
29	Cash	204.66		702.40

Fig 9.8

Bank Statement

19——		Debit £	Credit £	Balance £	
March 1	Balance			150.00	Cr
6	Sundries		75.00	225.00	Cr
10	213486	30.00		195.00	Cr
13	213487		17.00	212.00	Cr
15	Credit transfer – B Egg		16.00	228.00	Cr
18	213488	15.00		213.00	Cr
31	Charges	10.00		203.00	Cr

Bank Account

19——		Debit £	Credit £	Balance £
March 1	Balance b/f			150.00 (Dr)
6	Cash	75.00		225.00
8	A Roe		30.00	195.00
13	W Wing	17.00		212.00
16	T Salmon		15.00	197.00
28	R Bird		29.00	168.00
31	R Nest	39.00		207.00

Fig 9.9

5

William Tanner received the following bank statement on 31 May 19—:

19—	Debit £	Credit £	Balance £
May 1 Balance			332
7 110119	102		230
11 Cash		518	748
18 Credit transfer investment dividends		600	1348
19 110121	340		1008
26 Direct debit insurance	78		930

William Tanner checked the statement against his cheque counterfoils and found that cheques numbered 110118 for £235 and 110120 for £136 had not been presented.

The names of the payees of the cheques are:

110118	S Lyle
110119	N Faldo
110120	C O'Connor
110121	K Brown

As William Tanner has not written up his cash book for the month of May 19— you are required to:

a write up the bank columns for that month

b balance the bank columns, and reconcile that balance with the amount shown on the bank statement at the end of the month (*RSA BKI*)

6

On 28 February 19— the bank column of W Payne's cash book showed a debit balance of £600.

A bank statement written up to 28 February 19— disclosed that the following items had not been entered in the cash book:

a the sum of £1500 received from P Jones by credit transfer

b the transfer of £1000 from Payne's private bank deposit account into his business bank account

c bank charges £180

When the bank statement was further checked against the cash book the following items were discovered:

a cheques drawn in favour of creditors totalling £8300 had not yet been presented

b cash and cheques £4100 had been entered in the cash book but not yet credited by the bank

c a cheque for £50 drawn by W Payne in respect of drawings had been correctly entered in the cash book but debited twice in the bank statement

You are required to prepare as at 28 February 19—.

a A statement showing the adjusted cash book balance.

b A bank reconciliation statement showing the balance appearing in the bank statement. (*RSA BKI*)

7 🗄️ **Priority**

You receive the statement (Fig 9.10) from the bank on 15 September 19— in connection with Task 7 of Unit 9.1.

a Bring the bank account up to date.

b Prepare a statement to reconcile the difference between the new up-to-date balance in the bank account with the balance shown on the bank statement.

c Inform Sarah Faulkner of the amended balance of cash at the bank and explain why the previous figure you gave her was not up to date.

Fig 9.10

P Faulkner & Sons
Chestnut Avenue
Southampton
SO2 4AG

Midland Bank plc
SOUTHAMPTON

Statement of Account

19—   Sheet 221   Account No. 12345678

	DEBIT £	CREDIT £	BALANCE £
SEP 1 BALANCE BROUGHT FORWARD			11628.30 C
1 SUNDRIES		3124.00	14752.30 C
4 CT – BELL & SONS		235.00	14987.30 C
5 300120	2831.50		12155.80 C
6 DD – ROYAL INSURANCE	186.24		11969.56 C
6 300121	2490.00		9479.56 C
8 SUNDRIES		3469.22	12948.78 C
8 CHARGES	32.00		12916.78 C
9 300123	46.00		12870.78 C
10 300122	720.00		12150.78 C
12 300125	862.50		11288.28 C

9.3 Recording petty cash

It is the practice of Faulkner to pay all money received into the bank, and all payments over £10 have to be made by cheque. There are, however, many items of less than £10 which a business has to pay for at regular intervals, such as window cleaning, small items of stationery (pens, pencils, postcards, etc) and tea and coffee. These small payments are paid in cash and entered in a Petty Cash Book with columns to analyse the expenditure before posting it to the expense accounts in the nominal ledger.

The advantages of using a petty cash book are:

1 Many small items are grouped together under main headings such as stationery or travelling expenses and only the total is posted to the ledger, thus reducing the number of postings.
2 The bank account (or cash account if one is used) is not filled up with these small items.
3 It allows the work of handling small items of cash to be delegated to a petty cashier and leaves the chief cashier to deal with larger items.

Faulkner uses the 'imprest' system of recording petty cash which has the following features:

1 The imprest (or float) at Faulkner is £50. It has been estimated to be sufficient to cover the petty cash expenditure for one month and is the amount which the petty cashier has in the cash box to start the month.
2 During the month payments are made from the £50 imprest. All expenditure must be covered by a petty cash voucher (Fig 9.11) or a receipt. This voucher must be signed by the person receiving the money and authorised by a responsible official such as the chief cashier. The vouchers and receipts are numbered and filed numerically for audit purposes.
3 At the end of the month the petty cashier receives a sum of money from the cashier to reimburse the amount spent. The system is designed to give control of petty cash expenditure because the size of the balance (the imprest) is fixed at the beginning of the period and can never be more than that. If the imprest is £50 and at the end of the month there is £11 left, the petty cashier receives cash for £39 to restore the imprest.
4 The petty cash can be checked *at any time*, even if the petty cash book is not up to date because:

Petty cash vouchers + cash held = imprest

Example

There was £10.50 in the petty cash box on 1 October, so the petty cashier was given a cheque for £39.50 to cash to make up the 'imprest' to £50. During October the following payments were made after being confirmed by petty cash vouchers:

19—			Amount £	VAT (included) £
Oct	3	Cleaning materials	1.65	0.21
	8	Bus fare to Winchester	1.37	
	9	Biros and pencils	3.25	0.42
	10	Tea and sugar	1.50	
	10	Milk	1.20	
	14	First aid kit for office	6.85	0.89
	17	Small bottle aspirins	0.40	0.05
	19	Newspapers	2.20	
	21	Window cleaning	6.70	0.87
	23	Large manilla envelopes	1.43	0.18
	28	Donation to Salvation Army	2.50	
	31	Bus fare to Mayflower Park Exhibition	1.30	

The example of a petty cash book in Fig 9.11 illustrates:

1 The opening balance of £10.50 brought forward from September.
2 The amount received £39.50, which is debited to make up the imprest to £50.
3 The entry of each payment in the 'Total payment' column and also the analysis to the appropriate expense columns of 'Cleaning', 'Travelling expenses', 'Stationery', 'Office expenses', 'Subscriptions and donations', together with the entry of VAT in the 'VAT' column where VAT is included in the payment.
4 The totalling of the analysis columns which 'cross balances' with the total payments of £30.35.
5 The entry of the closing balance of cash £19.65 contained in the petty cash box which, when added to the expenditure of £30.35, equals £50, i.e. it agrees with the imprest of £50 – a process which is called balancing off.

To calculate the balance:

Subtract total payments from imprest (total receipts)

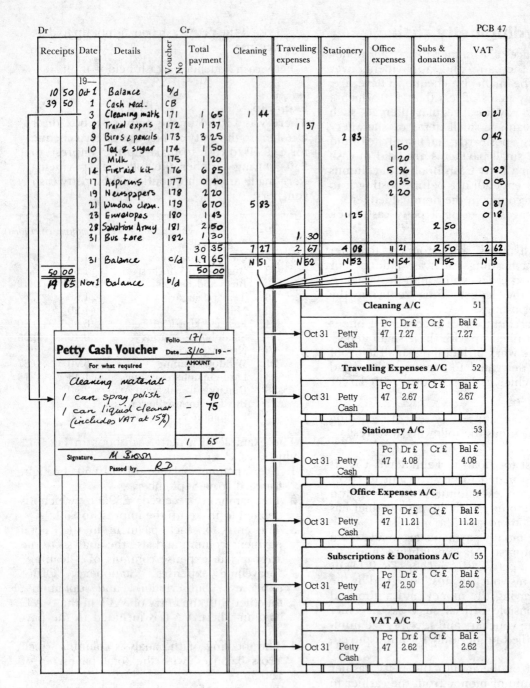

Fig 9.11 Petty cash book

To restore the imprest:

Subtract closing balance of cash from imprest = total payments

6 The bringing down of the balance of £19.65 on 1 November.

7 The posting of the analysed (credit) columns to the debit of the relevant nominal ledger accounts, which is similar to the postings from the cash payments journal for expenses, except that with the petty cash columns only one posting is required for each expense for the month. In this example 12 items have been reduced to six postings.

Guidelines for the security of petty cash;

- Check sums of money carefully before handing them over.
- Lock the cash in a cash box and keep it in a locked safe.
- Locate the keys to the cash box and safe in a secure place which is only accessible to the petty cashier and their supervisor.
- Never leave the office unattended with the cash box unlocked.
- Ensure that every payment of cash is supported by an authorised petty cash voucher.
- Make regular checks of the petty cash account and cash to ensure that the petty cash vouchers received + the cash held in the box = the imprest.

TASKS

1
Enter the following items from petty cash vouchers into P Faulkner & Sons' petty cash book for November, analysed into cleaning, travelling expenses, stationery, office expenses, subscriptions and donations, and VAT. Total the columns, cross balance, balance off on 30 November, bring the balance down on 1 December and post to the relevant accounts in the nominal ledger.

On 1 November the balance was brought forward from the petty cash book in Fig 9.11 (PCB47).

On 2 November a cheque was received and cashed to make up the imprest to £50.

19–			£
Nov	3	Donation to Oxfam	5.00
		Cleaning materials (VAT included £1.50)	11.50
	9	Taxi fare for Miss Jones (ill) (VAT included £0.60)	4.60
	13	Tea bags, coffee, 2 lb sugar	4.87
	14	Envelopes (VAT included £0.28)	2.20
	19	Newspapers	2.30
	23	Milk	1.12
	24	Scissors for office (VAT included £0.30)	2.30
	25	Adhesive tape (VAT included £0.12)	0.92
	30	Flowers for Miss Jones (ill in hospital) (VAT included £0.75)	5.75

2
R G Baldwin's petty cash book is kept on the imprest system, the amount of the imprest being £50.

a Enter the following transactions in the petty cash account, balance the account on 30 November, total the analysis columns and post the totals to the appropriate accounts in the nominal ledger:

19–			£
Nov	1	Balance in hand of petty cashier	16.40
	1	Cash received from chief cashier to restore the imprest (*work this out for yourself*)	
	6	Paid travelling expenses	5.50
	8	Purchased paper clips (including 79p VAT)	6.10
	10	Purchased cleaning materials	3.00
	15	Purchased typewriter ribbon (including £1.20 VAT)	9.20
	18	Purchased postage stamps	3.00
	22	Purchased office tea and sugar	3.50
	29	Paid for windows to be cleaned (including £1.12 VAT)	8.62

b Carry down the balance of cash in hand on 30 November and restore the imprest on 1 December.

Receipts		Date	Details	Voucher /Folio No	Total payments		Motor expenses		Office expenses		Postage		Purchases		Travelling expenses		VAT	
		19—																
7	37	JAN 1	Balance	b/f														
92	63	2	Cash recd	8														
		3	Petrol & oil	1	7	63									6	64	−	99
		4	Stationery	2	3	21			2	79							−	42
		5	Postage stamps	3	3	12					3	21						
		10	Travel exes	4	6	43							6	34				
		13	Envelopes	5	4	51					3	92					−	59
		18	Window cleaning	6	1	80			12	−							1	80
		24	Salesmen's parking fees	7	5	−									5	−		
		28	Newspapers	8	25	−			25	−								
		30	Purchases	9	12	10							10	53			1	57
			Initial towel	10	7	70	1	00									6	70
					88	50	1	00	39	79	7	13	16	87	11	64	12	07
		30	Balance	c/d	11	50												
100	−				100	00												
15	10	Feb 1	Balance	b/d														
84	90	2	Cash recd	CB														

Fig 9.12

3

The petty cash book (Fig 9.12) contains a number of errors. Rewrite the book in a correct manner and comment on the effect of the errors.

4

Greaves (Builders) Ltd keep their petty cash on the imprest system with a £100 float and analyse its expenditure into: stationery, travelling expenses, telephone expenses, miscellaneous expenses, and deductible input tax (this last item is to record the VAT element in any expenses paid through petty cash).

Enter up the petty cash book from the following details, balance off at the end of the month, restore the imprest on 1 July, and state where the items would be posted to in the ledger.

19—			£
June	1	Balance in hand (float)	100.00
	2	Paid for envelopes (VAT included 28p)	2.20
	3	Paid travelling expenses	5.00
	5	Paid telephone expenses (VAT included £3.00)	23.00
	8	Bought first aid kit (VAT included 71p)	5.50
	10	Paid for biros (VAT included 18p)	1.38
	16	Paid travelling expenses	7.00
	22	Bought string (VAT included 7p)	0.55
	23	Paid for tea, milk & sugar	5.00
	25	Bought 2 tins glue (for use on buildings) (VAT included £1.27)	9.77
	30	Paid cleaning bill	15.00
	30	Paid for cleaning materials (VAT included 12p)	0.99

5

Daniel Clarke operates an accounting system of paying all receipts into the bank and making all cash payments (under £20 each) out of petty cash. Higher amounts are paid by cheque and entered in the cash book. The petty cash float of £100 is restored at the end of each month.

At the close of business on 31 January 19— Daniel Clarke's cash at bank balance was £561.60 and his petty cash balance was the imprest amount of £100. During the month of February 19— his transactions involving the cash and petty cash books were:

Payments out of petty cash

19—		Details	Voucher No	£
Feb	1	Postage stamps	400	12.00
	2	Window cleaning	401	16.00*
	3	Taxi fare	402	2.50*
	4	Coffee	403	5.15
	10	Aerogrammes	404	4.80
	17	Cleaning materials	405	13.60*
	18	Bus fare	406	0.75
	22	Greetings card	407	1.10*
	24	Correcting fluid	408	2.75*
	25	Postal order	409	4.34

*VAT at the standard rate to be added.

Bank paying-in book counterfoil entries

19—			£
Feb	4	Cheque from L McDonald	262.00
		Cash sales	53.49
	10	Cheque from P Jarrett in full settlement of £120 owed by him	108.00
	17	Cash sales	340.00
	22	Cheque from J Lewis	1490.00
	28	Cash sales	846.50

Cheque counterfoil entries
19—

		£
Feb	1 British Gas for heating	862.50
	8 R Smith in settlement of £200 owed to him	180.00
	18 Meadow Dairies Ltd for milk supplied to the office	24.50
	22 R Cox in part-payment of outstanding account	100.00
	28 Petty cash to restore imprest	?

You are required to write up:

a the petty cash book with appropriate analysis columns;

b the cash book, indicating clearly the name of the ledger account to be debited or credited in respect of each entry.

6 📥 **Priority**

You are in charge of petty cash at P Faulkner & Sons.

a Examine the petty cash vouchers (Fig 9.13 on pages 133–4) and, if they are in order, enter them in the petty cash book in Fig 9.14. If any of the vouchers are unacceptable, write memos to those people who have requested the money, pointing out the reason(s).

b Today (30 January) you are reimbursed with £1.20 for bus fares spent when you delivered a document to the printer. Also, you are asked to purchase a pack of six aerogrammes from the post office. Prepare petty cash vouchers for these two items, arrange for their authorisation and enter them in the petty cash book.

c Balance the book at 31 January 19—, carry down the balance and prepare a cheque on 1 February 19— for signature by the Accountant to restore the imprest.

d Post the analysis column totals to the appropriate accounts in the nominal ledger at 31 January 19—.

Petty Cash Voucher
Folio 187
Date 27-1-19—

For what required	VAT amount	Amount incl. VAT
Biscuits		1 40
Coffee		1 30
		2 70

Signature W.Cap
Passed by J Russell

Petty Cash Voucher
Folio 188
Date 28-1-19—

For what required	VAT amount	Amount incl. VAT
Correcting fluid	60	1 26
	60	1 26

Signature J Wyatt
Passed by S Faulkner

Petty Cash Voucher
Folio 189
Date 28.1.19—

For what required	VAT amount	Amount incl. VAT
3 dusters		6 30
		6 30

Signature R Mace.
Passed by J Russell

Fig 9.13

Petty Cash Voucher

Folio _190_   Date _29-1-19-_

For what required	VAT amount	Amount incl. VAT
Contribution to Wild Life Fund		5 00
		5 00

Signature _J T Bull_
Passed by _Hawkins_

Petty Cash Voucher

Folio _191_   Date _29-1-19-_

For what required	VAT amount	Amount incl. VAT
ADHESIVE TAPE	— 13	1 03
	— 13	1 03

Signature _R. Martin_
Passed by _____

Petty Cash Voucher

Folio _192_   Date _29.1.19-_

For what required	VAT amount	Amount incl. VAT
Postage stamps		5 00
		5 00

Signature _S. Watson_
Passed by _J Russell_

Fig 9.13 (cont'd)

Petty Cash Book

Dr Receipts	Date 19—	Details	VN	Total payments	Cleaning	Travelling expenses	Stationery and Postage	Office Expenses	Subs & donations	Cr VAT
12 32	Jan 1	Balance	b/a							
37 68	1	Cash received	CB14							
	2	Taxi fare	183	3 50		3 50				
	10	Envelopes	184	4 60			4 00			0 60
	18	'Get well' card	185	0 75				0 75		
	23	Postal order	186	0 91			0 91			

Fig 9.14

Assignment – Unit 9

Situation: You have been asked by the Social Committee of your firm to organise an outing to a concert and to include a meal at a restaurant on the way there. Past and present members of staff are to be invited to take part. Use your own location for the setting of this project (i.e. the place where the concert takes place, the restaurant, etc). You are expected to use your initiative in making the necessary plans for this event.

a Write a memo to the Personnel Manager requesting the firm to give a subsidy for this activity and pointing out the importance of social events of this kind for the morale and welfare of staff.

b Draft a letter to staff giving full details of the outing, with a tear-off slip for staff to return to you with their remittance if they wish to take part.

c You are required to keep a special current account at the bank and a petty cash account with an imprest of £50 for the payment of items below £10. The Social Committee has allocated you £100 to open your bank account. Enter the items shown here (Fig 9.15) in the appropriate books.

Fig 9.15

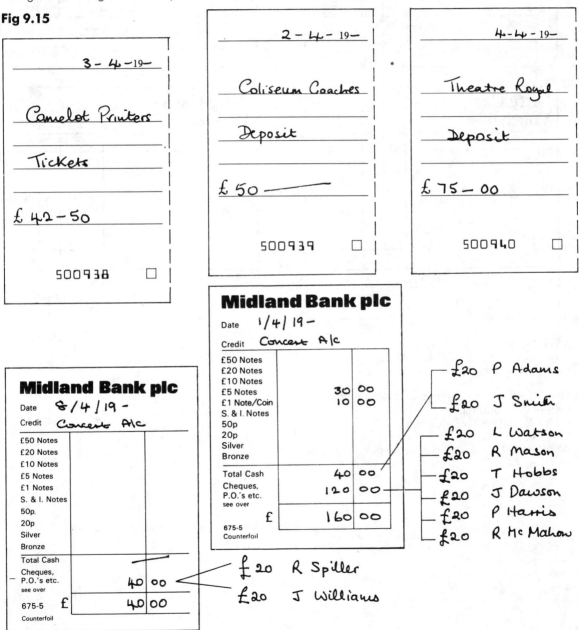

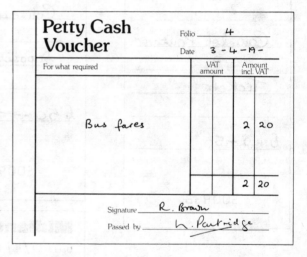

Petty Cash Voucher

Folio _____ 1 _____

Date _____ 1 – 4 – 19 – _____

For what required	VAT amount	Amount incl. VAT
Postage stamps		3 00
		3 00

Signature _____ R. Brown _____

Passed by _____ L. Partridge _____

Petty Cash Voucher

Folio _____ 2 _____

Date _____ 2 – 4 – 19 – _____

For what required	VAT amount	Amount incl. VAT
Telephone calls		– 85
		– 85

Signature _____ R. Brown _____

Passed by _____ L. Partridge _____

Petty Cash Voucher

Folio _____ 3 _____

Date _____ 2 – 4 – 19 – _____

For what required	VAT amount	Amount incl. VAT
Accounts stationery		1 12
Typing paper		3 50
		4 62

Signature _____ R. Brown _____

Passed by _____ L. Partridge _____

Petty Cash Voucher

Folio _____ 4 _____

Date _____ 3 – 4 – 19 – _____

For what required	VAT amount	Amount incl. VAT
Bus fares		2 20
		2 20

Signature _____ R. Brown _____

Passed by _____ L. Partridge _____

Fig 9.15 (cont'd)

d On 10 April 19— you receive a statement from the bank (Fig 9.16). Prepare a statement to reconcile the bank statement balance with your bank account balance.

e What amount of cash is held in your petty cash box on 10 April?

```
                          Midland Bank plc
Concert Organiser
                          Statement of Account

                              DEBIT      CREDIT       BALANCE
19—     Sheet 001   Account No. 12349876   £          £

APR  1 BALANCE BROUGHT FORWARD                        100.00 C
     1 200001                    50.00                 50.00 C
     1 SUNDRIES                             160.00     210.00 C
     7 200002                    50.00                160.00 C
     8 200003                    42.50                117.50 C
```

Fig 9.16

TO SUM UP
FINANCIAL DATA

Cash book   *Source document*
Dr   cash and cheques received   bank paying-in slip
Cr   cash and cheques paid   cheque counterfoil

Day book for discounts:
Dr   discount allowed
     Total posted to Discount Allowed Account Dr
Cr   discount received
     Total posted to Discount Received Account Cr

Petty cash book   Imprest = cash + vouchers
Dr   cash received
Cr   cash paid (entered twice)   petty cash voucher

Bank reconciliation statement
Update cash book: Dr   credit transfers
                   Cr   standing orders
                        direct debits
                        bank charges

Reconciliation statement:
    Opening balance = closing balance on bank statement
    Add: money paid in but not credited
    Deduct: unpresented cheques
    Closing balance = final updated balance of bank account

10 The payroll

Introduction

In many industries the employees' pay (wages or salaries) forms the largest element in the cost of production and therefore it is essential to keep accurate records and control over payment.

There is no difference in the method of recording pay, whether salaries or wages, but it is customary to pay salaries monthly by cheque or credit transfer, whereas wages are normally paid weekly in cash.

At Faulkner the cost of the materials used in production and the cost of wages last year were of equal value.

10.1 Calculating gross pay

In order to calculate pay, a record must be kept of the time spent at work by each employee. At Faulkner this is done by means of a clock card which each employee inserts in a time recording (or clocking-in) machine at the time of entering and leaving the workplace. An example of a clock card is given in Fig 10.1.

For costing and checking purposes, a record may be kept of the time spent by each employee on each job; this is done on a daily time sheet.

Each week the clock cards are passed to the wages clerk, who also obtains the daily time sheets and checks that employee's time and job hours agree before making out the wages. Once the hours are agreed, the wages are calculated and then entered in the wages records.

The clock card illustrated in Fig 10.1 relates to Mr T Rawlings for the week ended 13 April 19—. This card, along with the cards for all the other employees, is collected from the clocking-

in machine racks at the end of the week and handed into the wages office. A calculator is useful for multiplying the number of hours by the rate of pay per hour. Each day's total is calculated to the nearest quarter of an hour.

In this example, Mr Rawlings spent 8 hours 38 minutes at work on Monday and he is credited with 8.75 hours, as the 8 minutes in excess of 30 is over half way to the next quarter, allowing him to claim 15 minutes. This employee is paid at the rate of £5 per hour for a 38-hour week and time and a half (£7.50 per hour) thereafter, which is regarded as overtime. These amounts are calculated on the clock cards in the wages office. In the case of Mr Rawlings, he has worked a total of 41.50 hours of which 38 are paid at the rate of £5 per hour (£190.00) and 3.5 hours at £7.50 per hour (£26.25), giving him a total gross wage for the week of £216.25.

The clock cards provide the information to be entered in the wages records and on the pay slip which the employees receive with their pay.

PERFORMANCE CHECK
When checking clock/time cards and calculating gross pay:
- identify all discrepancies and take appropriate action to correct them
- ensure that only correct clock/time cards are authorised for payment
- complete all essential information legibly
- make accurate calculations
- complete tasks within the required deadlines

CLOCK CARD

No 15   Name: T RAWLINGS

Week ending: 13 April 19—

Day	In	Out	In	Out	TOTAL HOURS
M	0800	1201	1302	1739	8.75
Tu	0758	1200	1300	1730	8.50
W	0802	1202	1301	1800	9.00
Th	0810	1200	1301	1731	8.25
F	0801	1203	1258	1601	7.00
TOTAL					41.50

	£
Ordinary time: . . . 38 hrs @ £5.00 (up to 38 hours)	190.00
Overtime . . . . . . 3.5 hrs @ £7.50	26.25
TOTAL GROSS WAGES	216.25

Fig 10.1 Clock card

TASKS

1

Calculate the gross pay for each of the following employees whose basic rate of pay is £4 per hour for a 38 hour week; time and a quarter for the next four hours and time and a half thereafter:

B Brown	38 hours	D Davis	44 hours
C Capable	39 hours	E Evans	40 hours

2

The employee whose clock card No 18 is given in Fig 10.2 is paid at the rate of £5.20 per hour for a 42-hour week; time and a quarter for the next 6 hours; and time and a half thereafter. Calculate his gross weekly wage.

3

a Calculate the daily and weekly total hours worked, the amount of pay for ordinary time and the amount of pay for overtime for the employee whose clock card No 3 is given in Fig 10.3. The current rate of pay is £4.80 per hour for a 38-hour week and time and a half thereafter, which is regarded as overtime.

b From 1 November a new pay scale was negotiated increasing the basic pay to £5.40 per hour for a 36-hour week. What difference will this make to Mr Bull's gross pay if he works the same number of hours as above?

CLOCK CARD

No 18   **CLOCK CARD**

Name S WATSON

Week Ending 4 June 19-—

Day		In	Out	In	Out	Total
AM	M	0800				
PM			1201	1300	1800	
AM	Tu	0759				
PM			1230	1330	1730	
AM	W	0802				
PM			1202	1300	1900	
AM	Th	0758				
PM			1201	1300	1800	
AM	F	0800				
PM			1230	1330	1900	
AM	S	0830				
PM			1230	1300	1700	
AM	Su					
PM						

Ordinary time	
Overtime	
Total wages	
Less Nat Ins	
Income tax	
Amount paid	

Fig 10.2

CLOCK CARD

No 3   Name: J T BULL

Week ending: 8 October 19-—

Day	In	Out	In	Out	TOTAL HOURS
M	0730	1201	1302	1700	
Tu	0728	1158	1300	1701	
W	0731	1202	1301	1659	
Th	0740	1201	1304	1712	
F	0730	1202	1303	1604	
TOTAL					

	£
Ordinary time: . . . . . hrs @ (up to 38 hours)	
Overtime . . . . hrs @	
TOTAL GROSS WAGES	

Fig 10.3

4

a Check the daily and total hours given in the clock cards in Fig 10.4 and if any card is incorrect return it to the Wages Clerk with a note of explanation.

b After amending any incorrect totals, calculate the total gross wages for each of the employees, using the rates of pay given in Task 1. (*Continued: Task 6, Unit 10.2.*)

CLOCK CARD

No 1   Name: B BROWN

Week ending: 10 April 19—

Day	In	Out	In	Out	TOTAL HOURS
M	0800	1200	1301	1700	8.00
Tu	0755	1201	1300	1630	7.75
W	0801	1205	1300	1631	7.50
Th	0750	1204	1330	1710	8.00
F	0800	1203	1300	1600	7.00
TOTAL					38.25

£

Ordinary time:............ hrs @ . . . .
(up to 38 hours)

Overtime..................... hrs @ . . . .

TOTAL GROSS WAGES

CLOCK CARD

No 5   Name: C CAPABLE

Week ending: 10 April 19—

Day	In	Out	In	Out	TOTAL HOURS
M	0750	1200	1301	1730	8.75
Tu	0755	1203	1300	1630	7.75
W	0758	1210	1300	1730	8.75
Th	0750	1201	1310	1645	7.75
F	0755	1200	1308	1600	7.00
TOTAL					39.00

£

Ordinary time:............ hrs @ . . . .
(up to 38 hours)

Overtime..................... hrs @ . . . .

TOTAL GROSS WAGES

CLOCK CARD

No 6   Name: D DAVIS

Week ending: 10 April 19—

Day	In	Out	In	Out	TOTAL HOURS
M	0800	1200	1300	1630	7.50
Tu	0800	1204	1301	1730	8.50
W	0805	1206	1259	1635	7.50
Th	0758	1200	1258	1645	7.75
F	0801	1201	1304	1601	7.00
TOTAL					38.25

£

Ordinary time: .... hrs @ . . . .
(up to 38 hours)

Overtime..................... hrs @ . . . .

TOTAL GROSS WAGES

CLOCK CARD

No 7   Name: E EVANS

Week ending: 10 April 19—

Day	In	Out	In	Out	TOTAL HOURS
M	0805	1200	1300	1730	8.50
Tu	0801	1203	1302	1800	9.00
W	0802	1209	1310	1700	8.00
Th	0800	1200	1300	1630	7.50
F	0755	1203	1300	1605	7.25
TOTAL					40.25

£

Ordinary time: .... hrs @ . . . .
(up to 38 hours)

Overtime..................... hrs @ . . . .

TOTAL GROSS WAGES

Fig 10.4

5 Priority

Write a memo in reply to this telephone message (Fig 10.5). The hours worked by the office staff in week 19 were as follows:

J Brown	38
J T Bull	39.50
W Cap	41
R Martin	38.50
T Rawlings	40
L O Watson	41.50
S Watson	39.50
J Wyatt	38

Staff work a basic 38-hour week.

Fig 10.5

Telephone Message

TIME RECEIVED __0930__   DATE __10. 8. 19 —__

FROM __Peter Faulkner__

For Accounts clerk

There seems to be a great deal of overtime being worked by the office staff. What was the average amount per person for last week (week 19)? Can you suggest how we might reduce this?

RECEIVED BY __W Cap__

10.2 Calculating and recording pay

Income tax and national insurance are statutory deductions, i.e. required by law. There are, however, other deductions which are voluntary, such as savings and social club subscriptions.

Savings and social club contributions are *fixed* deductions which do not normally change from one week to the next, but income tax and national insurance are variable deductions linked to gross pay and may vary from week to week. The variable amounts are calculated each week or month and recorded on a deductions working sheet (form P11), as illustrated in Fig 10.6 (or on an alternative pay form) in the following manner:

National Insurance contributions – form P11

1 Enter the total amount of gross pay in column 1a.
   Example for Week 3: £197.50
2 Refer to the National Insurance contribution tables to find the total of employee's and employer's contributions payable on the amount of gross pay. Enter the combined amount in column 1b and the employee's amount in column 1c. An alternative method of calculating National Insurance is to use appropriate percentages.
   Example for Week 3: £197 = £38.41 (1b)
   $\qquad\qquad\qquad\quad$ = £17.77 (1c)
3 Columns 1d and 1e are completed for employees 'contracted out' from the state scheme.

4 Enter any statutory sick pay in column 1f.
5 Enter any statutory maternity pay in column 1g.

Income tax

1 Calculate the total amount of gross pay due to the employee *less* pension/superannuation contributions on which there is tax relief and enter it in column 2 (see page 143).
   Example for Week 3:
   £197.50 – £9.50 = £188.00
2 Add the amount in column 2 to the total of all previous payments made to the employee since 6 April and enter the new total in column 3.
   Example for Week 3:
   £188.00 + £387.25 = £575.25
3 Refer to Tax Table A (free pay)* to find the amount of free pay to which the employee is entitled according to his/her code number and enter it in column 4.
   Example for Week 3: Code No 294 = £170.16
4 Subtract the 'free pay' in column 4 from the total pay to date in column 3 to arrive at the amount of taxable pay, which is entered in column 5.
   Example for Week 3:
   £575.25 – £170.16 = £405.09
5 Calculate the total tax due by referring to the 'taxable pay' in Tax Table B and enter this sum in column 6.*
   Example for Week 3:
   £405 = £101.25
6 Subtract the amount of tax already deducted from the total tax due to date in column 6, to

Deductions Working Sheet P11   Year to 5 April 19

Employer's name	P FAULKNER + SONS

Tax District and reference

716 300 B MR 29 82 14 B

<table>
<tr><td colspan="3">Complete only for occupational pension schemes newly contracted-out since 1 January 1986. Scheme contracted-out number</td></tr>
<tr><td>S</td><td>4</td><td></td></tr>
</table>

National Insurance Contributions *

Earnings on which employee's contributions payable 1a	Total of employee's and employer's contributions payable 1b	Employee's contributions payable 1c	Earnings on which employee's contributions at contracted-out rate payable included in column 1a 1d	Employee's contributions at contracted-out rate included in column 1c 1e	Statutory Sick Pay in the week or month included in column 2 1f	Statutory Maternity Pay in the week or month included in column 2 1g	Month no
£ 216.25 190.00 197.50	£ 42 10 37 05 38 41	£ 19 48 17 14 17 77	£	£	£	£	6 April to 5 May **1**
							6 May to 5 June **2**
							6 June to 5 July **3**
							6 July to 5 Aug **4**
							6 Aug to 5 Sept **5**
							6 Sept to 5 Oct **6**
			SPECIMEN				6 Oct to 5 Nov **7**
Total c/forward	Total c/forward	Total c/forward	Total c/forward	Total c/forward	Total c/forward	Total c/forward	

P11

Fig 10.6 P11 deductions working sheet
(Crown Copyright)

Employee's surname *in CAPITALS*		First two forenames			
RAWLINGS		TREVOR			

National Insurance no.	Date of birth *in figures*			Works no. etc	Date of leaving *in figures*		
	Day	Month	Year		Day	Month	Year
RO 42 38 4 9	18	05	47	10			

Tax code †	Amended code †				
294	Wk/Mth in which applied				

PAYE Income Tax

Week no	Pay in the week or month including Statutory Sick Pay/ Statutory Maternity Pay 2	Total pay to date 3	Total free pay to date as shown by Table A 4	Total taxable pay to date Ø 5	Total tax due to date as shown by Taxable Pay Tables 6	Tax deducted or refunded in the week or month *Mark refunds 'R'* 7	For employer's use
1	206 75	206 75	56 72	150 03	37 50	37 50	
2	180 50	387 25	113 44	273 81	68 50	31 00	
3	188 00	575 25	170 16	405 09	101 25	32 75	
4							
5							
6							
7							
8							
9							
10							
11							
12							
13							
14							
15							
16							
17							
18							
19							
20							
21							
22							
23							
24			SPECIMEN				
25							
26							
27							
28							
29							
30							

* You must enter the NI contribution table letter overleaf beside the NI totals box - *see the note shown there.*

† If amended cross out previous code.

Ø If in any week/month the amount in column 4 is more than the amount in column 3, leave column 5 blank.

give the amount to be deducted from the employee's pay, and enter it in column 7.
Example for Week 3:
£101.25 − £68.50 = £32.75

If the employee has worked a short week, the total tax shown by the tax tables may be less than the tax already deducted; in that case the wages clerk must refund the difference to the employee instead of making a deduction and enter the amount of refund in column 7 with the initial 'R'.

Note: The figures quoted above are correct at the time of going to press but later editions of the NI and Tax Tables will give different amounts.
* These Tax Tables are included in *Finance: First Levels of Competence Lecturer's Manual*.

The gross pay calculated from the clock cards, or a standard wage or salary if the employee is paid at an agreed amount, together with the deductions, is recorded in the following documents:

- Payroll (see Fig 10.10).
- Employee's pay record sheet (see Fig 10.8), which may replace the deductions working sheet.
- Pay advice slip for the employee (see Fig 10.9) to advise them of the amount of pay and deductions for the week or other period.

The principal stages in the procedure for paying wages in cash are as follows:

	Payroll Ref No*
Enter gross pay, i.e. basic pay plus overtime, bonus, etc, calculated from the clock card.	1
If a pension/superannuation contribution is paid which qualifies for tax relief, it is entered and deducted from gross pay.	2
Calculate and enter the national insurance contributions for employee, employer and the combined amount for employer and employee (see page 141).	3
Calculate and enter income tax (see page 141).	4
Enter the fixed deductions payable.	5
Total and enter the deductions.	6
Subtract the total deductions from gross pay to arrive at net pay which is entered.	7

* Reference numbers relate to the payroll in Fig 10.10.

At this stage the employee's pay record sheet and pay advice slip are completed and, when the pay records of all employees have been compiled, the payroll is totalled and entries made in the relevant ledger accounts (see Fig 10.11), as follows:

	Payroll Ref No
Total gross pay	8
Total the pension contributions. These are paid to the Pension Fund and credited to the Bank Account.	9
Total the combined national insurance contributions. Each week the Inland Revenue Account is credited and the Wages Account debited. The contributions are paid once a month to the Board of Inland Revenue.	10
Total the employees' national insurance contributions. This is a deduction from gross pay.	11
Total income tax payable. Each week the Inland Revenue Account is credited with income tax payable (less any amounts refunded). The employer holds this total until the end of the month and then pays it to the Board of Inland Revenue.	12
Total the savings paid. This is paid to a Savings Account and credited to the Bank Account.	13
Total the social fund contributions. The total deducted is paid to the Treasurer of the Social Fund and credited to the Bank Account.	14
Total the total deductions column. This must equal the totals of columns 11, 12, 13 and 14. This process of cross-casting is an essential check on the accuracy of the work of the wages clerk.	15
Total the net payment column. This is the total sum which must be drawn from the bank for payment of wages and it must equal the gross pay (less pension contributions) (17) less total deductions (15) – another check on the accuracy of the calculations.	16
The employer's national insurance contributions are totalled and added to the gross pay in the Wages Account (Dr column).	18

The number of coins and notes required for each employee is calculated and totalled, an exercise known as 'coining'. The total net pay for the five employees listed on the payroll in Fig 10.10 is £583.28, which is calculated in a coining summary (Fig 10.12) and withdrawn from the bank in the appropriate notes and coins, as shown in the cash summary (Fig 10.12 also).

After collection from the bank, the cash is sorted into the required amounts in accordance with the pay advice slips. The money is not inserted into the wage packets until the total has been sorted correctly and the amounts rechecked by a second member of staff. The employees are required to sign for their pay packets. The procedure outlined above is suitable for the payment of wages in cash when the entries are made manually. There will be variations in the procedure for payment by cheque or credit transfer.

Computerised payroll

When a computer is used to calculate and prepare wages, the employees pay record sheets are stored on disk and updated each week or month. The income tax deductions and national insurance contributions are also stored so they can be extracted from the computer's 'memory' and the payroll and pay advice slips are printed out together with a cash analysis to indicate the number of notes and coins required from the bank. The input to the computer can either be keyed in on a terminal or provided automatically by an electronic time recording system.

Typical menus and sub-menus for wages applications include those shown in Fig 10.7.

When an 'exception' payroll is used only non-standard payments and deductions need to be input into the system; the employees automati-

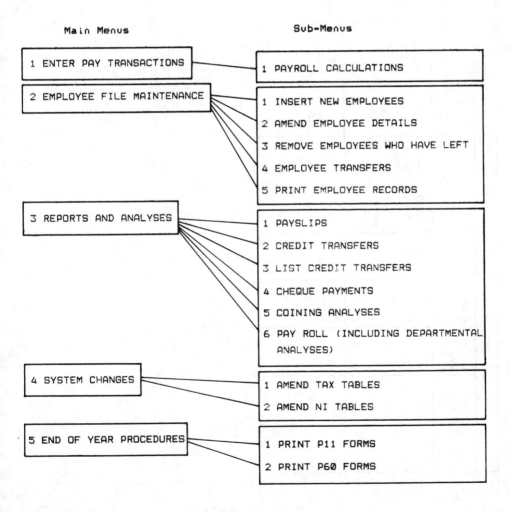

Fig 10.7

INDIVIDUAL PAY RECORD

Surname: RAWLINGS   Forenames: TREVOR

Address: 49 Hill Lane, Southampton, SO4 2DW

Date started: 1.1.75   Date left:

Date of birth: 18.5.47   Works No. 15

Occupation: Accounts Clerk   Department: ACCOUNTS

National Insurance No   RO   42   38   4   9

Wk No.	Date 1.4.19—	Basic 38 hrs @ £5	Overtime Time and a half	Basic	Over-time	GROSS PAY	Pen-sion	GROSS PAY for tax purposes	Income tax refund	Total employer's and employee's contbn	Employer's contbn	Employee's contbn	Income tax payable	Savings	Social fund	Total	NET PAYMENT
				£	£	£	£	£	£	£	£	£	£	£	£	£	£
1	13.4.19	190.00	26.25	190.00	26.25	216.25	9.50	206.75	—	42.10	22.62	19.48	37.50	5.00	1.00	62.98	143.77
2	20.4.19	190.00	—	190.00	—	190.00	9.50	180.50	—	37.05	19.91	17.14	31.00	5.00	1.00	54.14	126.36
3	27.4.19	190.00	7.50	190.00	7.50	197.50	9.50	188.00	—	38.41	20.64	17.77	32.75	5.00	1.00	56.52	131.48

Table sections: Earnings (Basic, Overtime, GROSS PAY, Pension 5% basic wage, GROSS PAY for tax purposes, Income tax refund); National Insurance Table A — Nat Ins (Total employer's and employee's contbn, Employer's contbn, Employee's contbn); Income tax code 294; Deductions (Income tax payable, Savings £5 pw, Social fund £1 pw, Total, NET PAYMENT)

Fig 10.8

cally receive their basic pay and their normal standard deductions, such as union subscriptions, savings, etc.

Weekly or monthly payroll calculations are performed on Menu 1 (Enter pay transactions) as follows:

1 Previous pay, tax details, etc. held on the employee master file, are brought forward.
2 Gross pay is calculated and entered.
3 Income tax is calculated and entered.
4 National insurance contributions for employer and employee are calculated and entered.
5 Deductions in **2** and **3** and any other deductions are totalled and deducted from gross pay to arrive at net pay.
6 The employee master file is updated with the entries made in **2**, **3**, **4** and **5**.

These calculations can then be printed on the appropriate forms by switching over to the following sub-menus:

3.1 payslips
3.5 coining analyses
3.6 payroll

A computerised payroll holds a record on a master file for each employee with the following data:

- employee's name
- clock card/employee number
- pay rates
- hours worked or standard pay
- pay to date
- income tax to date
- code number
- other deductions, including pension, savings, etc.

PAY ADVICE		
Name: Mr Trevor Rawlings		Works No: 15
Week No: 1	Date: 13.4.19—	Code No: 294
		£
Earnings: basic pay		190.00
overtime		26.25
other		—
Total gross pay		216.25
Less pension		9.50
Gross pay for tax purposes		206.75
Less deductions:	£	
Income tax	37.50	
National insurance	19.48	
Savings	5.00	
Social fund	1.00	
Other	—	
Total deductions		62.98
NET PAY		143.77

Fig 10.9

PAYROLL

Week ending: 13.4.19—

Employee	No	Basic pay	Over-time	GROSS PAY	Pension	GROSS PAY for tax purposes	Income tax refund	National Insurance Total employee's and employer's contbn.	Employer's contbn.	Employee's NI	Income tax payable	Savings	Social fund	Total	NET PAYMENT
		①		⑧	⑨	② ⑰		③ ⑩	⑱	⑪	④ ⑫	⑤ ⑬	⑭	⑥ ⑮	⑦ ⑯
		£	£	£	£	£	£	£	£	£	£	£	£	£	£
S T Pratt	14	175.00	—	175.00	8.75	166.25	—	34.13	18.34	15.79	28.25	—	1.00	45.04	121.21
T Rawlings	15	190.00	26.25	216.25	9.50	206.75	—	42.10	22.62	19.48	37.50	5.00	1.00	62.98	143.77
L O Watson	17	150.00	6.00	156.00	7.50	148.50	—	28.16	14.08	14.08	23.50	—	1.00	41.58	106.92
S Watson	18	95.00	15.00	110.00	4.75	105.25	—	15.46	7.73	7.73	13.00	1.00	1.00	22.73	82.52
J Wyatt	19	190.00	—	190.00	9.50	180.50	—	37.05	19.91	17.14	25.50	8.00	1.00	51.64	128.86
TOTALS		800.00	47.25	847.25	40.00	807.25	—	156.90	82.68	74.22	127.75	17.00	5.00	223.97	583.28

Fig 10.10

Payroll totals as given in the payroll (Fig 10.10)

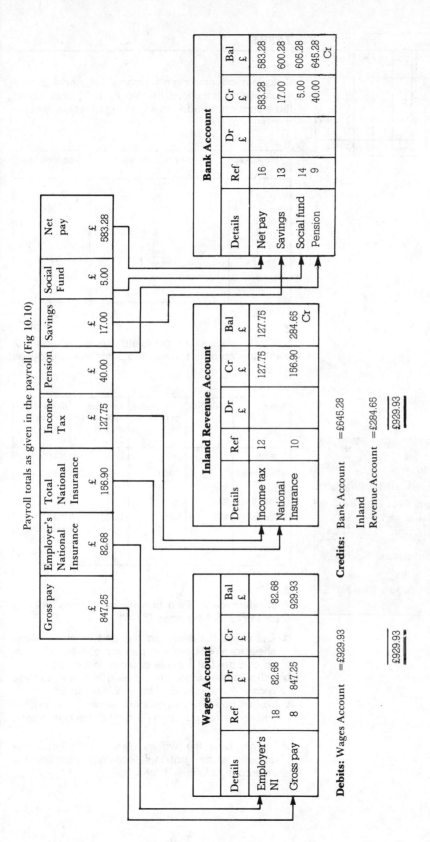

Gross pay	Employer's National Insurance	Total National Insurance	Income Tax	Pension	Savings	Social Fund	Net pay
£	£	£	£	£	£	£	£
847.25	82.68	156.90	127.75	40.00	17.00	5.00	583.28

Wages Account

Details	Ref	Dr £	Cr £	Bal £
Employer's NI	18	82.68		82.68
Gross pay	8	847.25		929.93

Debits: Wages Account = £929.93

£929.93

Inland Revenue Account

Details	Ref	Dr £	Cr £	Bal £
Income tax	12		127.75	127.75
National Insurance	10		156.90	284.65 Cr

Bank Account

Details	Ref	Dr £	Cr £	Bal £
Net pay	16		583.28	583.28
Savings	13		17.00	600.28
Social fund	14		5.00	605.28
Pension	9		40.00	645.28 Cr

Credits: Bank Account = £645.28

Inland Revenue Account = £284.65

£929.93

* Any statutory sick pay and maternity pay paid out is deducted from National Insurance before this is paid to Inland Revenue.

Fig 10.11 Procedure for posting wages

Coining Summary

Net payments £	£20	£10	£5	£2	£1	50p	20p	10p	5p	2p	1p
121.21	6				1		1				1
143.77	7			1	1	1	1		1	1	
106.92	5		1		1	1	2			1	
82.52	4			1		1				1	
128.86	6		1	1	1	1	1	1	1		1
583.28	28	–	2	3	4	4	5	1	2	3	2

Cash Summary

				£
28	@	£20	=	560.00
2	@	£5	=	10.00
3	@	£2	=	6.00
4	@	£1	=	4.00
4	@	50p	=	2.00
5	@	20p	=	1.00
1	@	10p	=	0.10
2	@	5p	=	0.10
3	@	2p	=	0.06
2	@	1p	=	0.02
				————
	TOTAL		=	583.28

Fig 10.12 Coining and cash summaries

PERFORMANCE CHECK

When preparing pay records:

- complete records accurately and legibly
- use the correct documents and transfer totals to the appropriate ledger accounts
- make accurate calculations
- follow cash security/confidentiality procedures at all times
- complete tasks within the required deadlines

TASKS

1

Calculate an employee's income tax and national insurance contributions for Weeks 1–10 and record the entries on a deductions working sheet. Their code number was 278L.

Week No	Gross pay in the week £	Amended code
1	120	
2	120	
3	120	409H
4	120	
5	135	
6	135	
7	100	
8	100	
9	140	
10	140	

2

You are required to complete the entries on tax deduction cards for Week No 5 for the employees listed:

Name	Code No	Gross wages up to week No 4 £	Tax paid up to week No 4 £	Gross wages in week No 5 £
J Martin	308L	640.00	100.50	160.00
S Saunders		700.00	121.25	175.00
Weeks 1–4	278L			
Week 5	409H			
L Turner	430H	820.00	122.25	220.00 (increased from £205 this week)

3

With reference to John Brown's deductions working sheet in Fig 10.13 (pages 151–2):

a Complete the entry on the deductions working sheet for Week No 6. A pension qualifying for tax relief is paid at the rate of 6 per cent of gross pay.

b What circumstances could lead to this employee receiving the refund of tax in Week No 5?

c Explain how the wages clerk would know (1) the amount of free pay, and (2) the total tax due in each week.

d Explain how the wages clerk would know the amount of the national insurance contributions entered in columns 1b and 1c.

Employer's name	P FAULKNER & SONS
Tax District and reference	716 300B MR 29 82 14 B

Complete only for occupational pension schemes newly contracted-out since 1 January 1986.
Scheme contracted-out number

S	4						

National Insurance Contributions *

Earnings on which employee's contributions payable 1a	Total of employee's and employer's contributions payable 1b	Employee's contributions payable 1c	Earnings on which employee's contributions at contracted-out rate payable included in column 1a 1d	Employee's contributions at contracted-out rate included in column 1c 1e	Statutory Sick Pay in the week or month included in column 2 1f	Statutory Maternity Pay in the week or month included in column 2 1g	Month no
£	£	£	£	£	£	£	
200	38 99	18 04					6 April to 5 May **1**
200	38 99	18 04					
200	38 99	18 04					
200	38 99	18 04					
200	38 99	18 04					6 May to 5 June **2**
190							
							6 June to 5 July **3**
							6 July to 5 Aug **4**
							6 Aug to 5 Sept **5**
							6 Sept to 5 Oct **6**
			SPECIMEN				6 Oct to 5 Nov **7**
Total c/forward	Total c/forward	Total c/forward	Total c/forward	Total c/forward	Total c/forward	Total c/forward	

P11

Fig 10.13 P11 for John Brown (Crown Copyright)
(continued overleaf)

Employee's surname *in CAPITALS*		First two forenames		
BROWN		JOHN		

National Insurance no.	Date of birth *in figures*			Works no. etc	Date of leaving *in figures*		
		Day	Month	Year		Day	Month	Year
TW 38 69 7 4	8	12	1949	2			

Tax code †	Amended code †					
284	430					
	Wk/Mth in which applied	5				

PAYE Income Tax

Week no	Pay in the week or month including Statutory Sick Pay/ Statutory Maternity Pay 2	Total pay to date 3	Total free pay to date as shown by Table A 4	Total taxable pay to date Ø 5	Total tax due to date as shown by Taxable Pay Tables 6	Tax deducted or refunded in the week or month *Mark refunds 'R'* 7	For employer's use
1	188 00	188 00	54 79	133 21	33 25	33 25	
2	188 00	376 00	109 58	266 42	66 50	33 25	
3	188 00	564 00	164 37	399 63	100 00	33 50	
4	188 00	752 00	219 16	532 84	133 25	33 25	
5	188 00	940 00	414 35	525 65	131 50	1 75 R	
6							
7							
8							
9							
10							
11							
12							
13							
14							
15							
16							
17							
18							
19							
20							
21							
22							
23							
24							
25							
26							
27							
28							
29			SPECIMEN				
30							

* You must enter the NI contribution table letter overleaf beside the NI totals box - *see the note shown there.*

† If amended cross out previous code.

Ø If in any week/month the amount in column 4 is more than the amount in column 3, leave column 5 blank.

4

a Prepare a payroll, employee pay record sheets and payslips for Week No 2 for the five employees in the payroll given in Fig 10.10. Note that the entries have been completed for T Rawlings in his pay record sheet (Fig 10.8) and that the data required for the other employees is given in the employee records (Fig 1.6 in Unit 1). The employees are paid at their weekly pay rates for ordinary time plus the following overtime payments:

S T Pratt – no overtime
T Rawlings – completed
L O Watson – £12
S Watson – £20
J Wyatt – £15

A pension qualifying for tax relief is paid at the rate of 5 per cent on basic pay.

b Make out a coining analysis and cash summary for the payment of wages.

c Prepare the cheque to withdraw cash from the bank to pay the net wages.

d Complete the wages account, inland revenue account and bank account with the necessary entries for the week's wages

5

Prepare T Rawlings' pay records for Week No 4 by:

a calculating his gross pay from the clock card given in Fig 10.14;

b calculating his net pay and completing his pay record sheet (Fig 10.8);

c completing his pay advice slip.

6

Use the checked and amended clock cards in Task 4 of Unit 10.1 and the employee records (Fig 1.6) to carry out the following tasks:

a Prepare a payroll, pay advice slips and individual pay record sheets for the four employees for Week No 1. The employees pay 5 per cent of their basic pay for pension.

b Make out a coining and cash summary for the payment of wages.

c Prepare the cheque to withdraw cash from the bank to pay the net wages.

d Complete the wages account, inland revenue account and bank account with the necessary entries for the week's wages.

7

Rachel Martin receives a basic wage of £3.50 per hour for a 38-hour week. Hours worked in excess of 38 are paid at time and a half except for hours worked on a Saturday which are paid at double time. During the week ending 20 April she worked a total of 44 hours, 4 of which were on Saturday. The deductions from her pay were:

Income tax: 25% of all earnings in excess of £50 per week.
National insurance: 10% of gross pay.
Pension: 6% of basic pay (excluding overtime).
Savings and Social Club: as in Fig 1.6.

You are required to calculate Rachel Martin's gross pay and prepare her pay advice slip for the week ending 20 April 19—.

CLOCK CARD					
No 15			Name:	T RAWLINGS	
Week ending: 3 May 19—					
Day	In	Out	In	Out	TOTAL HOURS
M	0800	1200	1301	1700	
Tu	0755	1205	1300	1631	
W	0801	1205	1300	1633	
Th	0751	1204	1330	1710	
F	0800	1203	1300	1631	
TOTAL					
					£
Ordinary time:...... hrs @ £5.00 (up to 38 hours)					
Overtime .... hrs @ £7.50					
TOTAL GROSS WAGES					

Fig 10.14

8

a Make out a cash analysis showing what you will collect from the bank to pay the following wages:

£	£	£
82.25	75.16	120.45
105.14	110.23	80.84
148.99	78.11	105.26

b What statutory deductions must be made from wages?

c How are national insurance contributions calculated and entered?

9

You are the general clerk of a retail store employing four shop assistants who are paid in cash weekly, one week in arrears. The net wages for the week ending Saturday, 20 June 19—, which will be paid on 26 June 19—, are as follows:

	£
T Bell	82.79
R Carter	123.14
T King	85.18
R Telman	98.10

You are required to calculate the number and denominations of coins and notes required to pay the wages of the four men. The owner of the business will not pay with notes greater than £10 and insists that at least one £1 coin should be present in every packet.

10

a Use a computer wages package to prepare employee pay record sheets, payroll and pay advice slips for Weeks 1–3 in respect of the following employees, using the data supplied in Fig 1.6, Fig 10.10 and Task 4:

Employee	Overtime paid in Week No 3 £
S T Pratt	—
T Rawlings	7.50
L O Watson	12.00
S Watson	7.50
J Wyatt	—

b Use a spreadsheet package containing the data supplied in the employee records (Fig 1.6) to calculate the following:

1 The current weekly and annual gross wages (excluding overtime payments and salaries paid to the proprietors).

2 The effect of a 5 per cent increase in wages on the annual wages bill for all employees.

3 The effect on the annual wages bill of a 7.5 per cent increase in wages for operatives and a 5 per cent increase for all other employees.

11 Priority

Trevor Rawlings calls in to see you to say that he has received notification from the tax office that his code number has been increased from 294 to 400 in Week 5. He asks you what effect this will have on his basic pay and whether there will be any reduction of previous tax payments. You agree to look this up and let him have a note explaining the situation.

Assignment – Unit 10

1 Work in groups to research and discuss the following topics:

Group 1
Income tax is deducted on a 'pay as you earn' basis. Would you rather pay tax in a lump sum once a year? Are there any advantages of this PAYE system for the employee, the employer and the state? What does income tax pay for?

Group 2
How does the payment of income tax differ from the way in which you pay for local government services? What major services are provided by your local county council and district council? What is the relationship of your school/college with the county council?

Group 3
National insurance is deducted on a 'pay as you earn' basis. Would you rather pay NI in a lump sum once a year? What benefits do you gain from paying NI? What action do you and your employer need to take when you are away from work through illness?

Group 4
When you begin full-time employment:
a What documents do you need to supply?
b Will you have to pay national insurance and income tax?
c Are you obliged to join a trade union?
d What information would you expect to be given in a contract of employment and when would you expect to receive it?

Group 5
Compare a computerised system for the preparation of wages with a manual method. What security measures are required for each method? Would P Faulkner & Sons benefit from computerising its payroll? Do you have any legal rights of access to personal data held on computer files? Are there any health problems involved in using VDUs?

2 Check your conclusions with your tutor and give an oral presentation of your findings to the rest of the class.

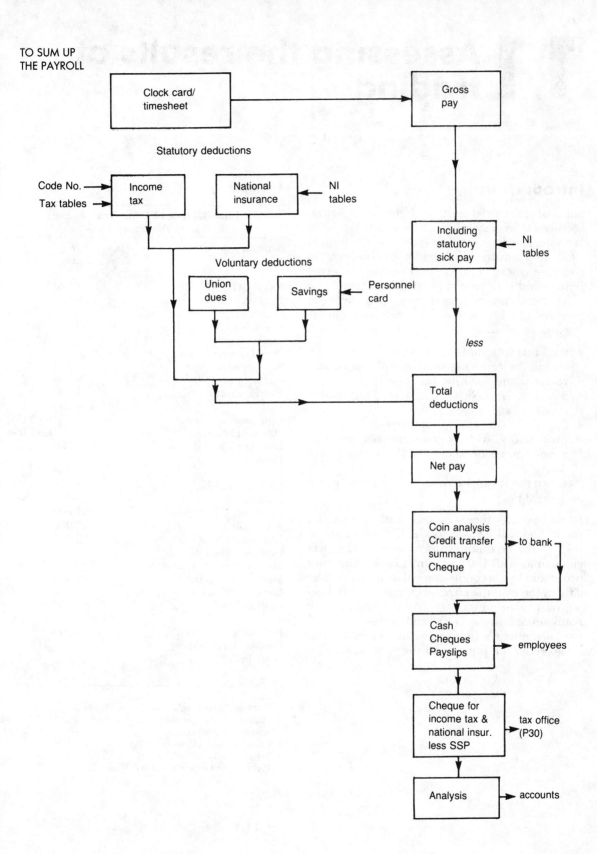

11 Assessing the results of trading

Introduction

Successful financial control of any organisation is crucial to its survival and future development. We shall now look at final accounts – the figures used to measure the results of trading, to compare these results with estimates/target figures and with results for previous years.

A sound accounting system provides the owner(s) of a business with a means of identifying and controlling:

- the finances of the business month by month, by revealing the amounts spent and received and for what purpose
- liquidity, i.e. cash flow and working capital ratios
- the return on capital employed
- profitability, such as gross and net profit as a percentage of sales, mark up and profit margins

(See also the various accounting functions given on page 2.)

In examining these figures and accounting ratios, you will be able to identify the relationship of the accounting documents in the previous units with final accounts, i.e. trading and profit and loss accounts and balance sheets. The data in the examples are taken from the following trial balance extracted from the books of P Faulkner & Sons at 31 December 19–5, the last day of the firm's financial year. (Turn to Unit 7.1 to recall the purpose of the trial balance.)

Example

Trial Balance of P Faulkner & Sons
at 31 December 19–5

Accounts	Dr £	Cr £
Stock (1.1.19–5)	3 500	
Debtors	8 400	
Creditors		3 600
Purchases	159 150	
Sales		505 100
Purchases returns		6 150
Sales returns	5 100	
Carriage inwards	2 300	
Carriage outwards	4 000	
Wages	152 100	
Commission received		3 000
Discount received		2 000
Discount allowed	4 500	
Rent	48 000	
Rates	7 500	
Lighting and heating	4 750	
Salaries	33 000	
Insurance	3 800	
Advertising	5 000	
Interest on loan	5 000	
General expenses	6 500	
Machinery and equipment (at cost)	240 000	
Motor vans (at cost)	32 000	
Bank overdraft		1 650
Cash in hand	50	
VAT		150
Drawings	25 000	
Capital (1.1.19–5)		188 000
Bank loan		40 000
	749 650	749 650

Notes:
1 Stock on 31 December 19–5 was £5,900.
2 Machinery, equipment and motor vans are to be depreciated by 10% on cost.
3 Rates prepaid £1500.
4 Rent accrued £2000.
5 Lighting and heating accrued £250.

Fig 11.1

11.1 Calculating gross profit

In order to make a profit, a business must buy or manufacture goods and sell them at a higher price than it pays for them. In the first year of manufacturing the Faulkner Resteasy Camp Beds cost £10 each to make and were being sold for £15 each, resulting in a profit of £5 on each one sold. During the whole of the first year 100 of these beds were sold, resulting in a sales figure of:

	100 × £15 =	£1500
The cost of sales was:	100 × £10 =	− £1000
Providing a profit of:		£500

There were 20 left in stock at the end of the first year and these were brought forward as opening stock for the second year, when a further 120 were made for the same cost; the selling price was not changed and 110 were sold. The second year's figures show:

Opening stock (20 × £10) £200		Sales (110 × £15)
Add Manufacturing cost		= £1650
(120 × £10)	£1200	
Cost of goods offered		
for sale (140 × £10)	£1400	

If the cost of goods offered for sale (£1400) is deducted from the sales of £1650, it would appear that a profit of only £250 had been made. This is not, however, the true profit figure, because if 110 were sold at a profit of £5 each (sales £15 each, less stock £10 each), then the profit would be £550 (i.e. 110 × £5). The difference between the £550 and £250 figures is £300 and this is explained by looking at the value of the closing stock (the stock at the end of the second year). As 140 were available for sale and only 110 were sold, there should be 30 (i.e. 140 − 110) in stock at the year end. This gives a stock figure of £300 (i.e. 30 × £10). The stock figures at the beginning and at the end of a trading period are, therefore, essential in calculating profit.

In trading account form these calculations appear as follows:

Trading Account of P Faulkner & Sons
for the year ended 31 December 19—

	Dr		Cr
	£	£	£
Sales			1650
Less Returns*			—
			1650
Less Cost of sales:			
Opening stock (1/1/19—)		200	
Add Purchases	1200		
Less Returns*	—		
		1200	
Carriage inwards*		—	
Wages*		—	
		1400	
Less Closing stock		300	
(31/12/19—)			
			1100
Gross profit			550

* These items, although not required for this example, are inserted to indicate how they would be treated if they were included in a more detailed trading account.

It will be seen that the trading account is used as a means of calculating gross profit. Gross profit is the excess of the selling price over the cost price plus any direct expenses in acquiring the goods, such as carriage inwards and wages.

When the figures for sales, purchases and cost of sales are used in calculating percentage margins and rates of turnover they should be net, i.e. sales should have sales returns deducted; purchases should have purchases returns deducted; cost of sales should have added to it any costs which affect the cost before being offered for sale. These include carriage inwards, i.e. transport costs in bringing goods into the business (but not carriage outwards), wages paid in making or improving the goods such as bottling, blending, etc.

Percentage margin

This simply means the percentage of profit and it can be expressed in two ways:

1 On cost – when it is called **mark-up**
2 On the selling price (sales) – when it is called **margin**

The percentage margins involved in selling the Faulkner Resteasy camp beds are:

$$\text{Mark-up} = \frac{\text{Gross profit} \times 100}{\text{Cost of sales}} = \frac{\overset{1}{\cancel{550}} \times 100}{\underset{2}{\cancel{1\,100}}} = 50\%$$

$$\text{Margin} = \frac{\text{Gross profit} \times 100}{\text{Sales}} = \frac{\overset{1}{\cancel{550}} \times 100}{\underset{3}{\cancel{1\,650}}} = 33\tfrac{1}{3}\%$$

The same answers will be obtained if the cost per unit (i.e. each camp bed) is used:

$$\text{Mark-up} = \frac{\text{Gross profit} \times 100}{\text{Cost of sale}} = \frac{\overset{1}{\cancel{5}} \times 100}{\underset{2}{\cancel{10}}} = 50\%$$

$$\text{Margin} = \frac{\text{Gross profit} \times 100}{\text{Selling price}} = \frac{\overset{1}{\cancel{5}} \times 100}{\underset{3}{\cancel{15}}} = 33\tfrac{1}{3}\%$$

This formula is also used to calculate *gross profit as a percentage of total sales*, i.e. the amount of gross profit for every £100 of sales.

Rate of turnover

Turnover is another term for sales and the rate of turnover indicates how quickly stock is being moved (or sold). A business becomes more efficient when it speeds up its rate of turnover, i.e. the number of times the average amount of stock is sold in a year.

To calculate rate of turnover use this formula:

$$\frac{\text{Cost of sales}}{\text{Average stock}}$$

Note: Average stock = $\dfrac{\text{opening stock} + \text{closing stock}}{2}$

Faulkner's rate of turnover for the second year for Resteasy camp beds was:

$$\frac{1\,100}{(200 + 300) \div 2} = \frac{1\,100}{250} = \underline{\underline{4.4}}$$

Example

The complete trading account for P Faulkner & Sons, using the data given in the trial balance (Fig 11.1), is as follows in Fig 11.2:

Trading Account of P Faulkner & Sons
for the year ended 31 December 19–5

	Dr		Cr	
	£	£	£	£
Sales			505 100	
Less Returns			5 100	
				500 000
Less Cost of sales:				
Opening stock (1.1.19–5)		3 500		
Add Purchases	159 150			
Less Returns	6 150			
		153 000		
Wages		152 100		
Carriage inwards		2 300		
Cost of goods offered for sale		310 900		
Less Closing stock (31.12.19–5)		5 900		
			305 000	
Gross profit			195 000	

Fig 11.2

TASKS

1

At 1 January 19—, Brian Jenkins had 1500 articles in stock which had cost him £2 each. During the month of January, he purchased 2000 more articles at the same price. He sold 2500 at £3.00 each and 100 at £2.50 each.

a Draw up a simple stock record to show the number of items in stock at the end of the month.
b Prepare his Trading Account for the month of January to show clearly the cost of sales and gross profit. (*RSA BKI*)

2

From the following figures which relate to the financial year ended 31 December 19— prepare the Trading Account of James Brown. The account should show clearly net purchases, cost of goods offered for sale, cost of sales and net sales:

	£
Purchases	18 500
Sales	30 350
Stock (1 January 19—)	2 100
Sales returns	350
Purchases returns	500
Carriage inwards	40
Wages	2 500
Stock (31 December 19—)	640

3

Calculate for Faulkner Resteasy camp beds for this year:

a the percentage margin and
b the rate of turnover from the following information (calculations to be correct to one decimal place):

Sales:	150 @ £15.75 (as per price list)
Opening stock:	30 @ £10.00
Production (purchases):	146 @ £10.50
Closing stock:	26 @ £10.50

4

Calculate the percentage margins and mark-up from Faulkner's price list in Fig 1.7 for each commodity, given the following cost prices:

Cat No	Cost £	Cat No	Cost £
734T	170.00	14SB	13.00
754T	140.00	15SB	12.00
774T	110.00	27R	18.00
523T	108.00	29R	13.00
553T	84.00	31R	10.75
583T	70.00	81C	10.50
13SB	13.50		

5

Use the data in Fig 11.3 to calculate:

a rate of turnover
b gross profit as a percentage of sales (calculations to be correct to two decimal places).

Trading Account of P Morrison & Sons
for the year ended 31 December 19–1

	Dr		Cr	
	£	£	£	£
Sales			68 000	
Less Returns			460	
				67 540
Less Cost of sales:				
Opening stock (1.1.19–1)		4 200		
Add Purchases	38 000			
Less Returns	520			
		37 480		
Wages		14 000		
Carriage inwards		340		
Cost of goods offered for sale		56 020		
Less Closing stock (31.12.19–1)		3 800		
			52 220	
Gross profit			15 320	

(*Continued: Task 7, Unit 11.2.*)

Fig 11.3

6

Use a computer package to prepare a trading account for W Watson & Sons from the following figures which relate to the year's business ending on 31 December 19–:

	£
Stock (1 January 19–1)	20 800
Stock (31 December 19–1)	23 200
Purchases	83 000
Sales	129 400
Purchases returns	3 000
Sales returns	1 400
Carriage inwards	600
Factory wages	17 800

(*Continued: Task 6, Unit 11.2.*)

7  **Priority**

You are required to deal with the note (Fig 11.4) left for you by Sarah Faulkner:

```
Will you let me know the profit margin figure
(gross profit as a percentage of sales) from
last year's trading account (19–5). The previous
years' profit margins were:

19–1  —  25%
19–2  —  35%
19–3  —  32%
19–4  —  40%

I would like to see the 19–5 figure in a graph
showing the figures for the five years

SF.
```

Fig 11.4

11.2 Calculating net profit

Unit 11.1 dealt with the calculation of gross profit in a trading account and showed that the profit from sales was arrived at after allowing for the direct costs of buying or making the goods. In addition to these direct costs, a business has to pay overhead costs (referred to in Unit 1) such as administration expenses – rent, rates, lighting, heating, insurance, salaries of office and sales staff, etc – as well as distribution costs such as carriage outwards to customers and advertising. When the overheads are deducted from gross profit the business expects to make a net profit – but if the overheads exceed the gross profit, there will be a net trading loss.

All the expenses relating to the period during

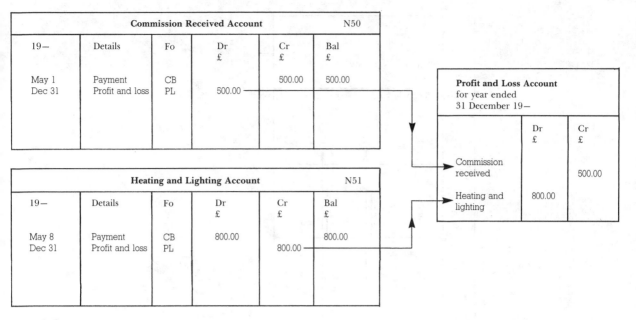

Fig 11.5

which the profit is calculated have to be 'written off' or transferred to the profit and loss account: the expenses to the Dr column and the income to the Cr column, as in the examples shown (Fig 11.5):

Accruals and prepayments

More often than not the amounts in the nominal ledger expense accounts do not match the period covered by the accounts when calculating profit. For example, there will usually be:

Accruals Amounts still to be paid for, variously described as 'due', 'owing', 'in arrears', 'outstanding' or 'accrued'. The accrual is added to the amount paid in order to arrive at the actual value of the expense, which is the sum transferred to the profit and loss account.

Example: In Faulkner's profit and loss account (Fig 11.7) £48 000 had been paid for rent, but a further bill of £2000 had been received and not paid (an accrual) and this is added to the amount paid.

Prepayments Any item paid for but not received/used, variously described as 'paid in advance', 'unexpired' or 'prepaid'. The prepayment is deducted from the amount paid to arrive at the amount used, which is the sum transferred to the profit and loss account.

Example: In Faulkner's profit and loss account (Fig 11.7) rates of £7500 were for the year expiring in April and £1500 was paid in advance on 31 December (a prepayment), so this is deducted from the amount shown as paid.

Depreciation

This is the loss in value of an asset over a period of time. When assets such as motor vehicles and equipment 'age' they undergo 'wear and tear' and lose their value; assets also lose value because of the passage of time or obsolescence. Depreciation should be regarded as a charge on the business for the use of its assets. (This concept can be compared with a business which hires some of its assets, such as a fleet of vehicles, in which the hire charge paid is debited to the profit and loss account.) Depreciation is a means of apportioning the cost of an asset against trading profits over the anticipated life of the asset. An estimate of the loss in value of the asset (an expense) is made and this amount is charged (debited) to the profit and loss account.

Example:

In Faulkner's profit and loss account (Fig 11.7) 10 per cent of the cost of machinery and equipment (£240 000) i.e. £24 000 is debited as a deduction from profit.

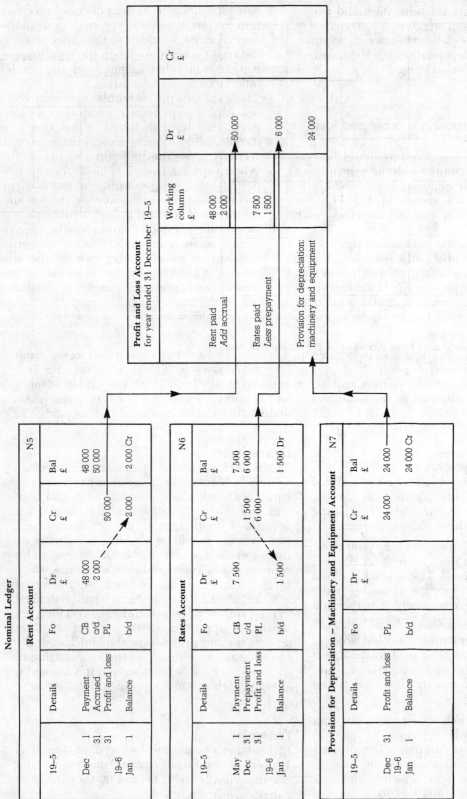

Fig 11.6

The ledger accounts for rent, rates and provision for depreciation are now illustrated (Fig 11.6), showing the adjustments for accruals, prepayments and depreciation and the transfers to the profit and loss account.

Guidelines for preparing a profit and loss account

1 The profit and loss account should be correctly titled and comply with the principles of double entry, like other accounts. The bracketed headings are shown in Fig 11.7 for guidance only and can be dispensed with when known.
2 It is normal practice to combine the trading account with the profit and loss account. The trading account is shown first with its result, i.e. the gross profit (see Fig 11.2); if you are asked to prepare a profit and loss account only, the gross profit figure will be supplied.

3 Any other income, such as discount received, rent received, interest received or commission received, is added to the gross profit in the credit column to obtain the total income; if there is no other income, omit the line for total income.
4 The expenses (i.e. revenue expenditure but not capital expenditure or drawings – see page 167) are deducted from the total income, after allowing for prepayments and accruals, to obtain the amount of net profit.
5 When working from a trial balance to prepare the trading and profit and loss account, it is recommended that you use the working column so as to clarify your calculations.
6 Details of the value of closing stocks, prepayments, accruals and depreciation are often supplied as notes at the foot of the trial balance. Closing stock (for example, of stationery and postage stamps) is deducted before the stock figure is transferred to the profit and loss account.

Trading and Profit and Loss Account of P Faulkner & Sons
for the year ended 31 December 19–5

	(Working column) £	(Dr) £	(Cr) £
Trading Account – see Fig 11.2			
Gross profit			195 000
Add: Commission received			3 000
Discount received			2 000
Total income			200 000
Less Expenses:			
Rent paid	48 000		
Add accrual	2000		
		50 000	
Rates paid	7 500		
Less prepayment	1 500		
		6 000	
Lighting and heating paid	4 750		
Add accrual	250		
		5 000	
Provision for depreciation:			
Machinery and equipment	24 000		
Motor vans	3 200		
		27 200	
Carriage outwards		4 000	
Salaries		33 000	
Insurance		3 800	
Advertising		5 000	
Discount allowed		4 500	
Interest on loan		5 000	
General expenses		6 500	
			150 000
Net profit			50 000

Fig 11.7

Profitability ratios

Net profit as a percentage of sales measures the amount of net profit for every £100 of sales. It is useful in comparing the cost of overheads in relation to sales revenue from one year to the next. The formula is:

$$\frac{\text{Net profit} \times 100}{\text{Sales}}$$

Example

Compare the net profit of £5000 made from sales revenue of £80 000 in 19–4 with a net profit of £6000 from sales revenue of £100 000 in 19–5:

$$19\text{–}4 \quad \frac{5000 \times 100}{80000} = 6.25\%$$

$$19\text{–}5 \quad \frac{6000 \times 100}{100000} = 6.0\%$$

Capital and revenue expenditure

All items of capital expenditure (expenditure on assets) are debited to their appropriate ledger accounts, but they are quite different from the expenditure involved in purchasing goods for resale. When Faulkner bought a new delivery van and a typewriter for the office, this was capital expenditure because they were purchased with the intention of keeping them for a long time and not for resale as part of Faulkner's daily business. Their purchase resulted in the firm acquiring additional assets to increase its earning capacity. This expenditure does not affect either the profit or the capital until provision is made for depreciation. In other words, Faulkner is neither better nor worse off as a result of these purchases as they have exchanged one asset (cash) for another asset (delivery van/office equipment).

Revenue expenditure (or overheads), on the other hand, are the day-to-day running expenses of the business such as rates, electricity, salaries and motor expenses. As these expenses are deducted from the firm's income, they reduce both the profit and the capital (the money put into the firm by the owner) and they are entered in the trading and profit and loss account.

Example

The purchase of a building for a new store (an asset) is capital expenditure but the cost of advertising to announce when it will be opened (an expense deducted from profit) is revenue expenditure.

The treatment of these two categories of expenditure and their effect on the business are very different and it is important for the accountant to distinguish revenue expenditure from capital expenditure.

TASKS

1
a Calculate the net profit as a percentage of sales from Faulkner's profit and loss account in Fig 11.7.
b In the previous year (19–4) the net profit of £60 000 was made from sales revenue of £400 000 with overheads of £100 000. Compare the profitability ratios for the two years. Which year was more successful and why?

2
The following trial balance was extracted from the books of Janet Martin at 31 December 19–1:

	£	£
Capital account (1.1.19–1)		8 208
Drawings	6 000	
Fixtures and fittings	1 600	
Insurance	1 418	
Rent and rates	2 480	
Wages and salaries	3 800	
Discounts allowed and received	880	420
Trade debtors and creditors	2 502	2 508
Stock (1.1.19–1)	3 016	
Purchases and sales	18 080	32 340
Cash in hand	420	
Cash at bank	2 180	
Purchases and sales returns	1 010	640
Postage and stationery	520	
Carriage outwards	210	
	44 116	44 116

From this trial balance and from the notes given below, you are required to prepare the trading and profit and loss account of Janet Martin for the year ended 31 December 19–1.

Notes:
a Stock 31 December 19–1 £3220.
b Wages and salaries accrued at 31 December 19–1 £130.
c Rates are prepaid on 31 December 19–1 £230.
d There is a stock of stamps to the value of £28 at 31 December 19–1.

3

The following balances were extracted from the books of C Williams on 31 December 19–1. You are required to prepare his trading and profit and loss account for the year ending 31 December 19–1.

	£
Purchases	62 000
Sales	94 000
Stock (1.1.19–1)	21 000
Carriage inwards	120
Carriage outwards	110
Sales returns	600
Purchases returns	400
Discounts allowed	120
Discounts received	240
Insurance	320
Heating and lighting	2 400
Rates	1 500
Office expenses	1 200
Wages and salaries	5 010
Stationery	1 800
Telephone	640

You are required to take the following into consideration at 31 December 19–1:

		£
a	Closing stock	18 500
b	Insurance paid in advance	40
c	Heating and lighting bills accrued	200
d	Rates prepaid	300
e	Stock of stationery supplies	350
f	Telephone charges accrued	210

4

R Parker's gross profit for the year ending 31 March 19–1 is £22 500. His trial balance on that date includes the following balances:

	£
Salaries	8 420
Rent	840
Motor vehicle expenses	350
General expenses	380
Insurance	150
Heating and lighting	1 400
Drawings	1 800
Capital	64 000

The following additional information has to be taken into consideration:

Rent in arrears at 31 March 19–1 was £160.

Insurance includes an annual premium of £144 which was due on 1 January 19–1 and paid in full on that date.

General expenses includes the purchase of office stationery and at 31 March 19–1 there was a stock of stationery valued at £180.

You are required to:

a Write up the ledger accounts for rent, general expenses and insurance, showing appropriate transfers to the profit and loss account.

b Prepare the profit and loss account for the year ending 31 March 19–1.

5

State whether the following transactions involving P Faulkner & Sons are capital or revenue expenditure, giving reasons for your answers:

a Payment of rent for premises.
b Purchase of a new copier for the printroom.
c Purchase of new tyres for a motor van.
d Purchase of computer software for computer.
e Payment for painting the stores.
f Payment of annual fire insurance premium.
g Purchase of coffee vending machine for canteen.
h Payment for electrical repairs to machinery in the workshop.

6

As a continuation of Task 6 in Unit 11.1, use a computer package to prepare the profit and loss account of W Watson & Sons for the year ending 31 December 19–1 from the following details:

	£
Office salaries:	
Payments during 19–1	2 220
Owing 31 December 19–1	640
Discounts allowed	480
Discounts received	1 000
Carriage outwards	240
Rent	4 800
Heating and lighting	1 600
Telephone	1 800
Office expenses	460
Motor vehicle expenses	760
Insurance:	
Payments during 19–1	2 600
Prepaid 31 December 19–1	600

(*Continued: Task 6, Unit 11.3.*)

You have been attached to P Morrison & Sons on one day a week to help out with the accounts as they are short of staff. Deal with the task shown in Fig 11.8. The trading account was completed in Task 5 of Unit 11.1. (*Continued: Task 7, Unit 11.3.*)

Profit and Loss Account of P Morrison & Sons

for the year ended 31 December 19–1

	£	Dr £	Cr £
Gross Profit			15320
Add Discounts received			250
Total income			15270
Less Expenses:			
Office salaries	8880		
less amount owing	200		
		8680	
Discounts allowed		100	
Carriage outwards		80	
Heating and lighting		460	
Insurance		280	
General expenses		120	
Rates	1050		
Add amount prepaid	50		
		1100	
Interest on loan		450	
			11270
Net Profit			4000

Please check my calculations and working in this Profit + Loss A/c. If you find any errors, please correct them and rewrite the account. PM.

Fig 11.8

11.3 Interpreting the balance sheet

A balance sheet is not an account and therefore does not contain transfers from any of the ledger accounts. It is generally defined as: *a statement of how a business stands at a certain point in time.* It is a summary of all ledger balances after calculating profit.

The balance sheet illustrated in Fig 11.9 is in a vertical format; the practice of displaying the assets and liabilities in a two-sided format is seldom used today.

Marshalling the assets
This is the process of arranging the assets in order and in groups.

Assets

The possessions of a firm or person are divided into two categories (fixed and current) and the totals of each group are shown in the balance sheet:

Fixed assets   The possessions which are acquired with the intention of keeping them for a considerable time; they are acquired by capital expenditure and include such items as buildings, machinery, motor vehicles, computers, office furniture, etc.

Current assets   These include items in current use, such as stock-in-trade, debtors and money.

Liabilities

The debts owing by a firm or person (excluding the capital – see below). They can also be divided into two groups and the totals of each group are shown in the balance sheet:

Long term   These include liabilities which do not have to be met in the immediate future, such as mortgages and long-term loans.

Current   The debts which have to be met in the near future, such as creditors, VAT and short-term loans.

Capital

Capital is the amount invested in the business by the proprietor(s) and it is the difference between the total assets and total liabilities. It represents the value of the firm's net assets owing to the owner(s). In a company, capital would consist of shares paid for by the company's shareholders.

Procedure for drawing up a balance sheet

1 The title should contain: the title of the document (Balance Sheet); the business name; the date on which the balances were extracted.
2 List the fixed assets first with the net values in the right-hand column; where depreciation is involved this should be shown as illustrated in Fig 11.9 by using the analysis columns and deducting it from the previous value. Total the net 'book' values of the fixed assets.
3 List the current assets in the order indicated and total them.
4 List the current liabilities in the order indicated and total them under current assets.
5 Deduct the current liabilities from the cur-

rent assets to arrive at the working capital, which should be entered in the right-hand column. Working capital is the amount of net current assets available for the immediate needs of the business.
6 Add working capital to the fixed assets to arrive at total net assets.
7 In order to check the balance sheet and show how the business is financed under '*Represented by*' enter the previous capital; add the net profit; deduct the drawings; and the amount remaining is the new amount of capital on the date of the balance sheet. (*Note:* Drawings do not affect the business trading figures and they should not be entered in the profit and loss account; they can be in the form of goods or cash taken out of the business by the owners.)
8 List the long-term liabilities and add the total to the new capital figure.

Capital and drawings accounts

The capital account records the amount invested in the business by the proprietor, with additions in the form of net profit and deductions accounted for by drawings. It has a credit balance as the capital is a liability which the firm has to the owner(s). Any profit made by the firm increases the capital and likewise any loss made by the firm reduces the capital. This is shown in the completion of the double entry cycle, when the net profit from the profit and loss account is transferred to the credit column of the capital account.

For convenience a record of drawings is kept in a drawings account until such time as a balance sheet is prepared. The drawings account is debited each time the owner draws out cash or goods for his/her own use; the total of all the drawings is transferred by a debit entry in the capital account and this amount appears in the balance sheet as a deduction from capital.

The capital and drawings accounts shown on page 168 illustrate the effect of drawings and profit on the capital invested by the proprietor, and the figures relate to the example given in Fig 11.9.

Computerised final accounts

In a fully-integrated, computerised system the totals from the purchases and sales ledgers are posted automatically to the nominal ledger to

Capital Account						N14
19—	Details	Fo	Dr £	Cr £	Bal £	
Jan 1	Balance	b/d		188 000	188 000	
Dec 31	Net profit	BS		50 000	238 000	
Dec 31	Drawings	N15	25 000		213 000 Cr	

Drawings Account						N15
19—	Details	Fo	Dr £	Cr £	Bal £	
Dec 1	Balance	b/d	24 500		24 500	
Dec 20	Payment	CB	500		25 000	
Dec 31	Transfer to Capital Account	N14		25 000	—	

allow for the preparation of trading and profit and loss accounts and balance sheets.

Balance sheet of P Faulkner & Sons
as at 31 December 19–5

	Cost £	Depreciation £	Book value £
Fixed assets			
Machinery and equipment	240 000	24 000	216 000
Motor vans	32 000	3 200	28 800
	272 000	27 200	244 800
Current assets			
Stock	5 900		
Debtors	8 400		
Rates prepaid	1 500		
Cash in hand	50		
		15 850	
Less Current liabilities			
Creditors	3 600		
VAT accrued	150		
Rent accrued	2 000		
Lighting and heating accrued	250		
Bank overdraft	1 650		
		7 650	
Working capital			8 200
Total net assets			253 000
Represented by:			
Capital (1.1.19–5)	188 000		
Add Net profit	50 000		
	238 000		
Less Drawings	25 000		
Capital (31.12.19–5)		213 000	
Long term liabilities			
Bank loan		40 000	
			253 000

Fig 11.9

Analysing the balance sheet figures

1 Return on capital employed

Formula:
$$\frac{\text{Net profit} \times 100}{\text{Capital (opening)}}$$

Example: $\dfrac{10\,000 \times 100}{200\,000} = 5\%$

Purpose: To indicate to the owner(s) the percentage return for the capital invested in the business.

2 Current ratio

Formula:
$$\frac{\text{Current assets}}{\text{Current liabilities}}$$

Example: $\dfrac{7500}{2500} = 3{:}1$

Purpose: To show the relationship between current assets and current liabilities, i.e. the number of times current liabilities can be met by current assets.

3 Acid test ratio

Formula: $\dfrac{\text{Current assets} - \text{Stock (closing)}}{\text{Current liabilities}}$

Example: $\dfrac{7500 - 3750}{2500} = 1.5{:}1$

Purpose: To check the ability of the business to meet its current debts from the liquid assets which can be used for this purpose. The minimum should be 1:1.

PERFORMANCE CHECK
As for Unit 11.1.

TASKS

1

a Calculate the following performance ratios for P Faulkner & Sons' balance sheet for the year 19–5 in Fig 11.9.

1 return on capital employed
2 current ratio
3 acid test ratio
(Calculations to be correct to two decimal places.)

b Compare the above figures with those for the previous year, based on the following 19–4 figures:

	£
Net profit	60 000
Opening capital	200 000
Current assets	12 320
Current liabilities	8 400
Closing stock	3 800

2

Owen Williams prepared the following trial balance at 31 December 19— after drafting his trading account:

	£	£
Trade debtors	9 300	
Trade creditors		11 650
Bank		4 500
Capital		48 300
Rent and rates	2 600	
Drawings	9 000	
Freehold premises	30 600	
Heat and light	1 650	
Wages and salaries	7 550	
Cash in hand	1 700	
Motor vehicle expenses	2 500	
Carriage outwards	800	
Motor vehicles	5 200	
Advertising	2 000	
Gross profit		21 000
Stock 31 December 19–1	12 550	
	£85 450	£85 450

You are given the following information:
a Provide for carriage outwards owing £200.
b An electricity bill for £300 for the quarter ended 31 December 19–1 had not been paid.
c The advertising expenditure shown above includes £1600 for a television contract due to commence on 1 January 19–2.

You are required to prepare the profit and loss account for the year ended 31 December 19–1 and a balance sheet as at 31 December 19–1. (*RSA BKI*)

3

George Price is the proprietor of a small business. He keeps his financial records on double entry principles and extracted the following trial balance on 31 May 19–2:

	£		£
Stock 1 June 19–1	7 000	Capital 1 June 19–1	85 000
Cash at bank	8 000	Creditors	3 700
Furniture and fittings	7 500	Sales	40 000
Premises	65 000		
Rates	1 600		
Purchases	30 000		
Heating and lighting	1 500		
Cleaning	1 700		
Packing materials	1 400		
Drawings	5 000		
	128 700		128 700

You are required to take the following into consideration on 31 May 19–2:

	£
a Stock on hand	9 500
b Rates paid in advance	400
c Stock of packing material	300

and prepare a trading and profit and loss account for the year ended 31 May 19–2 and a balance sheet at that date. (*RSA BKI*)

4

The following balances remain in William Dean's books after completion of the trading and profit and loss accounts for the year ended 31 May 19–2:

	£	£
Capital 1 June 19–1		124 000
Net profit for the year ended 31 May 19–2		13 800
Loan from John Dean		9 500
Trade creditors		1 950
Expense creditors		270
Premises	110 000	
Stock in trade	25 000	
Trade debtors	2 600	
Balance at bank	1 400	
Cash in hand	20	
Expense items paid in advance	500	
Proprietor's drawings	10 000	
	149 520	149 520

You are required to:
a Set out William Dean's balance sheet as at 31 May 19–2. Your balance sheet should show long-term and current liabilities: fixed and current assets.
b Write up William Dean's capital account as it would appear in his private ledger for the year ended 31 May 19–2. (*adapted from RSA BKI*)

5

You have now been put in charge of the ledger accounts at P Faulkner & Sons. The list of ledger balances at 28 February 19— is given in the trial balance below and the details which follow it. You are required to carry out the following tasks:

a Transfer the ledger balances as at 1 March into three separate ledgers, namely sales ledger, purchases ledger and nominal ledger (for accounts other than debtors and creditors). Enter the cash and bank balances on the same date in a cash book.

b Enter the transactions for March in the appropriate books, post to the ledgers, and extract a trial balance at 31 March.

c Prepare the final accounts for the quarter ending 31 March after taking into account:
1 Stock at 31 March 19— was valued at £8500
2 Prepayments: rates £857 and advertising £250
3 Accrued lighting and heating £1107

P Faulkner & Sons
Trial Balance at 28 February 19—

Accounts	Dr £	Cr £
Capital		100 000
Buildings	62 000	
Machinery and equipment	25 000	
Stock at 1 January 19—	10 000	
Delivery vans	4 400	
Wages and salaries	27 000	
Purchases	46 500	
Purchases returns		500
Sales		110 700
Sales returns	700	
Debtors } see separate	10 000	
Creditors } lists		4 000
VAT		800
Advertising	5 500	
Rates	2 000	
Office expenses	13 000	
Lighting and heating	1 500	
Cash at bank	8 388	
Cash in hand	12	
	216 000	216 000

Debtors at 28 February 19—

	£
J G Andrews	2 300
Bailey Brothers	3 000
Carters Sports	4 000
Edna Davies	700
	10 000

Creditors at 28 February 19—

	£
NKG plc	1 000
Tape Works Ltd	536
CIC plc	734
Fettlenold & Sons	1 730
	4 000

Transactions for March 19—

(All purchases and sales are on credit; all receipts and payments are by cheque, except where otherwise shown.)

			Goods £	+VAT £
March	1	Sold to J G Andrews	2 600	390
	2	Purchases from NKG plc	740	111
	3	Paid Southampton BC for rates £917		
	4	Received from J G Andrews £2300		
	5	Received from Bailey Bros £2536		
	8	Sold to Bailey Bros	3 100	465
	10	Withdrew cash from bank £50		
	11	Purchases from Tape Works Ltd	340	51
	15	Paid NKG plc £734		
	15	Paid Tape Works Ltd £536		
	15	Paid Fettlenold & Sons £1730		
	16	Paid in cash for advertisement in EW News £50		
	17	Sold to Carters Sports	4 300	645
	18	Paid lighting and heating £533		
	19	Paid for advertisement in *Guardian* £500		
	22	Purchases from CIC plc	920	138
	23	Received from Carters Sports £7164		
	30	Paid wages £3000		

6

As a continuation of Task 6 in Unit 11.2, use a computer package to prepare the balance sheet of W Watson & Sons at 31 December 19–1 from the following balances extracted from the accounts:

	£
Debtors	9 600
Creditors	5 800
Furniture and fittings	10 800
Motor vehicles	13 040
Freehold land and buildings	280 000
Stock (31.12.19–1)	23 200
Bank overdraft	3 000
Petty cash	200
Office salaries accrued	640
Insurance prepaid	600
Drawings	8 000
Capital	318 000

Following last week's work on P Morrison's profit and
loss account, your help is requested with the balance
sheet (Fig 11.10):

Balance Sheet of P Morrison & Sons

as at 31 December 19–1

	£	£	£
Fixed assets			
Premises		120 000	
Fixtures and fittings		20 000	
Office equipment		7 400	
Motor vehicles		12 600	
			160 000
Current assets			
Stock	3 800		
Debtors	4 800		
Salaries accrued	200		
Cash at bank and in hand	3 500		
		12 300	
Less Current liabilities			
Creditors	1 950		
Prepaid rent	50		
		2 000	
Working capital			10 300
Total net assets			170 300
Represented by:			
Capital (1.1.19–1)	170 400		
Add net profit	4 000		
	174 400		
Less drawings	8 000		
Capital (31.12.19–1)		182 400	
Add long term liabilities:			
Bank loan		3 600	
		186 000	

---

*I drew up the balance sheet as you suggested, but it
doesn't balance! Can you please help to spot where
I have gone wrong and make amendments where
necessary. Is the return on capital comparable with
bank interest rates? PM*

Fig 11.10

Assignment – Unit 11

Situation: You have a good idea to set up your own business and you are involved in making plans for it.

Tasks

a In a memo to your Tutor explain the type of business you have in mind and how you propose to start it.

b Draw up an estimated trading and profit and loss account and balance sheet for the first year of operation to support your proposals to the bank for a loan. Include any relevant performance ratios which you would aim to achieve.

c Role play (in groups) an interview with the bank manager to persuade the bank that you have a good idea for starting your own business and that you should be given a loan.

d What sources of advice and assistance are available when you are planning to start your own business?

e What legal rights and obligations would you establish with (1) your customers/clients and (2) any staff you may employ?

TO SUM UP
FINAL ACCOUNTS

Document	Calculates	Performance ratios
Trading account	Cost of sales Gross profit	Mark-up Profit margin Gross profit as a percentage of sales Rate of turnover
Profit and loss account	Overheads Net profit	Net profit as a percentage of sales
Balance sheet	Fixed assets Current assets Total net assets Long-term liabilities Current liabilities Working capital Final capital	Return on capital employed

12 Accounting for leisure

There are many organisations which do not trade for profit and exist in order to provide activities for those who choose to belong to them, such as cricket clubs, professional societies, churches, youth clubs and social clubs. Nevertheless they are involved in receiving income (very often in the form of membership subscriptions and donations) and paying expenses and, therefore, must keep financial records. The records may be no more than a summary of the cash book called a Receipts and Payments Account and/or, if a more formal record is required by the rules or the members, an Income and Expenditure Account (with or without a balance sheet).

12.1 Receipts and payments account

This account, illustrated in Fig 12.1, is a summary of cash received and paid during a given period and it shows the amount of cash in hand at the end of the period.

Procedure:
1 The account should begin with the balance of cash held at the beginning of the period, which will be the same as the closing balance of cash for the previous period.
2 The receipts are listed under appropriate headings, summarised, totalled and *added* to the opening balance of cash in **1**.
3 The payments are listed under appropriate headings, summarised, totalled and *deducted* from the total receipts calculated in **2**.
4 The final total in **3** provides the balance of cash at the end of the period, which should agree with the amount of cash in hand.

12.2 Income and expenditure account

This account, illustrated in Fig 12.2 is similar to a trading/profit and loss account, but the excess

of income over expenditure is called a *surplus* and this is added to an accumulated fund in the balance sheet (instead of calculating net profit and adding it to the capital account balance in the balance sheet). If the expenditure exceeds the income the resulting 'loss' is called a *deficit* and this is deducted from an accumulated fund in the balance sheet. The income includes all that is due (whether it is paid or not) for the period covered by the account and likewise the expenditure allows for accruals and prepayments.

Procedure:
1 If a closing cash figure is not given, prepare a receipts and payments account containing only actual *cash* receipts and payments.
2 Convert the receipts and payments account into an income and expenditure account by:
   a allowing for prepayments and accruals (especially subscriptions owing)
   b including only *revenue* expenditure and income: any capital expenditure (e.g. the purchase of a typewriter) or capital income (loans to the organisation) should not be included and should be placed in the balance sheet.
3 Calculate a net total for each item of income and expenditure; this may entail compiling a small receipts and payments account or it may even require a trading account, as in the case of refreshments in Fig 12.2.
4 List all items of income and total them.
5 List all items of expenditure, deducting prepayments and adding accruals, and total them.
6 Deduct the total expenditure from the total income to arrive at a surplus or a deficit.

12.3 Balance sheet

The format and purpose of the balance sheet for non-trading concerns is similar in many respects to the balance sheet explained in Unit 11.3 but with different terms used for capital (accumulated fund) and profit/loss (surplus/deficit) as illustrated in Fig 12.3.

Procedure:
1 List and total the assets. If required, separate fixed assets from current assets.
2 List and total the liabilities and subtract them from the total of assets.
3 Calculate the opening accumulated fund balance by deducting the liabilities from the assets at the beginning of the period, as illustrated in Fig 12.3.
4 Add the surplus or deduct the deficit from the opening accumulated fund balance to arrive at the closing accumulated fund balance. This should be the same as the answer in 2, i.e. assets minus liabilities.

Example 1

Mr P Faulkner encouraged his staff to meet together socially in the firm's Staff Association to promote good relationships between staff and maintain a high standard of morale. He therefore gave a grant of £1000 each year to the Association. On 1 January 19–1 the Staff Association's records contained the following entries:

	£
Cash in hand	210.00
Stock of refreshments	75.00
A creditor (Catering Supplies Ltd) for refreshments supplied	26.00

During the year to 31 December 19–1 the Honorary Secretary and Treasurer received and paid the following amounts:

Receipts:

	£
Grant from Mr Faulkner	1000.00
Subscriptions	1040.00
Proceeds from outings	271.00
Sale of refreshments	1440.00
Proceeds from discos	275.00

Payments:

	£
Cleaning materials	86.00
Part-time cleaner's wages	1300.00
Rent of rooms	312.00
Suppliers of refreshments	1250.00
New typewriter	420.00
Telephone, stationery, postage, etc	174.00

At the end of the year the Association owed £46 to Catering Supplies Ltd for refreshments supplied and had £120 of refreshments in stock. The income and expenditure account and balance sheet were prepared to present to the members at the annual general meeting to be held on 10 January 19–2. Note that in order to prepare these two documents it was first necessary to calculate:
1 Cash in hand at 31 December 19–1 in the receipts and payments account (Fig 12.1).
2 Accumulated fund at 31 December 19–1 illustrated in Fig 12.3.
3 Net proceeds from sale of refreshments for the year in the refreshments trading account in Fig 12.2.

Faulkner's Staff Association
Receipts and Payments Account
for the year ended 31 December 19–1

	£	£
Balance of cash in hand (1.1.19–1)		210.00
Add Receipts:		
Grant	1000.00	
Subscriptions	1040.00	
Proceeds from outings	271.00	
Sale of refreshments	1440.00	
Proceeds from discos	275.00	
		4026.00
		4236.00
Deduct Payments:		
Part-time cleaner's wages	1300.00	
Cleaning materials	86.00	
Refreshment supplies	1250.00	
Rent of rooms	312.00	
Typewriter	420.00	
Telephone, stationery and postage	174.00	
		3542.00
Balance of cash in hand (31.12.19–1)		694.00

Fig 12.1

Faulkner's Staff Association
Refreshments Trading Account
for the year ended 31 December 19–1

	£	£	£
Sales of refreshments			1440.00
Less cost of refreshments:			
Stock (1.1.19–1)		75.00	
Add: purchases paid	1250.00		
purchases owing (31.12.19–1)	46.00		
	1296.00		
Less: purchases owing (1.1.19–1)	26.00		
		1270.00	
		1345.00	
Less: stock (31.12.19–1)		120.00	
			1225.00
Net proceeds from sales			215.00

Faulkner's Staff Association
Income and Expenditure Account
for the year ended 31 December 19–1

	£	£
Income		
Grant from P Faulkner & Sons	1000.00	
Subscriptions	1040.00	
Proceeds from outings	271.00	
Proceeds from discos	275.00	
Proceeds from sale of refreshments	215.00	
		2801.00
Less **expenditure**		
Part-time cleaner's wages	1300.00	
Cleaning materials	86.00	
Rent of rooms	312.00	
Telephone, stationery and postage	174.00	
		1872.00
Surplus for the year		929.00

Fig 12.2

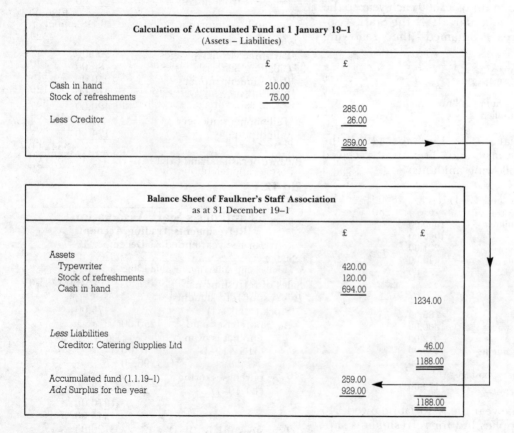

Calculation of Accumulated Fund at 1 January 19–1
(Assets – Liabilities)

	£	£
Cash in hand	210.00	
Stock of refreshments	75.00	
		285.00
Less Creditor		26.00
		259.00

Balance Sheet of Faulkner's Staff Association
as at 31 December 19–1

	£	£
Assets		
Typewriter	420.00	
Stock of refreshments	120.00	
Cash in hand	694.00	
		1234.00
Less Liabilities		
Creditor: Catering Supplies Ltd		46.00
		1188.00
Accumulated fund (1.1.19–1)	259.00	
Add Surplus for the year	929.00	
		1188.00

Fig 12.3

Example 2

Trevor Rawlings is the Honorary Treasurer of Littletown Youth Fellowship and at the end of the year (19–2) he is required to prepare a receipts and payments account, an income and expenditure account and a balance sheet for the annual general meeting.

The following is the balance sheet of the Littletown Youth Fellowship at 31 December 19–1 and a list of the receipts and payments made by the Treasurer during the year ending 31 December 19–2.

Balance Sheet of Littletown Youth Fellowship
as at 31 December 19–1

	Cost £	Deprec- iation £	Book value £
Fixed assets			
Minibus	6000		6000
Typewriter	250		250
Audio equipment	1000		1000
Games equipment	850		850
	8100		8100
Current assets			
Stock of refreshments	120		
Stock of stationery	20		
Membership subscriptions owing	30		
Cash at bank and in hand	90		
		260	
Less current liabilities			
Rent accrued		80	
			180
			8280
Accumulated fund (1.1.19–1)	8000		
Add surplus for the year	280		
			8280

Littletown Youth Fellowship
List of receipts and payments

	£
Receipts:	
Subscriptions	3000
Sponsored hike	350
Sale of refreshments at club nights	500
Disco proceeds	450
Payments:	
New audio equipment (purchased 10 December 19–2)	320
Rent of premises	720
Repairs to games equipment	120
Printing tickets for discos	110
Cost of refreshments for discos	120
Cost of refreshments for club nights	350
Light and heat	460
Minibus repairs	800
Petrol and oil	500
Stationery	80
Postage and telephone	90

Notes:

1 A stationery bill of £20 is outstanding.
2 Stocks at 31 December 19–2:

	£
Refreshments	100
Stationery	50

3 Membership subscriptions due £360.
4 The fixed assets are depreciated by 10 per cent on the book values at 1 January 19–2.

Documents **1**, **2** and **3** are prepared for the annual general meeting:

1 Littletown Youth Fellowship
Receipts and Payments Account
for the year ended 31 December 19–2

	£	£
Balance of cash at bank and in hand (1.1.19–2)		90
Add Receipts:		
Subscriptions	3000	
Sponsored hike	350	
Refreshments (club nights)	500	
Discos	450	
	4300	
		4390
Less Payments:		
Audio equipment	320	
Rent of premises	720	
Repairs to games equipment	120	
Printing	110	
Refreshments (discos)	120	
Refreshments (club nights)	350	
Light and heat	460	
Repairs to minibus	800	
Petrol and oil	500	
Stationery	80	
Postage and telephone	90	
		3670
Balance of cash at bank and in hand (31.12.19–2)		720

2 Income and Expenditure Account
for the year ended 31 December 19–2

	£	£	£	£
Income:				
Subscriptions		3000		
Less arrears from previous year		30		
		2970		
Add subscriptions due		360		
			3330	
Sponsored hike			350	
Club night refreshments:				
Sales		500		
Less cost of sales:				
Opening stock	120			
Add purchases	350			
	470			
Less closing stock	100			
		370		
			130	
Disco proceeds		450		
Less printing	110			
refreshments	120			
		230		
			220	
Net income c/f				4030

Income and Expenditure Account (continued)

	£	£	£
Net income b/f			4030
Less Expenditure:			
Rent of premises	720		
Less accrual	80		
(from previous year)		640	
Repairs to games equipment		120	
Light and heat		460	
Minibus repairs		800	
Petrol and oil		500	
Stationery:			
Opening stock	20		
Add purchases	80		
accrual	20		
	120		
Less closing stock	50		
		70	
Postage and telephone		90	
Depreciation: Minibus	600		
Typewriter	25		
Audio equipment	100		
Games equipment	85		
		810	
			3490
Surplus for the year			540

3   Balance Sheet as at 31 December 19–2

	Cost £	Deprec- iation £	Book value £
Fixed assets			
Minibus	6000	600	5400
Typewriter	250	25	225
Audio equipment	1320	100	1220
Games equipment	850	85	765
	8420	810	7610
Current assets			
Stock of refreshments	100		
Stock of stationery	50		
Membership subscriptions owing	360		
Cash at bank and in hand	720		
		1230	
Less Current liabilities			
Stationery accrued		20	
			1210
			8820
Accumulated fund (1.1.19–2)		8280	
Add surplus for the year		540	
			8820

TASKS

1

Prepare Faulkner's Staff Association's income and expenditure account and balance sheet for the year 19–2 from the information given in Example 1, the following receipts and payments and the adjustments in the notes:

Receipts	£
Grant from Mr Faulkner	1000
Subscriptions	1144
Proceeds from outings	320
Sale of refreshments	1621
Proceeds from discos	28
Proceeds from car rally	64

Payments:	£
Cleaning materials	125
Part-time cleaner's wages	1400
Rent of rooms	360
Suppliers of refreshments	1562
Filing cabinet (purchased on 1.1.19–2)	240
Donation to Children in Need	100
Telephone, stationery and postage	334
Secretary/Treasurer's Honorarium	300

Notes:

At 31 December 19–2:

1 Stock of refreshments valued at £247.
2 An invoice of £165 from Catering Supplies Ltd for refreshments was due to be paid.
3 Subscriptions owing from members £16.
4 Fixed assets are to be depreciated by 10 per cent on their book values at 1 January 19–2.

2

The following is a list of the receipts and payments made by the treasurer of the Mayfield Social Club during the year ended 31 May 19–2:

	£
Balance at bank 1 June 19–1	850
Subscriptions received during year	1200
Profit on sale of refreshments	410
Proceeds of whist drives and dances	175
Rent of hall paid during year	220
Purchase of new games equipment (regarded as revenue expenditure)	210
Cleaners' wages	520
Heating and lighting payments	175
Secretarial expenses	500
Purchase of new furniture	400

The following items are due for the year ended 31 May 19–2 but have not yet been paid:

	£
Rent of hall for one month	20
An electricity account for lighting	25

You are to prepare:

a The Mayfield Social Club's receipts and payments account for the year ended 31 May 19–2

b The Mayfield Social Club's income and expenditure account for the year ended 31 May 19–2 (*RSA BKI*)

3

The financial records of the Saints Hockey Club at 31 December 19–2 showed the following:

	£
Subscriptions received (£100 was owing for 19–2)	1200
Sports equipment	1360
Rent of club house (including a prepayment of £100 for 19–3)	1300
Bar stock at 31 December 19–2	120
Surplus for 19–2	400
Office equipment	600
Bank overdraft	80
Petty cash	20
Creditors for bar supplies	120
Insurance due for 19–2	200
Accumulated fund at 1 January 19–2	1500

You are required to prepare the balance sheet of the club as at 31 December 19–2.

Assignment – Unit 12

Situation: You are Assistant to the Honorary Treasurer of the Newtown Community Association.

Tasks:

a In the absence of the Honorary Treasurer you are asked to prepare a receipts and payments account, an income and expenditure account and a balance sheet for 19–2 from the following details:

Balance Sheet of
Newtown Community Association
as at 31 December 19–1

	£	£	£
Fixed assets			
Minibus		8000	
Office equipment		4000	
Games equipment		1500	
			13500
Current assets			
Bar stock	120		
Membership subscriptions owing	60		
Rent prepaid	100		
Cash at bank	1050		
Petty cash	50		
		1380	
Less Current liabilities			
Insurance accrued	120		
Electricity accrued	90		
		210	
			1170
			14670
Accumulated fund (1.1.19–1)		14000	
Add surplus for the year		670	
			14670

	£
Receipts	
Subscriptions	8400
Fete proceeds	4500
Whist drives	2000
Bar takings	8100
Payments	
New word processor	1000
Insurance	400
Rent	1600
Electricity	900
Repairs to minibus	400
Fete expenses	1400
Whist drive prizes and refreshments	1600
Goods for bar	5000
Wages of bar attendant	2000
Secretarial wages	4000
Petrol and oil	600
Office expenses	1200

Notes:
1 A bill for further repairs to the minibus is outstanding £60.
2 Membership subscriptions paid in respect of 19–3 £120.
3 Bar stock at 31 December 19–2 was £500.
4 Rent paid in advance £50.
5 The fixed assets are depreciated by 20 per cent on the book values at 1 January 19–2.

b When considering the year's activities at the Community Association's annual general meeting, how would you measure their effectiveness in relation to the final accounts?

c The Newtown Community Association caters for the leisure pursuits of people in your area and it has been suggested that, with increased automation in employment and a possible reduction in working hours/years, there will be even greater demand in future for such organisations. In a discussion with your colleagues consider what other effects an increased use of automation will have on office workers and prepare a summary of your findings.

TO SUM UP
ACCOUNTING FOR NON-TRADING CONCERNS

Receipts and payments account: summary of cash received and paid during the current year – but may relate to *any* year

Income and expenditure account: calculates surplus or deficit for the current year and includes all income (whether it is received or not) and all expenditure (whether it is paid or not)

Balance sheet: shows assets and liabilities at the end of the current year and the accumulation fund (capital) transferred from the income and expenditure account

Abbreviated answers (selected tasks)

Unit 1
1 a £100 000.
  b Profit 20p, wages 26p
    materials 26p, administration 20p, distribution 8p.
  c 20% this year; 15% last year. Yes, pleasing progress.

2 £4 per student.

Unit 2.1
1 a Stores requisitions.
  b Purchases requisition.

2 Purchases requisition for 100 metres of Cat No S801.

Unit 2.2
1 Orders to Darling & Son Ltd and Outdoor Fabrics plc.

2 Order to Tape Works Ltd.

Unit 2.3
1 a Delivery note from Outdoor Fabrics plc.
  b Goods received note for 100m of Grade A2 green tent cloth.

2 a Delivery note from Tape Works Ltd.
  b Goods received note for 20 bobbins of 5mm brown webbing.

Unit 3.1
1 a £586.45
  b £1680
  c £316.50

2 Net invoice price £346.23.

6 Total £1729.02, goods £1447.00, carriage £56.50, VAT £225.52.

7 Total £1459.57, goods £1228.30, carriage £40.90, VAT £190.37.

Unit 3.2
1 Total £457.29, goods £397.64, VAT £59.65.

2 a C/N net price £24.63

  b PRB: total   £24.63
       goods £21.42
       VAT   £3.21
  Account balances:
  Outdoor Fabrics   £484.25   Cr
  VAT   £63.17   Dr
  Purchases returns £21.42   Cr

Unit 3.3
1 a Wilkinson
  b 1 Dr invoices
    2 Cr payments/discounts/allowances
    3 Balance owing by Joyce
  c Debtor = Joyce
    Creditor = Wilkinson
    Amount owing: £327.50

2 Reconciliation statement:
  Balance as per statement
    (15.1.19—)   £88.29
  Deduct:
    Invoice error
    (A1162)   £10.00
    Payment   £53.00
                   £63.00
  Balance as per
  ledger account   £25.29

Unit 3.4
1 a Reverse Dr and Cr entries; all Cr balances.
  b Cheques: £
    Darling   303.77
    Insulation Supply   136.13
    CIC   242.49
  CPJ total   682.39
  Personal accounts:
    Cr payments, as above:
    all nil balances

2 Cheque: £156.78
  Balance: £111.72

Unit 4.1
1 Quotation.
2 Illustrated catalogue for caravans.

Unit 4.2
1 Confirmation of orders.
2 Order book.

Unit 4.3
1 Advice notes.
2 Advice note.

Unit 5.1
1 Aldous   £897.00
   Baldwin   £4048.00
   Coleman   1   £1524.55
            2   £20 658.60

2 Arnold   £181.12
   Attwood   £3491.40
   Bell   £13 506.75
   Brown   £258.75
   Charles   £144.90
   Coleman   £3300.50

7 Total   £20 883.42
   Goods   £18 159.50
   VAT   £2723.92

8 Total   £1633.37
   Goods   £1420.33
   VAT   £213.04

Unit 5.2
1 a Credit notes
   b Total   £66.70
     Goods £58.00
     VAT   £8.70

2 SDB: Total   £229.19
         Goods   £199.30
         VAT   £29.89
   SRB: Total   £43.70
         Goods   £38.00
         VAT   £5.70

Unit 5.3
1 Total £1673.11   Tents £277.35
   S'bags £422.08   R'sacks £461.61
   C'beds £293.84   VAT £218.23

2 Total £20 883.42   Tents £17 651.00
   R'sacks £225.00   C'beds £283.50
   VAT £2723.92

Unit 5.4
1 Chudleigh £2159.79 Dr
   Dreamland £5281.46 Dr

2 Chudleigh £1232.74 Dr

Unit 6.1
1 Aldous   Nil
   Andrews   Nil
   Arnold   £1655.10 Dr
   Bailey   £254.94 Dr
   Bostock   £55.19 Dr
   Carters   Nil

   Chudleigh £1232.74 Dr
   Coleman   £51.88 Dr
   Dreamland Nil
   Dunn   Nil

2 Leisure Products Nil
   CRJ £50 220.50

Unit 6.2
1 Receipt £55.19
   Bostock A/c Nil
2 Receipt £15.41

Unit 6.3
1 Paying-in slip £1196.34
2 Paying-in slip £50 220.50

Unit 7.1
1 TB £10 732.63
2 TB £3564.00

Unit 7.3
1 PL Control A/c £1223.60 Cr
   SL Control A/c £2185.28 Dr
2 PL Control A/c £4183.00 Cr

Unit 8
1 Stock control card balance: 600
2 Cost value £12 040
   NRV £15 170
   Lower of CV or NRV £11 990

Unit 9.1
1 Cash A/c £288 Dr
   Bank A/c £2100 Dr
   R A Brown A/c £160 Dr
   Palmer & O'Neill A/c £440 Cr
   Stationery A/c £34 Dr
   Motor expenses A/c £20 Dr
   Sales A/c £192 Cr

2 Bank A/c £1860.91 Dr
   Discount allowed A/c £34.12 Dr
   Discount received A/c £15.07 Cr
   VAT A/c £17.00 Dr
   Heating and lighting A/c £64 Dr
   Insurance A/c £108 Dr
   Building repairs A/c £52.18 Dr
   Motor expenses A/c £10.78 Dr
   Telephone A/c £50.44 Dr

Unit 9.2
1 Cash book balance (with amendments) £767.40
2 Cash book balance (with amendments) £213.00

Unit 9.3
1 Total expenditure £40.56
   Balance £9.44
   Nominal ledger accounts:
   Cleaning £10.00 Dr

Travelling expenses £4.00 Dr
Stationery £4.72 Dr
Office expenses £13.29 Dr
Subs/donations £5.00 Dr
VAT £3.55 Dr

2 Total expenditure £38.92
Balance £11.08
Travel expenses A/c £5.50 Dr
Stationery A/c £13.31 Dr
Cleaning A/c £10.50 Dr
Postage A/c £3.00 Dr
Office expenses A/c £3.50 Dr
VAT A/c £3.11 Dr

Unit 10.1
1 B   Brown £152
  C   Capable £157
  D   Davis £184
  E   Evans £162
2 S Watson £308.10

Unit 10.2
1
Week No	NI £	Income tax £
1	10.84	16.50
2	10.84	16.75
3	10.84	2.25 refund
4	10.84	10.25
5	12.19	14.00
6	12.19	14.00
7	7.03	5.25
8	7.03	5.25
9	12.64	15.50
10	12.64	15.25

(Using 1989 rates)

2
	Income tax £
Martin	25.25
Saunders	1.00 refund
Turner	34.25

Unit 11.1
1 a 900 articles
  b Cost of sales £5200
    Gross profit £2550

2 Net purchases £18 040.
  Cost of goods offered for sale £22 640.
  Cost of sales £22 000.
  Net sales £30 000.
  Gross profit £8000.

Unit 11.2
1 a Year 19–5 = 10%
  b Year 19–4 = 15%
    19–4 more successful:
    lower overheads

2 Gross profit £14 094
  Net profit £5334

Unit 11.3
1 a Year 19–5   1   26.60%
                2   2.07:1
                3   1.30:1
  b Year 19–4   1   30%
                2   1.47:1
                3   1.01:1

2 Net profit £5000
  Working capital £8500
  Balance sheet totals £44 300

Unit 12
1 Cash in hand (31.12.19–2) £450.
  Net proceeds from sale of refreshments £67.
  Deficit for year £46.
  Balance sheet totals £1142.

2 a Cash in hand (31.5.19–2) £610
  b Surplus £115